Community Policing

Community Policing

National and international models and approaches

**Mike Brogden and
Preeti Nijhar**

WILLAN
PUBLISHING

Published by

Willan Publishing
Culmcott House
Mill Street, Uffculme
Cullompton, Devon
EX15 3AT, UK
Tel: +44(0)1884 840337
Fax: +44(0)1884 840251
e-mail: info@willanpublishing.co.uk
website: www.willanpublishing.co.uk

Published simultaneously in the USA and Canada by

Willan Publishing
c/o ISBS, 920 NE 58th Ave, Suite 300,
Portland, Oregon 97213-3644, USA
Tel: +001(0)503 287 3093
Fax: +001(0)503 280 8832
e-mail: info@isbs.com
website: www.isbs.com

© 2005 Mike Brogden and Preeti Nijhar

First published 2005

ISBN 1-84392-005-0 (paperback)
    1-84392-006-9 (hardback)

British Library Cataloguing-in-Publication Data

A catalogue record for this book is available from the British Library

Project managed by Deer Park Productions, Tavistock, Devon
Typeset by GCS, Leighton Buzzard, Bedfordshire
Printed and bound by T.J. International Ltd, Trecerus Industrial Estate, Padstow, Cornwall

**To
Maureen Cain**

Contents

Acknowledgements

In a text which aims to cover a multitude of both academic sources and legal jurisdictions, only a few of those who have contributed (in differing ways) to this volume can be acknowledged. However, primary place must be given to one police constable of the new Northern Ireland Police Service. That problem solving community police officer, at a time when Catholic houses in North Belfast were being nightly firebombed by sectarian opponents, revealed in her social construction of a garden fence in South Belfast (see page 225) the central absurdity of one key aspect of community oriented policing. We thank her for that local lesson in the application of COP and for the inspiration of this text. Police discretion is also at the centre of the new COP. In North Wales, the practices of the popularly titled 'Traffic Taleban' reinforced a critical perspective. Contributions by police officers were, of course, not just local. One of the authors will not forget the image of Captain Evan Corbett of the late and unlamented South African Police proffering lollipops to bemused local children from a column of armoured police vehicles in a community policing tour of Soweto in 1993. On the other hand, it would be wrong to ignore the practices of many individual police officers – a former Nebraskan and CIVPOL officer represents (on the OSCE coach from Prilep to Skopje in 2004) one amongst many, as do former officers such as Keith Humphreys in Caernarfon and Keith Bryett (of many different places!).

It will be obvious from the above that not all contributors to this volume have done so positively. However, there are many others whose research and insights have been essential to the production of this critical text. The following academics must represent a much larger number of their fellows. In the United States it would be impossible to avoid the erudite work of Peter Manning and the historical analyses of Samuel Walker. Though we disagree with his optimism, one must recognize the major works of David Bayley and of course those of his transnational colleague, Clifford Shearing – Clifford is a Utopian – this book is an exercise in dystopianism! Long-term academic opponents, from Tank Waddington to Maurice Punch, have converged as welcome new bedfellows.

The book draws on a range of original revisionist studies – for example, Frank Leishman on Japan, and 'KC' Wong in China. Given that much of this text is a critique of the function of so-called 'development assistance', the one context in which external police research funding has been of major significance has been in South Africa where the quality of research from the Institute of Security Studies in Pretoria and from their colleagues at the Institute of Criminology of the University of Cape Town is partly the product of wise overseas investment. In Northern Ireland, where the dogma of a conservative Human Rights culture has sidelined critical sociological studies, Graham Ellison is aware of the value of his own work and comradeship, as are those of local contributors to Statewatch. The emerging studies of policing in South America are a key reference point. It would be churlish to ignore the many papers by Rachel Neild and Otwin Marenin in the United States, although like others, they will not agree with all the arguments in this text. Back in Britain, no serious student of policing can manage without the helpfulness of the librarians of the Bramshill Police College.

The usual round of comrades and suspects will forgive the anonymous recognition of their more direct assistance – only they know what they have had to put up with (as do Richard and Annie from Bryn Felin). To those should be added the initial teaching and laconic writings of the late Steve Box and the welcome reemergence of Julienne Ford. But like many other critical studies within policing and the wider sociology of law in the UK, none of this could have emerged without the long-term insights, scholarship, and comradeship of the person to whom this volume is dedicated.

Melin Cadnant
Llandegfan

Chapter 1

Globalizing community-oriented policing (COP)

... two emerging philosophies – community-oriented policing and problem-solving policing ... such notions as police-community reciprocity, decentralisation of command, re-orientation of patrol, and generalised rather than specialised policing are commending themselves to police executives around the globe. At first thought, this is rather surprising. Why should police executives with such different cultures, different economies, and different traditions as Oslo, Tokyo, London, New York, and Santa Anna, be advocating similar reforms?

(Skolnick and Bayley 1986 p. 17)

Introduction

Community policing has been the buzzword in Anglo-American policing for the last two decades. But it comes in all shapes and sizes. From the specifics of problem-solving by the local beat officer to the grand philosophy of a policing that is community sensitive, accountable, and transparent, it has not and will not be subject to clear definition. Public commentators – perhaps now more in the rhetoric of the mass media than in some of the nuances and refinements of official police discourse – generally treat community policing as a euphemism for a particular concept of police-civil society relations. Whatever the intent of local structures – from Police Community Forums to *ad hoc* campaigns like Crime Stoppers, from beat patrols to the optimism of Neighbourhood Watch Schemes (NWS) and to the specifics of Sector Policing, it appears to be most generally defined by its negative.

It is not military-style policing with a central bureaucracy obedient to directive legislation which minimises discretion. It is not policing that is autonomous of public consent and accountability. It is not policing that is committed primarily to reactive crime-fighting strategies. It is not policing that is measured by output in terms of professional efficiency. Rather it is policing which is determined by strategies, tactics and outcomes based on community consent. In this text, whatever the nuances of local usage, we shall use it as a generic term that implies a style and strategy of policing that appears to reflect local community needs.

As we shall discuss in the following pages, COP has become an important vehicle for police transformation in *failed* societies – that is societies such as those of the former Soviet bloc where the political systems have collapsed and new state structures are experiencing major birth pangs. Community policing is also important because it is a key component of an export drive from the West in the development of new policing structures in *transitional* societies – that is countries which might once have been described as 'Third World' or (optimistically) as 'developing', which are being forced by economic and social exigencies (such as rising recorded crime rates) to construct new safety and security agencies.

In Britain, community policing has become adopted in the popular parlance of the public, of the media and of politicians. In that discourse, it is imbibed with a mythical appeal in several senses. It appears to be a reincarnation of the old 'bobby-on-the-beat' – the foot patrol police officer who in the distant past appeared to use pragmatic commonsense in dealing with issues of local crime and disorder. Most British police forces no longer use the term of community policing in their policy development – specific strategies of *problem–solving policing* and of *intelligence-led policing* have replaced the community policing discourse. Further, most policing experts would argue that problem-solving now represents a quite distinct form of policing from that of COP (Bullock and Tilley 2003)[1]. But in public presentations, problem-solving is normally included under the rubric of community policing, resonating in a consensual policing style to which the public can relate directly. However, in practice, in Britain and in parts of Western Europe, community policing philosophies have often been displaced with local community safety contracts and secondly, with forms of tiered policing[2], such as local warden schemes (although some might regard them as necessarily included within the community policing mission).

In the United States, community policing (or as we shall refer to throughout this text, community oriented policing [COP]) represents the dominant ideology of policing as reflected in a myriad of urban schemes, in funding practices, and in research publications. COP represents the new orthodoxy in North American policing policy-making, strategies and tactics. But it is in *failed* and *transitional* societies that COP is the new cargo cult, as the Western missionaries promote a policing elixir that will resolve a range of social ills. Where such societies are characterized by rising recorded crime rates, by delegitimation of older criminal justice agencies and, where economic investment is handicapped by foreign investors' fears of social instability, police reform is perceived as the essential bedrock of social and economic progress. In that theatre of social change, COP is cast to play a key role.

Exporting policing

Despite the enormous sums spent on this COP export process, we have little evidence of its impact or indeed of the effect of international exchange and trade in police values, ideologies, policies and technologies (Marenin 1998). Apart from a few pathbreaking studies, there is little evidence of the motives of the often misnamed donor countries, of the nature of the commodity, of the conditions of delivery, of the processes of installation in the 'host' society, of the reactions of the recipients and of their agents, and of the consequences of installation. There is, however, one invaluable study of the export of COP to Kenya (Ruteere and Pommerolle 2003). There are also several briefer accounts appearing that problematize local acceptance of Western policing in Eastern Europe.

Of course, policing export to non-Western societies is not a new practice as the long legacy of colonial policing instructs us[3] and in the post World War II attempts to transplant US policing to the defeated Axis powers. British colonial practices, in particular, are well documented. But it is a century since one Robert Baden Powell arrived back in Cape Town from Dublin Castle with plans for the new South African Constabulary in his knapsack (Brogden 2005). Exporting policing today is a little different from the then British East African police with Irish Constabulary (IC) senior officers, Punjabi inspectors, Somali constables, and with new recruits learning their duties from the IC Instruction Book! (Brogden 1987). It is also distinct from 30 years ago when United States police aid and advice flowed through the Office of Public Safety (OPS) as an instrument of foreign policy to prevent the encroachment of socialist ideas and rule in contested Latin American societies (Marenin 1996).

In the last decade, policing strategies and materials have become a major part of the export drive from the West to failed and transitional societies. In a replay of colonial days when the police institution was often the first to be implanted to safeguard imperial trade, new policing is being driven by donor interest and also – and this is new – customer demand.

The motives of the exporters are mixed. They include versions of the 'thin blue line thesis' as apparent in the *law and development movement* of the 1970s[4]. The police institution is seen as the key to stability, in a period of rapid social change, while new legitimacies are created for other state institutions. In the words of key proponents of community policing internationally, police reforms became the axis of an effort to dismantle authoritarian structures and to move from 'regime policing' to 'democratic policing'. The establishment of democratic policing is regarded as the foundation of the security and stability necessary for the consolidation of democracy and for a fertile environment for economic development (Ziegler and Neild 2002). More recently, Call (2003) has distinguished between Human Rights, peacekeeping, law enforcement, economic development and democratization motives[5].

COP represents an historically-legitimated model for export, given the conservative ideologies of Anglo-American policing structure, which locate the origins of such community policing in a Peelite tradition. This perspective represents the police institution as a bulwark against the 'forces of darkness'. Community policing is the salvation. Call and Barnett (1999) in their analysis of the United Nations Civilian Police (CIVPOL) suggest a new perception by the international community, that of a relationship between domestic security and international security (especially since 9/11). Internal schisms may have international effects. In the words of the American Justice Department:

> Why are the police so important in the development of democratic societies? The police are different from any other government entity. Of all government functions, the policing function is arguably the most visible, the most immediate, the most intimately involved with the well-being of individuals and the health of the communities.
>
> (Travis 1998, p. 2)

Donor countries may offer community policing as part of a larger package of police 'reform' in order to guarantee a degree of stability. If one can establish 'efficient' policing structures, so the argument goes, other cognate state institutions are given the space and time to develop new legitimate structures. The police 'hold the line'. The thin blue line thesis – and its modern versions – holds that when society is undergoing major social change, policing is the one institution that can maintain stability until other elements of the state apparatus are able to establish legitimacy.

There are other well-meaning motives, with COP perceived as the elixir to solve Human Rights issues. Police export is also a profitable business in which private multinational corporations as well as individual entrepreneurs straddle the world in a quest for a market share of law enforcement commodities.

Several types of agency are involved in the process. Individuals contribute. So do policing agencies, NGOs, national governments and private corporations.

> The motivation for the involvement of individual police forces can vary from the practicalities of having to cooperate with the recipients of assistance in the future on common crime problems, to individual police officers perceiving such help as an opportunity to provide philanthropic assistance to 'fellow' police officers.
>
> (Beck 2002, p. 23)

Rank-and-file police officers from the West apparently spend vacations in transitional societies delivering community policing training with missionary zeal. For example, Captain John Deangelis (of the USA Egg Harbour Police) has been entrepreneurially selling domestic violence and community policing courses in Lithuania and Estonia. Old apparatchniks and retirees are reincarnated in a new guise as community policing missionaries. Thus the consultancy of George Fivaz and Associates (Pty) aimed to contribute to COP development at an international conference in Bangkok sponsored by the United States government. Fivaz, the former head of the South African Police CID and Mandela's choice for transitional Commissioner, was described as an international expert on community policing, with fellow board members consisting of pensioned members of the apartheid SAP establishment[6].

Bi-lateral police exchanges – sometimes state-sponsored sometimes not – convey the message. Foreign policy programmes with wider concerns support COP schemes, often promoted through training schemes by Western academies. For example, Fijian and Jamaican police officers attend COP courses at the British Bramshill Police College. Russian police officers undertake tuition at police academies in the United States. The St Petersburg Academy draws on the Metropolitan Police's expertise on community policing. The Dutch police exchange community policing experience on a routine basis with officers from Hungary, from Poland and from the Czech Republic. Amongst many other ventures, staff from Washington State Spokane Community Policing Institute cross the North Pacific to develop COP on Russia's Sakhalin Island. The British police aim to develop community policing in Bulgaria's city of Plovdiv[7]. The Toronto Police have been encouraging COP in Lithuania. Norwegians, Dutch and Canadians teach community policing in Prague. The United States' International Criminal Investigative Training Assistance Program (ICITAP) has promoted COP as part of a larger police reform programme in countries as diverse as Ghana, El Salvador and Indonesia.

Typically, the city of Novgorod is twinned with Rochester (New York). In a two-year programme, Rochester acted as community policing host for Russian officers while sending COP trainers to the Russian city (variously offering a menu of Neighbourhood Empowerment Teams, Crime Stoppers, restorative justice, and a truancy programme). Similarly, the Greenfield Wisconsin police are linked with Simferopool, encouraging community-based policing initiatives. In a separate programme, Michigan State University is linked with Lviv, aiming to develop a Community Police Centre as a resource base in the Western Ukraine. The University of South Carolina hosted senior Muscovite police for the same purpose. In the late 1990s, COP trainers (financed by the US State Department) were seconded to Poland to teach Polish police Chicago's community policing model.

> Poland's police force is a national force, one hundred thousand officers strong, and despite the differences, officials feel that what works in Chicago can work in Poland.
>
> (Haberfeld, Walancik and Uydess 2003, p. 17)

Such COP exchanges, of course, are not limited to relationships between Western and failed and transitional societies. There are glossy accounts of intra-Western exchanges over COP. French police visiting their colleagues in Surrey reportedly commended the way that British communities are involved in the community policing process through the NWS and community forums – unlike in France. Other French police officers hosted by the Kent police were apparently impressed by the Canterbury police, which 'had an additional 35,000 pairs of keen Neighbourhood Watch eyes and ears to alert them to anything untoward,' (*Mercian News*, June 2002). Merseyside Police boast of the export potential for their Neighbourhood Policing after a visit by two German community constables including '... the opportunity to go out on evening patrols with Huyton's Neighbourhood team as they undertake a Knowsley-wide operation to tackle youth disorder on

Mischief Night'[8]. Under ubiquitous community safety initiatives, cities in Western Europe regularly exchange wide-ranging experiences and practices over local security issues – for example, between Utrecht and Newcastle.

Well-intentioned NGOs promote community policing internationally. The New York-based Vera Institute has a long legitimate history in developing democratic policing and has been foremost in encouraging COP in transitional societies. COP elixirs have been adopted in NGO Human Rights' discourse – the answer to Human Rights problems in transitional society is invariably community policing. Thus a recent UN Conference on Human Rights in Southern Europe portrayed COP as the Human Rights response to the treatment of Roma minorities[9]. An otherwise highly competent report on crime and the problems of policing transitional societies[10] recommends New York-style COP as the solution for countries as varied as the Ukraine and Argentina. The University of Ottawa Human Rights Centre promotes COP as the antidote to the appalling level of police and civilian death rates in Sao Paulo[11].

In Nigeria, a polyglot group of donors encouraged COP. For example in August 2001, the United States Agency for International Development (USAID) commenced work with the British Department for International Development (DFID) to help develop community policing and police reform. The South African NED Bank donated $25,000 to develop that programme. In Kenya, COP was launched with NGOs (including the Vera Institute) assistance, multi-national and local business inputs, and professional contributions – from the Ford Foundation to British police and academic staff (*The Nation* [Nairobi], 22 April 2001[12]), in liaison with the Nairobi Central Business District Association. This project was encouraged and supported by the NGO Saferworld in tandem with the Kenya Institute of Public Administration.

Policing for profit is also a major contributor to the process – whether sold by local entrepreneurial agencies or by private corporations. David Brodie of Brodie Consulting Services in Maryland sells COP from Brazil to Hungary[13]. A former Metropolitan Police Officer and his partner established themselves as COP advisers in South Africa, on the basis of UK experience, before later locating themselves in Northern Ireland as experts on COP in South Africa (!). At a more commercial level, the American DynCorp (in an initiative which remains curious to many Europeans) includes COP in its CIVPOL mandate in the former Yugoslavia. Private companies sell and promote COP like they sell other goods. The international conglomerate ITT promotes a community policing award to countries where the schemes are reportedly a success (*sic!*)[14]. Policing export and import occurs frequently within a commercial ideology in which in South Africa and elsewhere, there is a '... redesignation of the community as customers' (Oppler, 1997).

Finally, and critically, COP policing is being undertaken by international organizations such as the United Nations and the European Union. In part, this stems from those organizations' wider remits – as with transnational co-operation under the umbrella of bodies such as Interpol, Europol, and CIVPOL. Functionally specific organizations such as the World Bank and the IMF increasingly require transitional societies to either develop or to reform policing in a COP direction in order to receive economic assistance. The Organisation for Security and Co-operation in Europe (OSCE) undertakes many such ventures – for example, encouraging COP in Croatia by sending Croatian officers to observe community policing in the Sussex force[15]. It has recently advertised for Western police officers with experience of implementing community policing in their own countries to develop community policing in Macedonia and Serbia. National policing may be determined by agencies over and beyond the nation-state.

But the key problem of such unilateral policing export is illustrated by local police officers in a Central Asian republic. Generalized police packages – from community policing to anti-terrorism priorities – often suit sellers rather than consumers.

> The Kyrgyz police are used to international organizations offering training and there is a lot of cynicism towards such offers. One former senior policeman said 'International organizations love to do training in drug trafficking ...We don't need training in drug trafficking. We need training in how to solve social conflicts' ... Training is necessary ... but it must be focused on the needs of the police and society, and not on the interest of the donors[16].

As Beck comments

> ... the problem with many of these forms of assistance ... (include) ... 'we have this available so you can have it.' Potential recipients with very few resources are highly unlikely to refuse any offer but there is a real danger with such an approach that the agenda for assistance is set more by what is available rather than by what is needed.
>
> (Beck 2002, p. 237)

Dixon (1999) has described as a 'criminal justice cringe', the assumption that transitional and failed societies, amongst others, should necessarily follow the Anglo-American path in terms of policing and wider criminal justice issues. The process has occurred irrespective of local requirements. Fruhling (2002), analyzing South American police imports from the United States, has noted the major problems that occur when Western models of policing are superimposed on countries with quite different social, economic and political realities. Whatever its actual content, the structures of NWS, of community forums, of problem-solving policing, and of beat patrols – like many other policing strategies, are promoted irrespective of local exigencies and realities. The West determines the policing programmes to be adopted[17].

The globalization of COP

As an export, COP has a unique appeal. It resonates as a value-free commodity, unencumbered with the trappings of economic and political interest. Otherwise critical commentators on policing reform by donor agencies may suspend their critical faculties. Community policing is often portrayed as devoid of the kind of cultural impediments that characterise other policing models. For example, Call and Barnett (1999) acknowledge the dangers of trying to transplant a single model without attention to local traditions and circumstances. But they simultaneously view COP as sundered from such petty impediments. COP is an emblematic international creed.

A globalization of elements of ill-considered community policing is occurring within the larger process of police export and import. For example, at an Abu Dhabi Conference[18], experts from Arab countries, and from Singapore, Taiwan, France, Britain, United States and Canada recommended the implementation of community policing, within Sharia and local cultural values, to reduce crime. Similarly, 'even South Africa and Brazil are amongst jurisdictions seeking Ontario Provincial Police expertise on community policing'[19]. A seminar[20] selling Singapore-style community policing was attended by police officials from South Africa, Bangladesh, Brunei, China, India, Indonesia, Laos, Malaysia, Maldives, Mongolia, Nepal, Papua New Guinea, Philippines, Solomon Islands, Sri Lanka and Vietnam.

Senior officers such as Superintendent Roy Fleming of the former Royal Ulster Constabulary flit from advising on community police development between countries as far apart as Mongolia, Sri Lanka and Macedonia. A retired London Metropolitan police officer talks of his mission to ameliorate the conditions of the Roma people in Bulgaria through COP, embodying the 'real basis of the "British bobby on the beat" ' as the core of that project. Bulgarian officers came to London to observe the policing of Afro-Caribbean and Bangladeshi communities – apparently on the assumption that they were the nearest peoples that Britain could find to the Bulgarian Roma[21] (!). In Nepal, a country with few telephones and a looming Maoist guerrilla war, the UK Department of International Development (DFID), supported by agencies from Singapore and Japan, funds a policing solution with a detailed community policing programme including Police-Community Groups of Public Safety, Community Forums, Lay Visitors, and problem-solving policing under the guidance of a retired senior officer of the Metropolitan Police – as well as elements of the British Police and Criminal Evidence Act![22].

There are many idiosyncratic attempts to develop COP in apparently alien contexts. In the Indian province of Tamil Nadu in India, Prateep (1996) has attempted to implant a variant of COP, 'Friends of the Police' concept, to help to project the 'right image' of police. Perhaps the most remarkable example has been the attempt by the Soros-funded Constitutional and Legal Policy Institute (COLPI)[23] to promote community policing in Mongolia through the expertise of two senior Royal Ulster Constabulary (RUC) officers. Support for police reform is a major programme in COLPI's work.

> An encouraging example is the community policing project in Mongolia, which has already gained international recognition, and which has resulted in remarkable changes in the Mongolian Police department. It has led to a substantive change in relations between the public and the police. Thanks to the new way of policing, the Mongolian police have achieved some remarkable successes in preventing and solving crime[24].

Remarkably after a short period (according to COLPI), Mongolian community policing had been an extraordinary success (judged by falling recorded crime rates). Simultaneously, the United States Justice Department's Community Policing Consortium was attempting (in a series of seminars) to sell COP to the apparently barren community policing field of Northern Ireland! In Rio de Janeiro, where '... on average, seven civilians and two policemen are killed every week ... one man is trying to change things ... Major Antonio Caballero's quest to introduce community policing in areas where he and his men put their lives at risk every day...'[25]. In El Salvador, a USAID-funded community policing project was adopted nationwide in 2003. Similarly, the Washington Office on Latin America (WOLA) is promoting community policing in Brazil and El Salvador[26]. In that diffusion process (Monkkonen 1981), spurious claims are made about success elsewhere. Kenyan police officers and Human Rights activists have travelled to learn about community policing from their compatriots in India and in South Africa who reportedly claim, despite substantial evidence to the contrary, community policing successes[27].

Sometimes there is reverse missionary work '... the cosy koban, Japan's answer to community policing, may be small but its potential is great – as America is discovering' (*Economist*, 7–13 August 1999). The Milton Eisenhower Foundation promoted the development of the Japanese koban in the United States as early as 1988 with koban schemes established in Boston, Chicago, Memphis, Little Rock, Los Angeles, Philadelphia, Columbia and San Juan.

> The koban idea slipped into America largely unnoticed in the 1990s along with a boatload of other Japanese imports. It was carried in by American police officials who had journeyed to Japan in search of some explanation for the island's low crime rate[28].

But generally, community policing diffusion is a one-way process, from Anglo-American societies to those countries deemed to have failed or to be in a process of transition.

For example in Nairobi, trainers from the UK's National Police Training College claimed success in Belfast.

> I was able to share my practical experience of consultation and partnership policing programmes in North Belfast. The students quickly discovered that even though Nairobi and Belfast seem worlds apart, the problems facing the police and the community in both cities are very similar … Belfast was written off as a no-hope scenario. But this really can work.[29]

Independently of problems of practice, the resistance to the new ideals of Western policing has often related to different perceptions of the level of development and transition. '… Police in the new democracies of central and Eastern Europe do not necessarily have to "do what the West did best" ' (Koci 1996 p. 9). The COP Western model is often unrelated to the requirements of former members of the Eastern bloc. For example, some Western countries have higher recorded crime rates than their Eastern counterparts. But the latter were informed that higher crime rates – and the Western policing response to that phenomenon – was the price they had to pay for their new freedoms. This caused feelings of resentment

11

and frustration on the part of the public, and became the forum of contentious debate (Koci 1996). In Slovenia, more police officers on the street (as promoted by COP) simply created a false sense of security, one that had little effect on recorded crime. The police regarded the imported community models as relating to peculiar Western problems not to those of Slovenia (Zvecik 1996). In any case, the COP tenets had been tested before the arrival of the Western experts. Many such attempts to transfer knowledge to Eastern European countries are '... so general and so shallow that they do not bring anything new' (Dvorsek 1996 p. 5). *Ad hoc* offerings of COP ignore what has gone before. As a Taiwan commentator pointed out during a trial of COP in Taipei's Shilin district, it was not the first such initiative. The lessons of a previous failure to implant COP had been forgotten (*Taipei Times*, 11 November 1999).

Of course, not all donor assistance is directed at community policing. The South African experience is the best documented and probably the most salutary about the optimistic reconstruction of policing in a transitional society[30]. Since 1994, South Africa has enjoyed significant donor assistance across the core departments of the criminal justice system. But the spread of contributions was diverse and confusing. United States assistance concentrated on the training of specialist law enforcement. The Dutch invested in youth justice. Belgium provided significant assistance for a five-year police restructuring programme, covering the design and development of community policing, public order policing, and to combat organized crime. The government of Denmark financed limited training but also contributed to more administrative projects such as printing and distribution of community policing booklets. Sweden committed itself to human rights and democracy training for the South African Police Service (SAPS) and the design of model police stations. Canada contributed over £2 million towards a marshalls' training programme. France, Germany, and the Netherlands have all invested considerable sums as have the Commonwealth, the European Union and the United Nations.

But the key contribution in South Africa was that of the UK (reflecting a traditional sphere of interest approach), directly committed towards various aspects of community policing. A UK and Commonwealth Advisory Team helped the SAPS to develop a new basic community policing level training programme, with some £10 million funding community policing projects in four South African provinces.

What the South African experience suggests is that while donor countries may direct their resources in developing policing in a transitional society, the preference is clearly for community policing. Community policing is both a band-aid for transitional governments as well as the panacea for all crime ills and the key building block of the new democratic state.

Why community policing?

To date, with the exception of van der Spuy (2000) in South Africa, Lia (2000) on Palestine, more theoretically by Marenin (1998, 2001), Call (2003), and by Neild (2002), we have little perceptive analysis of that export-import process – of the motives of the often misnamed donor countries, of the nature of the commodity, of the conditions of delivery, of the processes of installation in the 'host' society, of the reactions of the recipient institutions and their agents, and the consequences of installation. There are (as above) several accounts appearing that increasingly problematise the acceptance of external ideas on policing by local agencies in Eastern Europe. Individual reservations do occasionally surface. A former Spokane police chief, after a visit to Sakhalin Island, commented that the local Russian police might be required as patrol officers one day and off to Chechnya to fight as a military unit the next.

However, the attraction for the new policing at both state and popular level is obvious. In the face of major internal security problems, the choices of failed and transitional society choices are limited. Traditional deterrence approaches to crime have not worked. Imposing heavier sentences simply fills the jails to over-capacity. Existing paramilitary policing agencies have little legitimacy and are often underpaid and corrupt as well as grossly inefficient. The criminal justice system can do little more than furnish short-term relief through strategies of mass arrests, incarceration and incapacitation. Orthodox crime prevention practices have been largely unsuccessful.

In transitional and failed societies, as well as in the decaying urban metropolises of the West, community policing is portrayed as the only alternative. COP has become the antidote. Where, as in several recent African studies (for example, Hills 2000), state policing is viewed as maintaining a narrowly conceived public order on behalf of dominant elites, a dramatic shift in police models is regarded as the only alternative. Community policing is popular by default. There appears to be no alternative for societies under popular and international invest-ment pressure. In its many guises, COP is the band-aid plaster for local crime crises and for replacing corrupt, dysfunctional paramilitary policing. Community policing has been largely introduced as an antidote to crime problems, together with a fatalistic view that history requires an inexorable path of police reform. But it is often difficult to relate the official intentions of many of these schemes to their practical reality.

Preliminary doubts about COP

It is important in this introductory chapter to raise some homegrown caveats (anticipating the discussion in Chapter 3). Why is there a near-universal concern for police forces internationally to adopt community policing practices? That question is especially high on the agenda given the emerging criticisms in its countries of origin. While some of these critics make uneasy political bedfellows, they appear to have a point. As Skogan and Hartnett (1997) suggest, in their pathbreaking study of COP in Chicago, of the previous 11 experimental COP projects in six cities across the United States, only one survived. Take the detailed denunciation by the right-wing American Heritage Foundation in its allegations of the failure of community policing in the United States. Heritage called for the termination of the COP development in the United States primarily because it had failed to alleviate the victimization of communities that suffered most from violent crime and because its commitment to beat policing was an ineffective way to 'fight crime'[31].

Supporters of COP justifiably respond that the Heritage Foundation misrepresents some of the goals of COP and wrongly attributes to it strategies such as beat patrolling, which all enthusiasts might not accept as a necessary feature of community policing. Indeed, there are evaluations of specific localised community policing strategies such as targeted problem-solving policing that have been evidently effective. There are less partisan criticisms of COP than those that emerge from the Heritage Foundation.

But Heritage does have a point – especially given the millions of dollars in aid packages of community policing in failed and transitional societies. It is also curious that agencies with markedly contrasting politics – as in Kerala, in Eastern bloc countries, and Human Rights groups in Los Angeles (California Association of Human Rights Organisations 1999) – should reject community policing because they equate it with 'community spying'. That latter view may either be a perception of the community police as part of a larger state apparatus of control – or simply a civil libertarian theme that some aspects of civil society should remain private from state policing. There are some civil affairs in which the police presence may be a novel and unwanted intrusion. Further,

> ... 'what works' in community policing is relegated to a few initiatives highlighted in a few, selected cities across the country.

The vast bulk of the literature on community-oriented policing is anecdotal and more apt to read like propaganda.

(Taylor, Fritsch and Caeti 1998, p. 2)

Outline of the text

This text explores some of those features: from the initial promises of COP to its success and failures; from its sources in Anglo-American societies and in South Asia; and to its transplantation to more dependent societies. In this introductory chapter, we have illustrated some of the more idiosyncratic implants that have followed the international mushrooming of community policing. As a new policing creed, it is appearing haphazardly in the most unexpected jurisdictions. A combination of missionary zeal and local desperation for new solutions to a perceived policing crisis has determined COP as an antidote.

Part One considers the orthodox approaches to community policing – from Anglo-American societies and from Asia. Chapter 2 documents the conventional wisdom regarding community policing in the West. It relates, largely uncritically, its development as a break with traditional notions of crime-fighting, its assumed history, the varied schemes that can be located under the community policing rubric, and the developments of problem-solving. The chapter represents a beginner's guide to community policing orthodoxy. Chapter 3 deals with the conventional criticisms of COP in the West. It reveals the mythologies with which COP is imbued – the importance of discretion in problem-solving; its universal relevance; the problems of COP police discourse; its reliance on a particular reading of police history; the problems of relating to informal community methods of social control; the evidence over effectiveness; its assumptions that organizational resistance is due to aberrational factors rather than systemic; and its lack of sensitivity to its own insularity.

Chapter 4 considers quite different community policing models from the Pacific Rim. The koban system of Japan is widely recognised as a community policing system with quite different origins from that of the West. Singapore's current Neighbourhood Police Post (NPP) system has origins in the koban but has developed its own momentum and character. Less familiar is the indigenous Chinese system which draws on both Confucian philosophy and on Maoist doctrine, suggesting a quite different notion of community policing. Chapter 5 reverts to Europe. In Western Europe, policing systems quite different from the Anglo-American model, with major local variations, have been the core of legal order. Often state rather than locally-centred, with a primary view of the police function as safeguarding the state, reactions to Anglo-American COP have varied considerably. The chapter focuses on the importance of proximity policing and of local safety contracts, *inter alia*, comparing the Dutch interpretation of COP with that of countries with a markedly different Code Napoleon inheritance.

Part Two deals with the export of community policing to transitional and failed societies. South Africa, the subject of Chapter 6, presents a major case study of the attempt to transplant Western COP to a transitional society. Western zeal to export that model initially encountered local enthusiasm to import Western-style policing as part of a larger democratization project. The current view is that that implantation process has failed dramatically. Chapter 7 deals with more limited case studies of COP in transitional societies. Drawing on a range of materials, the chapter examines the apparent failure of those initiatives in nation states from Africa to the Asian sub-continent to Latin America. There are few success stories of community policing export and import. The succeeding chapter, 8, deals with COP transplant attempts in failed societies. While the major such effort has been in Poland, there are now many examples of the way instant COP solutions have been encouraged in the nations of Eastern and South-Eastern Europe. Again the evidence is of a general lack of success. COP is an alien creed even if adapted as in Poland into an older mythology. Chapter 9 returns closer to home. The relatively minute statelet of Northern Ireland is a unique case, where community policing has been represented as a solution, not to a crime crisis, but to a problem of sectarian policing. Like South Africa, it has enjoyed a major input by key community policing advocates. Unlike South Africa, the judgement over the success or failure of community policing remains on hold.

Finally, Chapter 10 considers the major dilemmas of COP highlighted throughout this text and wider concerns with democratic policing. Human Rights groups have emphasised progress through community policing as an arena for dealing with police partisanship. Such an emphasis may have contradicted alternative civil society demands for police to combat rising crime. Further, police structure and practices cannot be divorced from the social inequality inherent in policing – in mode of deployment, in choice of target and in criminalization. All societies, to varying extents, are characterized by a social history of policing directed against the poor. Policing has traditionally been targeted against those with least power and police resources, and often the same groups who perversely have the most need for policing services. Many community policing transplants have been targeted without reference to social context. How does one adapt Anglo-American notions to contexts in which they represent an alien breed, where the police are not so much a problem as irrelevant to the majority of the population (Hills 2000), and where there is minimal social capital with which to develop constructive police/community relations (Mendes 2004)? The chapter discusses these contradictions in unravelling the essential problematic nature of a community policing philosophy.

Inevitably, this study is both methodologically partial and partisan. It is partial in that it cannot do adequate justice to the vast wealth of targeted community policing schemes (although that notion may itself embody a deep contradiction) – such as in relation to drugs and house-hold abuse – which have mushroomed in recent years. Nor can it deal with all the major contributions to the debate about community policing that have been engaged in by scholars and police practitioners in the range of English-speaking countries. It also draws on a range of data of varying quality – does one newspaper report from Bangalore equal an official state police report on the same city for veracity on the truth of community policing in that province? A healthy scepticism, born of long experience, is directed at official accounts of the successes and wonders of community policing. The text is partisan in that in the post-modern age, it perceives the intrusions of state police authorities in civil society with a residual suspicion, born of universal scholarship on the history of state police institutions.

> Research on community policing, for the most part, is very heavily weighted toward the reporting of 'success stories' and seldom entails a reporting of lessons learned from failed efforts.
>
> (Lyons 1999, p. 89)

Finally, the text is selective but representative in its referencing. It cannot however do justice to the vast number of studies of community policing now available.

Notes

1 For a detailed summary of US evaluations of problem-solving policing, see http://www.popcenter.org/Responses/response-crackdowns_appendixb_summary.htm.
2 See the debate on tiered policing in Brodeur (1983), Brogden (1998), Johnston (2003), and Blair (2003).
3 See, amongst many others, Brogden (1987) and the collections in Anderson and Killingray (1991, 1992).

4 See Chapter 10.

5 Of the limited literature on this topic, Call's (2003) paper represents by far the most sophisticated analysis. Considered criticisms of the implantation of COP in transitional societies are now belatedly appearing. See, for example, N. Henderson, K. Davis, and C. Merrick, Community Policing: Variations on the Western Model in Developing Societies' *Police Practice and Research*, 4, National Institute of Justice, 2004. The most thoughtful recent and wide-ranging analysis of such police reforms appears in H. Groenewald and G. Peake *Police Reform through Community-Based Policing: Philosophy and Guidelines for Implementation* Seminar hosted by the International Peace Academy and Saferworld, New York, September 2004. The central problems with such new analyses is that they take COP as an unquestionable 'good' and fail to recognise its inherent problems in the countries of origin, before considering its development elsewhere. Further, many transitional societies seem to assume that the curious zero tolerance model of COP in New York is the standard to follow.

6 Intelligence No 375 27 2000.

7 www.parliament.the-stationery-office.co.uk/pa/cm200001/cmselect/cmfaff/318/... British-Bulgarian policing projects seem to have an infinite trajectory. See, for example, the earlier British police commitment in Bulgaria, Department of International Development Project, No 265-542-083, 1996.

8 Official Release, 30 November 2002.

9 See, for example, the conference on 'The Role of Community Policing in Building Confidence in Minority Communities' OSCE, Supplementary Human Dimension Meeting, Final Report, Vienna 28-29 October 2002.

10 International Crisis Group March 2003.

11 www.acdi-cida.gc.ca/cida_i.../fd80c1db1cc7dd7a1

12 See, in detail, Ruteere and Pommerolle (2003) and for a recent similar argument on Hong Kong in Lau (2004).

13 See the similar example of Community Patrol Services, Inc of Ontario http://strategis.ic.gc.ca/ccc

14 The Soros Institute, which financed a community policing initiative in Mongolia, claimed a success for the project within 12 months. That claim is very curious. See 'Interview with COLPI Director Arie Bloed' *Focus Newsletter*, 12 February 2002.

15 OSCE Press Release, 13 October 2002.

16 See the comments on the OSCE training programme reported at http://lists.partners.intl.net/pipermail/civilsoc/2003-July/001330.html

17 For example in Guatemala, attempts to implant COP from the United States were arbitrarily superseded by Spanish commitment to a radically different model based on the militarised Spanish Civil Guards. 70 ICHR 2002.

18 February 2000.

19 Community Police Development Centre Customizing Police Services 2001.

20 Singapore Conference on The Koban System of Japan and its Adaptation as the Neighbourhood Police Post System in Singapore, September 1999.

21 *CPRSI Newsletter*, April 1996 Vol. 2 No. 2.
22 UK Department for International Development (DFID), Community Police in Nepal, S. Males, 2000. Bizarrely, the British DFID has recently committed itself to the development of COP in war-torn Southern Sudan, as part of a larger police aid package.
23 *COLPI Newsletter*, Spring 2001, 4,1.
24 ibid. It is clearly difficult to assess claims such as this from COLPI. But no matter what the reputation of the Institute behind them, they lend themselves to considerable incredulity – how does a brief visit by a few non-specialist RUC officers almost spontaneously transform the Soviet-inherited Mongolian police? Marenin makes the important point that this evaluation – like many more local COP evaluations – was an evaluation of a *process* rather than of a *result* (private communication).
25 'Major Caballero wants to introduce the bobby-on-the-beat – community policing to Rio de Janeiro' *BBC Correspondent*, 11 January 2001. For a critical report of the use of COP in Rio see also www.BBC-news.bbc.c.uk/hi/englishj.adiovideo/programmesCorrespondentne.../1312855.st
26 WOLA, Public Security Program (2000).
27 See Chapters 6 and 7.
28 Maryland police chief quoted in ibid.
29 Inspector Jane Hunter quoted in *Financial Times*, 10 July 2001.
30 See Chapter 6.
31 S. 754 in A.M. Antionelli and P.B. Sperry (eds.) *A Budget for America Heritage Foundation*, 2001.

Part I

Community Policing – Models and Critiques

... a growing body of research has offered remedies ... under the umbrella of the term 'community policing'.... However, much of this literature is coming from the Anglo-Saxon world, which usually takes the London Metropolitan Police created by Peel in 1829 as a common point of reference. The fact that police forces in the English-speaking world are organised along similar legal and structural principles (such as a high degree of discretion granted to individual officers and a certain level of decentralisation) has almost obscured the fact that many other policing systems that do not necessarily share these features have been in existence for a much longer period of time.

(Dupont 2002, p. 1)

Chapter 2

Community-oriented policing: the Anglo-American model

Introduction

In this chapter we outline the basic premises of community policing as it appears in the myriad offshoots in Anglo-American societies. The first part of the chapter explores the reasons for the movement towards community police, especially the apparent failure of traditional 'crime-fighting' policing. It summarises the key reasons why advocates have promoted a new approach to policing in the modern state on the basis of the apparent failure of that traditional policing. The second part outlines the key themes and variations with the continuing promises as it extends internationally.

Searching for a definition of community policing is a will-of-the-wisp. That endeavour offers little prospect of finding a concept of universal applicability. Instead, as a preliminary, we use five general propositions as the central guidelines of community policing.

- Neighbourhoods or small communities serve as primary foci of police organization and operations.

- Communities have unique and distinctive policing problems that conventional police organizations and responses have not traditionally addressed.

- Community consensus and structures should guide police response to the community's crime and security problems.

- Policing should be both locally accountable and transparent.

- Police discretion is a fact and should be used positively to maximize community confidence in the police.

The development of these propositions has a long and convoluted history. But their articulation owes much to the contribution of Robert Trojanowicz[1]. They also depend upon the conjuncture in police development when finally it was appreciated that traditional modes of crime-fighting had simply failed. But central to the development of the community policing ideas is Goldstein's heuristic article on police discretion. Whilst many other authors have noted that in common law countries police officers have considerable latitude about whether or not to enforce the law, Goldstein (1960) shifted the emphasis in policing away from the negative – when not to enforce the law – but rather to the positive discretionary extra-legal resources in solving problems of public order facing the police officer, of which crime may simply be a surface manifestation. After discussion of these preliminary arguments and evidence we proceed in this chapter to distinguish between the principles and varied practices of *community oriented policing,* and the rather more specific character of *problem oriented policing* (POP).

Community policing – orthodox origins

Community policing ideology draws on both a *golden age* history – that sometime in the past the relationship between police and citizens was harmonious, and also on a *golden isles* view, that somewhere in the modern world, policing works well. In the first instance, the Anglo-American version of COP rests on the notion of the Tythingman of Saxon England and (in some accounts) the development of the professional police by Sir Robert Peel in 1829. In Japan, a similar ideology draws on the history of the koban, especially during its development by the Meiji regime in the middle of the nineteenth century. Golden isles justifications – it is greener on the other side of the fence – depend on where you are. Anglo-American tradition refers to the koban itself. Japanese society was viewed until recently at the epitome of community policing by consent. To former colonial societies, the West generally represents the context in which community policing works. Much of this text is devoted to unravelling these golden age and golden isles myths both in their countries of origin and especially in their use in failed and transitional societies. In this section, we are concerned with a formal account of the first theme as seen from the point of view of many Western police scholars and police officers.

A Peelite history

A tradition which stems from the development of the London Metropolitan Police by Sir Robert Peel in 1829 contains two central propositions, which sometime become confused. One theme is that it represented the *ideal of policing by consent*. Much has been written about this claim. The general view amongst police scholars (see Brogden 1982) is that that orthodox view seriously underrated the degree of opposition to the New Police. However, much of the present argument for the development of community policing appears to seek the return of that notional golden age. If that community consent did *not* exist in the way that it is sometimes portrayed, the misrepresentation of the past has negative implications for the attempt to legitimize community policing today – by reference to that Utopian situation.

Peelian tradition regarded policing as a practice by *citizens-in-uniform* and emphasized the *local community contact*. Much earlier English police history (some 800 years ago) is often cited as the source of good community policing practice. In that history, the origins of English policing lay in a particular functionary – the Tythingman (literally one who collects tithes, taxes). The latter was considered to be the original community constable. He was considered an equal amongst equals by his fellow citizens, and elected by them to serve as the policing (and taxing) officer for the district for a fixed period[2].

Critically, the only policing powers the Tythingman possessed were English common law powers of arrest and prosecution – i.e. the powers of every other citizen. As a citizen, *he* had the power both to arrest a perceived wrongdoer and also to take that person to court and to prosecute him. Thus the invention of community policing in English-speaking countries embellished this notion that the police officer was simply a local citizen-in-uniform, accountable to his fellows and conditionally appointed by them to arrest and to prosecute felons using citizen powers. The only difference between that first police officer and his fellows was that he was tasked directly with the major responsibility for arresting and prosecuting suspected persons. Police power stems from the community and only by intensifying that community interaction and obligation through the Tythingman precedent, can police legitimacy be sustained. The new Community Police Officer is seen in many Western police circles as the modern day reincarnation of the Tythingman.

The other historical source of community policing lies in the history of policing in the United States[3]. In this account, policing arose in colonial America from two sources – partly from the imported English system and partly from the immediate exigencies of the new independent states as a frontier society. Small towns in the post-colonial era slowly appreciated a need for law and order in the absence of a directive central state. Groups of citizens consequently developed forms of self-policing of their sovereign communities, and appointed certain of their fellows, accountable directly to them, to conduct such functions.

Recent origins

Recent development in community policing can be traced back to the early 1970s in the USA in debates over the effectiveness of traditional policing when the attention of scholars and practitioners alike questioned the proper role of the police in a democratic society (Zhao, Lovrich and Thurman 1995), especially after police failure in the American city riots of the 1960s and early seventies. Policing underwent a period of substantial self-assessment that left practitioners with a loss of confidence in traditional policing methods. Rising crime rates and widespread social disorder seemed beyond the ability of law enforcement to control.

Certain of the impetus for reform came from revelations in research and public inquiries on corruption, discrimination and violence. But there was also a limited reform movement arguing for a more socially responsive police. Research data had revealed that most police work comprised helping people rather than being concerned strictly with law enforcement (Punch 1977). Thirdly, this was succeeded by a debate informed by scholars such as Goldstein (1960) and Skolnick (1966) over police-citizen relations (from police discretion to police brutality), culminating in questions about the distinguishing features of community policing and whether or not community policing represented something real or merely a change in rhetoric (Mastrofski 1988). Scholars favourable to community policing reform referred to it as a 'quiet revolution in policing' (Trojanowicz and Bucqueroux, 1990).

Pragmatists argued that the specific nature of police work and the subculture surrounding it made it exceedingly difficult, if not impossible, to change (Manning 1988).

The failure of traditional policing – a conventional view

It was argued that community policing development was a reaction to perceived failures in traditional policing. In Western countries in the 1970s and 1980s, it was increasingly recognized that the normal practices of policing had 'failed to deliver the goods'. Police paymasters, practitioners, and academics believed that the time had come to alter their policies and practices. These reasons are rooted in the history of policing and of police research, during the last quarter of a century, in the changing nature of communities (especially with regard to apparent increases in social and ethnic divisions), and in the varying characteristics of crime and violence that affect those communities. In part, policing strategies that may have worked in the past no longer appeared effective.

Despite innovations in technology, in forms of organization, and in police training, recorded crime rates continued to rise independently of the increased costs of the modern police agencies. Police scholars, researchers and managers sought to find an alternative to simply 'doing more of the same' – to improving existing tactics. Politicians facing electoral challenge and disgruntled populations wanted answers to the appearance of 'law and order' problems on national political agendas. It appeared time to re-think the whole purpose of policing.

The research evidence

Proponents of community policing claim that traditional policing, with its emphasis on reactive crime fighting, has failed. For most police departments in the West, police work amounted to routine patrol, to emergency response, and to crime investigations. *Crime-fighting* was the simple focus of operations. All police strategies and operations, forms of organization, tactical deployments and specializations, rhetorically focused on the metaphorical 'war against crime'. Whatever technical improvements appeared in those crime-combating agencies, policing increasingly appeared unable to achieve that goal.

Box 2.1 *Key features of crime-fighting or traditional policing*

Crime fighting or traditional policing include the following features:
a. randomized two-person motorized patrols as the major uniformed police tactic;
b. reactive rather than preventative crime procedures – the emphasis upon fast response times;
c. minor infractions such as prostitution regarded as crime rather than as social problems while the major social problems are ignored;
d. criminal investigations given the highest status and work in communities is often given the lowest;
e. significant reliance on technology such as computerized investigations – contact with the public is often by electronic means rather than face to face;
f. a centralized command structure with little discretion for the rank and file.

Community policing innovations, in part, derived from key lessons learnt from that research. Policing scholars have furnished a devastating critique of the traditional crime-fighting model of policing:

- Doing more of the same does not have any measurable effect on the crime levels. Crime-fighting in traditional ways has finite possibilities. Simply increasing police budgets is unlikely to have any measurable effect on the volume of reported crime and in police drives against it.

- Car patrols have little effect on crime or on arrests. Randomized police patrol does not solve crime nor improve the prospect of catching suspects. Saturating areas with patrols cars at best simply displaces crime. Regular car patrols and speeding up their response to reported crimes does not result in more arrests or in more victim sanctions. Motorized patrols become too self-contained and remote, neither reassuring citizens enough to reduce their fear of crime nor engendering trust. Two-person patrol cars are no more effective at catching criminals (and indeed may actually generate more complaints against the police than do one-person cars).

- The majority of calls for police assistance are unrelated to serious crime. Perhaps quality of life issues rather than crime should be the new rationale for policing.

- The police already *deliver* a range of necessary social services. They may be a secret social service – open 24 hours a day to deal with social problems such as drunks needing attention, the homeless bereft on the city streets, and crimes of private space such as domestic disputes which may sometimes result in serious violence. Rather than these functions being a digression from the main police task of crime fighting, perhaps they should become more central.

- Police crime-fighting depended upon public support for information. A police officer stranded in the mobile response vehicle has little day-to-day contact with that public. Technology increased the distance between police and public and hindered necessary community contact. Detective work solves few crimes. Most crimes cleared up depended on information obtained by foot patrol officers – either directly from their own observation and street knowledge, or more commonly, from their daily interpersonal contact with the public. Good community relations are crucial for the flow of information allowing criminal investigation officers to be effective.

- A concern with the *fear of crime* may often be more of a problem than crime *itself.* Many people, rightly or wrongly, are so afraid of the potential of criminal depredations against them that they are unwilling to conduct their normal activities. Locks and safety measures imprison residents in their own homes. A crime-fighting police has enhanced this frequently unjustified fear. Fear of crime undermines neighbourhood cohesion and leads to the deterioration of social life in such communities.

- Foot patrol has the particular virtue not just of ensuring contact and cooperation from the public but also in reassuring the people and enhancing their quality of life, while such patrols may have little direct impact on crime and on arresting offenders. The visible patrol officer is more likely to contribute to reducing the fear of crime than the occasional sighting of a mobile response unit. While the research is contradictory on this finding, many researchers believe that whether or not foot patrol actually increases community safety, many residents actually believe that to be the case. A highly visible and accessible police presence may help reduce fear of crime within the community.

- Dealing with crime is an inter-agency problem rather than simply the prerogative of the police. Research showed that crime fear (with consequences for community quality of life) was linked to environmental conditions and to social cohesion. Dilapidated buildings, badly-lit streets, and lack of leisure space for young people, might all contribute to a general and often unjustified fear. Improving such conditions and facilities is often beyond the powers and resources of a local police organization. Only by working with other agencies, recognising them as co-partners in the production of personal security (Shearing 2003) rather than independently, could the police lessen community fears. Community policing provides the ideal rubric under which necessary inter-agency co-operation could evolve.

• Local knowledge was a neglected resource in policing. It was needed to specify and prioritise security needs, to diagnose problems, to implement remedies and to render justice in acceptable terms (Bayley and Shearing 2001).

In sum, the traditional way that police agencies dealt with crime neither reduced crime nor reassured the public. Traditional policing was reactive to crime rather than preventative. It was often ineffective at catching criminals. It failed to inspire the public, to obtain legitimacy and public support. In the 1980s the police in Western societies increasingly devoted more and more resources to traditional, bureaucratically safe, crime-fighting approaches that no longer worked – if they ever did (Bayley 1994). Reordering police tasks and procedures was the only possibility of making an effective impact on crime, and on public fear of crime.

Police discretion and community policing

Police discretion has been a major contribution to the mandate of community policing. It is impossible to enforce all laws all the time. Police officers always make choices and use their discretion. COP takes advantage of police discretionary powers to enable them to conduct a variety of tasks that were previously not regarded as falling within the orbit of traditional police work.

As we note above, there has long been a contradiction within the police officer's position in law – his/her discretionary powers – in common law countries. This recognition was a key ingredient in the development of COP. In common law countries, where the rules of public order were developed from local social mores and norms rather than being defined and written in a constitution by a central state, police officers' authority derived from the rights of citizens to exercise *original* powers of arrest and prosecution. For example, before the development of an organised police, under the Anglo-Saxon law of England if their property had been stolen citizens had a right to pursue the offenders (perhaps using the further power of the *hue and cry*, that required other citizens to join the pursuit), to arrest the felon and to prosecute him or her. It was their legal right to arrest the suspects and to take them to court and subsequently to prosecute them.

The only caveat against such action was that the citizens could be liable for damages if they carried out that arrest and prosecution powers vicariously – that being in full knowledge that the pursued had *not* carried out the theft, they wrongfully invoked the law. Much later when organized police were formed – classically in Ireland with the formation of the Dublin City Police in 1786 and the Metropolitan Police in 1829 – the governments of the day did not issue new instructions detailing the specific powers of individual police officers. The latter simply assumed the powers of ordinary people – that is citizens' powers. When an officer arrested someone and took him or her to court, he (they were all male) simply operated with the enabling powers and discretion of a citizen – a citizen-in-uniform – rather than the statutory powers laid down by the state. Like the citizen, the police officer was not required by law to pursue, to arrest and to prosecute. Discretion in beat practice was crucial. No citizen was required to pursue a suspect (unless, of course, the hue and cry power was invoked). Though much has changed since those days with regard to differences between citizen powers and police powers in common law countries (especially with more compulsion being built into the police arrest powers and responsibilities), police officers, like citizens, could exercise discretion in that process.

Much more recently, this discretion was built into the conduct of police forces generally (in the forms of requirements to the chief police officer in the organization to use his discretion) in England and Wales. In the much cited judgment by Lord Denning in the case of *Blackburn* v. *The Metropolitan Police Commissioner*[4], the judge decided in a major and binding precedent that police officers were of course required to enforce the law – that is to arrest and prosecute presumed malefactors. However, the judge recognized that total implementation was impossible – it is quite beyond the resource of a finite police organization to prosecute all the laws all the time. As long as there was no policy of ignoring particular laws all the time, police officers were to act selectively in their enforcement practice – they were in fact required – as in the common law practice of their duties to use their discretion[5].

Denial of discretion is a denial of the self-evident. The police officer is required to decide on what occasions he/she should use these powers for two major reasons.

What crimes an officer will be in a position to act upon depends upon where the officer is and what he is looking for, and this involves discretion. Second, if the officer comes upon a minor matter that is criminal, he has to decide whether it is worth his time, and the time of prosecutors and judicial officials, to process the matter.

(Heymann 2000, p. 154)

Two studies emphasized the importance of discretion in the trajectory towards community policing. Skolnick (1966) noted that imposing the rule of law – making sure that all laws are imposed at all times – is often a policing goal that may be incompatible with a second objective, that of maintaining public order. Bars that stay open too late in a city precinct may be ignored by patrol officers concerned with the impact of disorder if they were closed arbitrarily. Drunks on the street may be a nuisance but may also constitute little threat to public wellbeing and safety. Police officers regularly and legally use their discretion to 'turn a blind eye' because enforcing every minor piece of legislation (were it possible) could actually result in more disorder and law-breaking rather than less. Law enforcement and a commitment to public order may often be contradictory bedfellows.

Further, in a series of articles, Goldstein (1960) argued that the traditional negative view of police discretion failed to recognize its positive features. Discretion was an advantage in policing not an aberration. Police officers armed with professional knowledge rather than with limited legal rules could often provide better community-supported results. Policies which recognized the virtues of police discretion rather than its negative aspects actually enhanced police job satisfaction (and morale) in encouraging creativity in task performance. If police officers were simply automatons, conducting machine-like law enforcement, the job would be reduced to a mechanistic one that required no creativity, no imagination, and no application of professional skills. In other words, using discretion would make more use of police officers' professionalism – deciding what was important and what was not, and determining between the occasionally incompatible goals of law enforcement and order maintenance. It would make the function of the officers more creative and therefore also more satisfying.

These several elements – use of common law powers creatively, the recognized contradiction between order and law enforcement, and the contribution of discretion to more successful policing and to job satisfaction – paved the way for the community policing innovations. In particular, Trojanowicz and Bucqueroux (1990) drew heavily on Goldstein's analysis of police discretion, in contrasting the crime-fighting model with the new vision of community policing (see Box 2.2).

Box 2.2 *Differences between traditional policing and community policing*[6]

Traditional policing	Community policing
Reactive to incidents	Proactive in solving community related problems
Roles of police officers are limited to incident response	Roles of police officers are broadened to include identification and solving of problems
Focus of internal resources	Leverage on community resources.
Limited linkages with the community	Police work with extensive links with the community
Random patrols in cars to respond to crime	Visible patrols to interact with the community, i.e. foot patrols and bicycle patrols
Information from the community is limited	Information from the community comes from many sources
Organization is control-oriented, authoritative style or command and control style	Decentralization of authority and autonomy given to front-line officers
Rewards based on solving cases	Performance evaluation rewards based on service activities, crime prevention, satisfaction and sense of safety of the community

Problem-oriented policing

Apart from his pathbreaking work on police discretion, Goldstein is also credited with the development of what has become known as problem oriented policing (POP). Confusingly, problem oriented policing is often seen as identical with community policing. But they can mean different things.

Goldstein suggested that *problem resolution*, rather than reactive crime-fighting, constituted the true, substantive work of policing. He advocated that the police identify and address the root causes of problems that lead to repeat calls for service – calling for progress from the *crime fighting, reactive, incident oriented, tradition* to one that *actively addressed the problems that underlay the incidents*. The theory behind problem oriented policing is simple. Underlying conditions create problems which, if neglected, may give rise to crimes and to other undesirable consequences. These conditions might include the characteristics of the people involved (offenders, potential victims, and others), the social setting in which these people interact, the physical environments and the way the public reacts. A problem created in this way may generate one or more incidents. These latter, while stemming from a common source, may appear to be different. For example, social and physical conditions in a deteriorating apartment complex may generate burglaries, acts of vandalism, intimidation of pedestrians by rowdy teenagers and other incidents. These incidents, which come to police attention, are symptoms of the wider problems and will continue so long as the problem that creates them persists. By concentrating on *post facto* crimes, police lose their grip on possible solutions. They misuse resources and lose out in effectiveness. Prevention not reaction is the road to effectiveness. Concentrating on problems rather than on crime *per se*, the police become proactive rather than reactive. The objective of policing in enhancing security and order does not change but is pursued through dealing with underlying problems.

There are two key aspects to Goldstein's argument on the development of problem-solving policing.

First, making positive use of police discretion also involves appreciating that police officers often use other resources to maintain social order than simply resorting to legal powers. Police officers endowed with good common sense or learned ways of 'getting the job done' (the 'recipe book' of policing – Chan 1997) are often much more effective at dealing with community quality of life problems than are those who 'live by the book'. Professional police officers do not just bring to an incident knowledge of the law. They also draw on a variety of other information – such as where to shelter homeless persons on the streets at night, who can most effectively deal with the inebriated citizen (locking him or her up rarely benefits police, public, or drunk), and which agency can be called on to board-up a decaying property used by drug abusers. Problem-solving policing seeks to make use of the officer's varied skills and knowledge, not simply his/her rote learning of the criminal law.

Goldstein also argued that most people approach the police when they want a *problem solved* rather than a *perceived offender detained*. For example, noisy youths on a street corner at night might yield to arrest. But most people would rather that they vented their energy in a place that would not disturb others, than be arrested. The problem constructed by the community in this case is noise and disturbance, not crime. Goldstein proposed that police officers should approach such incidents as 'problems to be solved' rather than as potential crimes. In doing so, they would both gain public approval as well as providing a potential cure for the problem – in the example above furnishing an alternative recreational venue for the youths, rather than exacerbating it by conferring on them a criminal record.

Box 2.3 *Principles of problem-solving policing*

The problem-solving process can include:
i   *eliminating the problem entirely* – arresting, prosecuting and detaining a serial criminal;
ii *reducing the number of occurrences of the problem* – advising schoolchildren on avoiding talking to strangers;
iii *reducing the degree of injury per incident* – perhaps by ensuring that residents are advised on ways of utilizing crime prevention methods such as safety glass on exposed windows;
iv *improving problem-handling* – where the officer might familiarize him or herself with the range of agencies available to cater for citizens incapacitated by illness or inebriation;
v   *manipulating environmental factors to discourage criminal behaviour* – persuading the city authorities to place street lighting in a dark civilian underpass where citizens may feel threatened;
vi *mediation* – acting as an arbitrator between   local disputants – for example, between commuters who wish to park their cars in an inner city street and residents who wish to maintain the area as a place for their children to play safely.

Clearly, such an approach means elevating police discretion in choosing between alternative knowledge resources. Goldstein recognized that such discretion could be misused if influenced by the negative aspects of police culture. His response was to argue for greater police professionalisation so that that discretion could be influenced by professional codes of conduct rather than simply by the police culture (or the dictates of senior officers).

Box 2.4 *An historical approach to problem-solving policing*

[Police] officers are fast learning that dealing with criminals after the evil habits have been formed is a hopeless task as far as the eradication, or even the lessening of crime is concerned. If he would serve his community by reducing crime he must go up the stream a little further and dam it up at its source, and not wait until it is a rising torrent, uncontrollable and restless. Moreover, if he would succeed in his efforts, he must utilise to the fullest extent every helpful agency in the community such as schools, churches, recreation and juvenile departments, public welfare and employment bureaux, clinics, dispensaries, hospitals and fraternal and labour organisations ...

(Pioneer policewoman Alice Stebbin Wells in
Good Housekeeping, 1911)

The emphasis on *problems* rather than on *means* marks the key difference between problem oriented policing and many practices of community policing. Problem oriented policing defines the police role in terms of the nature of the problems and the range of choices available to resolve them. Consequently, problem oriented tactics are *situation specific* (that is, tailor-made to fit each problem), whereas community policing tactics are *universal* (force-wide general procedures are applied) for a given problem. A problem oriented agency will engage in a search for the information and resources that appears to be most effective at addressing it. A community policing department may apply the same set of tactics to all problems that come to its attention.

Box 2.5 *Problem-solving policing in a transitional society – a Jamaican example*

Take for instance, the traditional calls and response to the crime of robbery at a particular bus or taxi stand. In normal or traditional policing, the way its happened is that e.g. the Hunt's Bay police station gets the call for service, naturally after the crime has been committed. By the time the police officer arrives on the scene, the officer usually does little more than take a report, since the culprits are long gone. We might improve that wasteful situation with the problem oriented approach. A technique like crime-mapping would flag the department to the persistent problems at that particular stand. An officer skilled in problem oriented policing would investigate why that particular stand has so many robberies. He'd likely suggest one basic solution: remove the stand or change to a different location, without really tracking back to see if he had solved the problem. If no robberies were reported for that location, the officer would have reason to believe that the problem had indeed been solved.

(*Gleaner* 28 October 2001)

What community policing and problem-solving policing have in common is that they both require decentralization of police authority to patrol officers and to first line supervisors, and they both place great emphasis on collaboration between police and agencies in the community.

Corporate managerialism and the new policing

In the 1980s and 1990s, like many other state agencies, police organizations were persuaded of the virtues of the new public management (Leishman, Cope and Starie 1997). A new consumerist ideology led to a view of policing as a public service which should take account of the public's views in shaping policies, and treat citizens as clients and consumers. As customers buying a service, the public had a right to expect the police to engage in measurable performance and to be held more accountable for expenditure. The public wants attentiveness, reliability, responsiveness, competence, manners and fairness from the police as part of providing a quality service (Mastrofski 1988). New strategies such as that of 'broken windows'[7] and new technology appeared to demonstrate that the police could record successes in crime-fighting in limited contexts when specific targets were agreed with the public. Coupled with the ideology of consumerism was the belated recognition in police agencies that the public were not just consumers but they could also be victims with victim's rights. Taking account of the public meant appreciating that victims and potential victims had rights to be heard in determining policing goals and practices.

Recognizing victims' rights was also influenced by earlier academic work that pointed out that the police had long been involved in hidden non-confrontational services that (as above) had resulted in some academics labelling them as a 'secret social service'. Managerialism meant elevating non-crime facets of policing into a more total picture of police commitment to the new consumers.

The new managerialism was also informed by a financial imperative which committed all public services to a corporate model of ensuring that public organizations were to be measured in terms of their productivity in ensuring that public expectations could be justified in meeting citizens' goals. Such a financial input was not just a constraint but it could also be enabling in developing community policing. Being in tune with the public mood could mean more resources for policing, for example the strong support of community policing by the Clinton administration, signified by the passage of the Violent Crime Control and Law Enforcement Act in 1994, granting $30 billion over six years as subsidies to cities which constructed community policing[8]. By 2003 some 90,00 extra officers would have been deployed[9]. Financial support, limited in other public corporations, was to be expanded as the police committed themselves to a popular community policing strategy.

New developments were linked with schemes that appeared to offer more effective policing. A 'nothing works' philosophy could be reversed. If crime control was the police *raison d'être*, there were evident failings. In response to this academic finding, new-style mayors and police chiefs, notably Guiliani and Bratton in New York, showed that 'something could be done'. Adopting new policies, which combined so-called 'zero-tolerance' with flexible notions of community policing (Kelling and Coles 1996). 'Broken windows' suggested that police organizations could be reconstructed in 'fighting crime'; and that local policing of nuisances could improve the quality of life in communities. Whatever the real evidence about those results (Bowling 1999) and their mythological origin[10], somehow certain police forces in the USA in the early 1990s seemed to have stumbled on the formula of successfully combining crime control with selectively tackling social problems. Community policing New York-style apparently worked in reducing crime.

This version of COP seemed to tie both ends of the policing spectrum neatly together. You could attack crime and solve problems as part of the same strategy – fighting crime could now be connected to community sensibilities and accountability. Community policing has been marketed as successfully linking crime fighting and crime prevention. In doing so it had built incrementally on a variety of piecemeal initiatives. A variety of watch schemes had emerged. Crime prevention programmes such as education about home security and neighbourhood watch programmes have been accepted virtually universally as has the commitment to and permanent assignment of officers to fixed neighbourhood-level geographic areas (Zhao, Lovrich and Thurman 1995). Corporate ideologies in policing reflected a larger public mood. Community policing was the means by which such a new managerialism could be delivered to a community of consumers.

The key elements of community policing

It will already be evident that there are several different types of community policing. Different police agencies may interpret the concept in different ways. Rank and file police officers, operating within the framework of police culture, may give different weight to its practice than senior management officers. In this section, we need to clarify some of the basic propositions of community policing, the philosophy underlying it.

Central tenets

Community policing differs from traditional policing – what we have referred to as *crime-fighting policing* – in how the community is perceived in relation to the police, how much notice the police should take of local community needs and demands. While crime control and prevention remain important as policing objectives, community policing strategies use a wide variety of methods to address those goals. The ideal represents a synthesis of three components – community partnerships, problem-solving, and commitment to the policing of a limited area.

To develop partnerships, local police are urged to construct positive relationships with the community, to involve the community in the quest for better crime control and prevention, and to pool their resources with those of the community and local agencies to address the most urgent local problems. The partnerships themselves can be loosely located under two headings – consultative forums and watch schemes. Each involves varying direct dialogue between the police and locals, each requires cooperation by both parties. Problem-solving policing is the process through which the key concerns and priorities of communities are identified, and through which the most appropriate remedies to abate these problems are found and brought to bear upon the incidents. Local commitment is essential, including an enhancement of the old beat system in which a police officer was required to deal with problems in a limited geographical area, and to be conversant with the local inhabitants[11].

Nevertheless, community policing remains vaguely articulated in texts such as Trojanowicz and Bucqueroux. It is often described as a philosophy, a body of ideas, rather than a specific plan of action and implementation. As such, it is infused with several different strands of thought. Different policing organizations give more weight to some of these ideas than to others. Bayley (1992) has spelled out most clearly the key themes of community policing from which the following is drawn.

Community policing personalises policing – in the crime-fighting model the police have increasingly become anonymous stereotypes due to the influence of technology and such an emphasis on motor patrols. Community policing reverses this trend.

Community policing permits vital information gathering through face to face contacts – it enhances the quality of crime-fighting through street-level interaction and the information acquired from local people.

Community policing minimizes overreaction – by getting to know communities well, police are much less likely to overreact in encounters with the public, thereby diminishing hostile confrontations.

Community policing allows police officers to target potentially violent people – because community police officers know the local residents well, they are able to identify and isolate potentially violent or troublesome individuals who may be the source of disturbances.

Community policing enhances responsiveness – by establishing regular processes of consultation between local police commanders and communities, police actions can be more carefully aligned with the needs of communities, especially the (previously ignored) more mundane incidents, and intrusive matters (such as domestic disputes).

Community policing symbolizes commitment – the activities involved in consulting, adapting to, and mobilising, show the public that the police care about a community. It is the most effective way for a police agency to obtain public support.

Community policing develops informal social controls – by enlisting citizens in solving general community problems, it allows them to take more responsibility for their own destiny – by encouraging the development of tenants' groups, 'concerned parents' and so on.

Community policing contributes to the quality of the physical environment – by responding to the 'signs of crime' – dumped cars, dangerous abandoned buildings, rubbish-strewn vacant sites, graffiti-painted walls, and broken street lights – not merely do officers inhibit the growth of crime by attending to such details, they also improve the social and physical quality of local life.

Community policing helps to ensure a sense of wider democratic accountability – mobilising other government and voluntary agency resources to enhance the quality of life makes governments appear to be more responsive and accessible.

Community policing positions police to monitor racial and ethnic tensions and mediate conflicts between different local groups.

Variations in community policing

Community policing is the broad sweep of activities which can be conducted by a police service that wishes to develop a community approach to replace its previous crime-fighting mission. Several authors (as above) distinguish between community policing as a philosophy – hence the 'broad brush' approach which characterizes many different schemes – and problem-solving as a practice. However, common to all versions of community policing is the application of a standard set of tactics.

Community policing can operate independently of problem-solving. It is a creature with many different faces, encompassing varied approaches. Part of the confusion about it is that it does not consist of a direct plan for police action but provides an umbrella under which a variety of alternative schemes can flourish. Many different policing practices use the community policing label. O'Connor (2000) in the United States has listed some 40 different styles of police operation that have at various times been referred to as community policing (see Box 2.6).

All the schemes in Box 2.6 are based on the anvil of police and (some) citizen cooperation. While often divergent in practice, giving different emphasis to different aspects of police-community relations, they all operate under the rubric of community policing. From that maze of schemes, it is sometimes very difficult to distinguish what is the essence of community policing and what is simply a local *ad hoc* scheme with an intriguing acronym, and a short 'shelf-life'.

Box 2.6   *Examples of schemes under the community policing heading*

Adopt-a-Cop. Suburban type programmes in which community residents take care to treat their local beat officers like family members.

Beat Commander Systems. A police sergeant is given command of 20 officers including detectives who only investigate crimes in the beat command area, on permanent assignment and closely monitored for satisfaction and efficiency at improving resident satisfaction.

Community Resolution Programmes. Efforts at establishing interagency cooperation and coordination for delinquency prevention and control without relying upon schools, police or courts excessively; liaison and referrals with mental health and others social service agencies.

CPOP – Community Patrol Officers Programme. Use of volunteers or vigilante groups such as Guardian Angels to reduce the fear of crime.

Operation Safe Streets. A 'weed and seed' type programme in which police use undercover tactics to remove undesirable people, and then move in with community organizing and development tactics.

Police Mini-stations. Establishment of decentralized neighbourhood-based precincts in run-down storefronts around the city to guide confused citizens through the maze of municipal government regulations and handle complaints such as about uncollected garbage that requires attention from other agencies.

PACE – Police Assisted Community Enhancement. Refers to any sort of graffiti removal programme where criminal justice employees and citizens work together.

Crime prevention and community policing

While community policing has a wider brief than crime prevention, the latter remains a central feature of policing work. Certainly, in dilapidated housing estates in the West, as in transitional societies, crime prevention is given as its major justification. In the community policing context, crime prevention is regarded as not just a police responsibility but also as an activity that should be conducted in liaison with other agencies and more generally with the public. Bayley notes three key structures in the new COP crime prevention strategies.

Consultation through community forums. These panels are often diverse in composition, some representing geographical communities and other, special interest groups, such as shopkeepers, ethnic minorities, gay people, or those using a particular mode of transport. Generally, these panels serve four functions – they advise the police about local needs and priorities; they help the police educate other citizens about crime and disorder and enlist the cooperation of the public in dealing with those matters; the meetings allow residents to ventilate grievances against the police in face to face interaction and permit the police to respond, unimpeded by bureaucratic rules and practices; and the panels provide information to the police about the relative success of the latters' efforts – a form of community evaluation.

Adaptation, diversity and locality of decision-making. Community policing strategies recognize that crime and social order varies from district to district. Consequently, the police have reshaped command structures to provide appropriate flexibility. Normally, this involves decentralizing the command structures geographically and locating decision making powers and responsibilities much further down the police hierarchy – in effect, flattening the police pyramid of authority and delegating local powers.

Mobilisation. This process involves the development of crime prevention programmes that enlist the active support of the public such as Neighbourhood Watch schemes. They may include also schemes as diverse as marking property with personal identification to aid recovery; evening patrols by civilian youth workers to advise and caution youths who might get into trouble with the police, and counsel them after the event; and the development of inter-agency links as well as with housing departments to deal with vandalised property.

The intention of *crime prevention* problem-solving is to study the conditions that give rise to calls for police services; to draw up plans for remedying those conditions; and to take a lead in evaluating and implementing remedial action.

Box 2.7 *Examples of the problem-solving approach applied to crime prevention*

In Madison, Ohio, shopkeepers complained of mental patients hanging around a shopping mall. The police discovered that the number of the latter was exaggerated and such problem as existed was due to the patients not being advised on appropriate medications. Hence the resolution to promote a solution through Social Services.

In San Diego, the police initiated the removal of an obstructing wall (which concealed the view of an area of crime and robberies) near a trolley park under planning regulations, and replaced it with a transparent barrier which therefore made the trolley park less attractive to potential thieves. Success in such schemes is measured by the situational impact of the problem-solving device of the particular problem, in this case the immediate consequences with regard to theft in the trolley park.

(Bayley 1994).

In practice, very little of the community police officer's time is spent on crime-related work. Studies suggest that traditional crime-related activity occupies only about five per cent of an officer's time – as opposed to approximately a third in traditional crime-fighting policing. Community officers in different forces spend their time in a multitude of ways – organising block watches and tenant associations; conducting community safety campaigns; developing recreation programmes; providing crime prevention newsletters; recontacting victims to advise them about the status of their cases; conducting door-to-door surveys of citizens concerning quality of life issues; identifying and correcting environmental conditions; and assisting in alley cleanups and graffiti removal.

Overview

In this chapter, we have outlined key elements of the orthodox accounts of community oriented policing. COP represents a major attempt to transform traditional crime-fighting policing in several ways, especially in relation to developing community assent to new local policing practices. It seeks to convert the police organization by emphasizing the positive aspects of the discretionary powers of the local constable. In particular, it seeks to replace a reactive style of policing with one that is preventative, especially in its problem oriented aspects, in seeking to deal with the causes rather than the symptoms of social disorder.

There are different approaches and foci which appear in local policing practice. In some countries such as the UK, local forces have tended to discard the totality of COP, instead seeking to emphasise particular skills drawing on that eclectic body of knowledge, such as problem-solving and community beat management. But despite pragmatic adaptations, community policing as a philosophy remains very important because it resonates in several ways with the new 'consuming' public. It appears to represent a connection with the past, when policing was supposedly 'better'. It seeks to make local policing accountable to local citizens, especially to victims and potential victims, as well as to those who pay for police services out of their taxes. In some of its manifestations, such as in the broken windows approach, it appears to offer a more effective way of preventing minor disorder turning into serious crime.

To the vast majority of the public, community policing, devoid of its complexity, and encompassing a variety of schemes from NWS to community forums to police foot patrols, is an undoubted 'good'. That public reaction to COP is often the major driving force for its further development, whatever the reservations of many senior officers and of policing academics. It may be that the advocates of community policing have too cosy an image of the history of police-public relations, which they use to design future practices. Any attempt to revive what we called 'Peelian principles' of community police relations does not allow for the way society has changed in complexity since the time at which Sir Robert Peel wrote – some 180 years ago. In any case, is that notion of community policing really appropriate for a modern and often diverse and socially unequal society? Perhaps the real role of the police was always, and will be in the future, law enforcement based on legal powers – not acting as a kind of uniformed social worker as implicit in COP. It is to these and related issues that we turn in the next chapter before considering the models of community policing outside the Anglo-American sphere.

Notes

1 Trojanowicz's publications on community policing are numerous. Probably the most significant is R. Trojanowicz and B. Bucqueroux (1990).
2 In practice, the Tythingman was often appointed by the local suzerain to enforce the latter's laws on the local community.

3 See Walker (2000) for a critique.

4 See the discussion in Marshall (2004).

5 Although, as Heymann (2000), despite formal disavowals, high levels of police discretion are also evident in countries with a quite different civil legal procedure as in those nation-states whose criminal legislation derives from the Napoleonic Code.

6 Source 'Community policing in the Context of Singapore', 112th International Training Course Visiting Experts' Papers – Jamal Singh 2003.

7 'Broken windows' is commonly assumed to be a community policing strategy – but see Bowling (1999) and Heymann (2000) amongst many others. It is extremely difficult to understand such a process which deliberately seeks confrontation – albeit with a minority – rather than consent from all – as *communal* policing.

8 Some cynics would however suggest that this latter imperative allowed anything to happen in local policing because of the financial gains as long as somehow the rubrics of community policing could be used as the formal facade. COPS funds likely funded the movement towards COOPS in those agencies that were already accelerating their own local programmes rather than cause acceleration in that direction.

9 United States Justice Dept – see www.ojp.usdoj.gov/nij.

10 Kelling, one of the architects of the New York 'miracle' claimed origins of his policy in Sir Robert Peel and the founding of the Metropolitan Police in London in 1829 – see Chapter 3.

11 A curious myth – for evidence on the distance between such patrol officers and the local public in the early twentieth century British police, see Brogden (1991).

Chapter 3

Anglo-American community oriented policing: ten myths

... many of the ideas associated with community policing are largely myths about an imagined and idealized urban lifestyle, urban policing and the power of informal mechanisms of social control in a pluralistic, fragmented society. The nostalgic yearning for the reappearance of the big-hearted cop walking a beat and a return to a simpler age when the police were perceived as supportive and friendly rather than bureaucratic or repressive is based on a highly romanticized view of nineteenth century neighbourhood life that never existed.

(Robin 2000, p. 99)

Studies on the impact of community policing to date show little or no impact on crime, disorder, of fear reduction. What they do show is a positive impact on citizen attitudes towards the police and patrol officer attitudes to their jobs.

(Lyons 1999, p. 51)

Introduction

There is an aphorism in which the English cast aspersions on the Irish: 'When the Englishman in Dublin asks an Irishman the way to Skibbereen, the response is "If I was you, I wouldn't start from where you are now". If you were to design a community oriented policing structure from scratch, you wouldn't start from a blueprint of a paramilitary, hierarchical and often armed organization. Unfortunately, there is no blank sheet of paper. A key problem in a sceptical discussion of community policing is the general overview from Reiner a decade ago with regard to that practice, drawing on mainly British studies – that 'nothing works' (1992).

But too often in academic criticisms, the baby is thrown out with the bathwater – especially in policing studies. Community policing advocates have some responsibility because of the breadth of their claims[1]. A critique of community policing has to retain its undoubted positive elements. In some contexts, when crime is out of control, something must be done. In some locales, community policing, subject to a range of caveats, 'works'. Community policing, with all its warts, cannot be as bad as some of the agencies of state policing in transitional and failed societies. This chapter approaches the critique of COP in a positive manner. While much is flawed, much is also of value.

The community policing model has been criticised for lack of continuity with history (Kappeler 1996), flaws in its parent doctrines (Walker 1999), for serving as a legitimating tactic (Kappeler and Kraska 1998) and for its contradictory assumptions about a notional unitary community's welcome for the police as all-purpose problem solvers (Manning 1988)[2]. Even its assumption that crime-fighting policing has failed is open to challenge – after all the police have always been remarkably successful at solving certain serious crimes – from homicide to armed robbery (Manning 1988). However, we approach COP in a favourable light, dealing with self-criticisms by the advocates and also those which reflect larger concerns with social context and inequalities in power and resources of the client communities.

The ten myths of community policing

Community policing depends upon the qualified acceptance of a number of mythologies about police models and practices in Anglo-American societies. Some of those assumptions are held more strongly than are others. But insofar as they all contribute to the development and practice of COP, the future is bleak.

These mythologies include the following:

- *The myth of the community.* COP's basis is of a local organic community (or one combined by interest) available to be mobilized to liaise with the police to prevent crime and resolve problems of social order.

- *The myth of local accountability.* With the decline of local democratic community controls over the police, COP increases direct community involvement in policing issues. Community forums offer a more direct means of contact and consultation between community and police.

- *The myth of professionally-informed enhanced discretion.* The commitment to problem-solving policing increases police discretion over courses of action and over what resources can be used in that solution. Such discretion is constrained by professional codes.

- *The myth of the universal relevance of community policing.* COP is a flexible tool that can be used to advantage in most communities, independently of social class or of other social divisions.

- *The myths of police rhetoric.* Local crime surveys, in particular, demonstrate officially the general community support for the goals and practice of COP.

- *The myths of police history – Peelite origins, crime control and the technological mistake.* COP returns policing to the original principles of Sir Robert Peel, and his concern with the police as an agency of crime prevention on behalf of all the community. Not merely (as above) is COP a natural development of the original ideas of Peel, it represents the summit of the natural trajectory of policing in industrial societies, a convergence of policing ideas. Unfortunately policing in the past half century has diverged from that vision because it made technological mistakes in distancing itself from the public.

- *The myth of public support for COP.* COP is widely welcomed in the community and meets a ready demand by local people who wish to participate in the policing of their communities.

- *The myth of linking with informal networks of control.* COP allows the police to link with and revive the local informal community structures. It is consequently able to revitalize communities by dealing with the substance rather than with the formal character of community relationships.

- *The myth of organizational change in COP.* While most commentators recognize that the traditional forms of police organization are not conducive to the implementation of COP, such problems are not a major obstacle.

- *The myth of the Anglo-American model – the failure to recognize alternatives.* COP operates with an ethnocentric unilinear trajectory of police development. The initial public order policing gives way to crime-fighting policing which in turn begets community policing. COP is a natural outgrowth of police history.

Box 3.1 *Community policing in practice!*

In the beginning was the word and the word was 'community policing' and darkness fell upon the face of the police force.

And it came to pass that a task force delivered unto the Commissioner a plan and the plan began restructuring and there was much rending of garments and gnashing of teeth among the Constables, for they comprehended it not and were sore afraid.

And the Constables spake unto their Sergeants saying, 'Verily it is a heap of shit and it stinketh!'

And the Sergeants went unto their Superintendents and said, 'Verily, it is a pile of dung and none may abide the odour thereof.'

And the Superintendents spoke unto the Assistant Commissioners saying, 'It is a mound of fertiliser and none can abide its strength.'

And the Assistant Commissioners went unto the Deputy Commissioners and said, 'It is that which promotes plant growth and it is very powerful.'

And the Deputy Commissioners spake unto the Commissioner saying, 'This powerful, new plan will actively promote growth and efficiency within the police force.'

And the Commissioner looked upon it and smiled and saw that it was good. And it came to pass that community policing was implemented.

(quoted from Bayley 1992A)

The myth of the community

Criticizing the community assumptions of COP is an easy Aunt Sally. Few present police scholars and senior officers would argue that organic communities exist as tangible realities with whom the police can liaise and conduct local crime prevention and resolve quality of life issues. Nevertheless, because of its core importance to the philosophy of COP, it is useful to examine the basic community assumptions. It is also important, secondly, to consider the extent to which such a notional community actually created a demand for the strategies implicit in COP.

As a concept, community policing is subject to multiple interpretations as evident in Goldstein's formulation: '… any activity whereby the police develop closer working relations with the community and respond more effectively to citizens' needs and priorities' (1990, p. 23)[3]. Most authorities now clearly acknowledge that the theory of community policing (or philosophy as Bayley would have it) has been used to cover a variety of unrelated procedures and practices. There are remarkably varied uses in the literature – narrowly as proactive consultation between the community and multifunctional patrol officers required to solve local problems of crime and social disorder, to prevent crime, and to reduce the fear of crime; and community policing as a general programme of public-police cooperation to solve crime problems; to service broad community needs, and improve quality of life, with a wide definition of 'legitimate' police work, a decentralised police structure, and an interventionist problem-solving mandate. This lack of clarity is apparent in practitioner literature where it appears variously as: a geographically-based delivery of service through an interactive process between officers and citizens to identify and address crime and noncrime problems and disorder; a strategy of input and participation emphasizing crime prevention, fear of crime, physical and social decay and quality of life; and a philosophical problem solving partnership to address community issues.

In practice, key features of the orthodox model of community policing are often absent from community policing schemes (Ziembo-Vogl and Woods 1996). In that study of police departments in the United States with populations of 50,00 people and over, few of the key elements of the original Trojanowicz model were present. For example, 'identifying community policing as a guiding philosophy' was present in only 18 per cent of the departmental literature. Secondly, one key practice, permanency of beat assignment, was also conspicuously absent in the vast majority of cases.

Not merely is there confusion over the concept but it is difficult to recognize the actual community to which the programme is directed. There is no single community. Only a relatively few areas – from the new gated citadels of the wealthy, to the monoculture suburbs, to a minority of black ghettoes – can be perceived as possessing unitary cultural traits. They may be man-made[4], enjoy natural boundaries such as a river, or based on outdated police beat structures.

Nowadays, the singularity of 'community' has given way to the pluralities of communities: moral communities (religious, ecological, gendered); life style communities (of taste and fashion); communities of commitment (to person and non-person issues); contractual communities (compassed of subscribing consumers); virtual communities (joined together in cyberspace); and so on. Such communities are diverse, overlapping, pragmatic, temporary, and, frequently, divided from one another (Johnston 2000 pp. 54–55). To this list we can add ethnic communities (where race provides a central organising point); socio-economic communities (determined by class interest); and age communities (from the leisure pursuits of young to *inter alia*, the guarded communities of the wealthy elderly).

Community policing rests on the fundamental illusion of *the* community, a concept which mystifies and confuses more than it clarifies. It provides the illusion that something exists. Given that this concept is the core of COP philosophy, reliance on it offers a chimera rather than substance.

As Manning (1988), Klockars (1988) and many other friendly critics question, how can the police define who the community is and determine what community needs are? In most cases, however, urban social order is diverse, representing social and ethnic minorities and majorities, divisions between the young in public space and the elderly cosseted at home, between the gender-stratified territories of males and females, between shopkeepers and small business interest, their employees, the unemployed, and those who use the geographical territory of the supposed communities for particular interests (car parking, shopping and so on). Business people affected by a particular problem in community may not actually live in a fixed geographical area. Community interest groups may not fall into structured neighbourhoods.

In Skogan and Hartnett's (1997) Chicago study, the notion of community, the fundamental concept of COP, was based on the organizational efficiency and timetabling requirements of police beats. The designated areas bore little relation, if any, to 'natural' communities. The beats bisected school catchment areas and were consequently unable to deal with youth-gang delinquency that was school-based. Skogan advocates, as a partial solution, aligning police beats to normative community boundaries. But even that was problematic, frequently ignoring the other crosscutting schisms. Communities in community policing are ephemeral. In practice as well as theoretically, it is often extremely difficult to determine the boundaries and components of the notional community.

Questions over the existence of a community logically prompt further problems for COP. In the orthodox literature, community policing is the epitome of policing by consent. However, in a socially divided society, consent will only be provided by those who regard the police as upholders of their way of life, their standards and their property (Waddington 1999). Policing is only popular with those in the locality who expect to gain from its presence. Normally police action occurs against those marginal elements who have never consented to policing.

Those who are to be policed, whether 'moved on' on the city streets, arrested for minor suspected offences and so on, have already been excluded. If community policing depends on generalized local consent, it cannot work because policing in a coercive enforcement mode is, and always has been, utilised against those in the locality who do not consent to police action. Proponents of community policing often fail to recognize this dichotomy between those locals who support the police and those who do not, and between those who utilize the police as consumers of police services and those who are on the 'hard end' of policing. Many of the latter make little use of police services over the quality of life issues that are the bedrock of support in community policing. For example, if insurance companies are unwilling to insure property in socio-economically depressed areas there is often little point in local residents seeking police assistance in what may simply result in a financial claim for a minor theft. Where COP results in enhanced street policing, there are many groups in society who do not want a continued police patrol presence, which they interpret as harassment. The nature of the demand for police services depends on social class composition, on the age of the neighbourhood and its inhabitants, and on ethnic composition. A blanket COP view that police patrol may reduce citizen fears and increase citizen satisfaction is an over-generalization. In lower class neighbourhoods where police are often present, an increased police presence may not even be noticed.

Not all members of the public want the same police service or visibility. Ethnic minorities and the unemployed may be unaffected by attempts to reduce fear of crime. These groups may have realistic fears which community policing aimed at the fear of crime cannot calm. Further, any increased satisfaction with police response to non-crime incidents may not actually increase satisfaction because the same people are already pleased with police reaction. While community policing reflects a response to a notion that public fear stems from disorder more than from crime, that perception of disorder may be a problem for a section of the population and often unrelated to potential victimisation and crime. Social collectivities are differentially sensitive to local disorder. There is no 'natural' voice of the 'community'. Communities of interest are at best transient[5] and are only important in competition with those who challenge that interest.

The myth of enhanced local accountability

A core criticism of COP relates to the question of accountability

(Waddington 1999). Community policing is rooted in a theory of community rights and responsibilities under which communities have a right to influence police practices. Community policing requires that agency to take a much more proactive, and often leading role in community affairs. In the United States, this notion draws *inter alia* on earlier conceptions of Jeffersonian democracy. But it also derives from contemporary criminological perspectives such as Left Realism. Given the limitations of legal and professional regulation of policing, community activists have advocated local community accountability as an alternative means of addressing problematic police practices. Such a view is emerging at a time when increased centralization by states may be undermining local democracy. In a corporate age, local offenders and victims become consumers and clients of police services, like transport passengers, and supermarket customers are reduced to the banality of the commercial consumer with artificial rights and expectations, rather than a citizen with democratic rights independently of purchasing power (Brogden 1982).

In contrast to the previous reactive centrally-directed policing, COP offers a different kind of local accountability – through structures such as community forums, watch schemes, crime prevention panels, and preventative problem-solving strategies and proposes enhanced police-community partnerships. COP inexorably makes the police more proactive, more interventionist, in community affairs and therefore more dependent upon local cooperation and consent. In formulating these initiatives, police look to the community for broad authorization at the local level. The basic model for the new accountability structure of community policing represents mechanisms by which communities might exert control over the police, with respect to the establishment of policing priorities. The concepts of police accountability and community participation underlying these models ostensibly bolster police legitimacy while reducing tension between minorities and the police. Law becomes less important as legitimizing police authority to be replaced by community consent. Instead, police officers meet with community members not only to learn from their local knowledge about the most pressing problems in the neighbourhood but also to obtain their implicit agreement to act on such problems through enforcement and order-maintenance tactics. As COP allows communities to play a greater role in identifying and setting local police priorities, police and civilians act as partners. This partnership supposedly facilitates a reciprocal understanding that clarifies each party's expectations of the other regarding what policing is appropriate and how problems are to be resolved. Community policing thus allows politics, in the sense of police responsiveness and accountability to the community, to re-emerge as a basis for police legitimacy.

The criticisms of this local Utopian view are direct. In Crawford's (1998) sweeping terms in commenting generally on community safety schemes, community policing does not just ignore or indeed exacerbate issues of conflict, of diversity, and of difference, it also ignores issues of institutional representation, participation and democracy (Mastrofski 1988).

Firstly (as we illustrate in Part Two), the ideal of community accountability and consent remains vulnerable to criticism with respect to interest representation and to the limitations on community participation in critical decision-making. The extent to which community consent legitimizes local policing practices will depend in part on assumptions about community interests and community participation. In practice, the degree to which community involvement in for example Police Community Forums (CPFs) reflects the general community seems minimal. Community participation often mobilizes only a minority of the local population. But the actions and opinions of this small segment may legitimize local police practices for the community as a whole, failing to impose any significant accountability over the police. All the evidence on CPFs is that they tend to reflect only a minority view of the locale, that members increasingly see themselves as acting on behalf of policing interest, and that other minorities as well as some majorities are rarely involved in the forum deliberations. This may result in a greater pressure on the police to align with proactive initiatives from well-organized groups who have their own regulatory agenda. In this scenario, community policing is reduced to an exclusive cooperation deal between a limited sample of 'law-abiding' citizens and the police (Stenson 1999). In that respect, community policing will come to defend only very specific interests. For example, in the community safety context, local inter-agency networks of crime control often provide for a distancing rather than a vehicle of communication between citizens and police (as with other safety agencies).

> Promising to honour democratic participation and self-regulation of the citizenry, free of paternalist and bureaucratic tutelage, the new multi-agency networks seem to turn out to provide less participation and more diffused regulation.
>
> (Van den Broeck 2002, p. 184)

When developing community policing initiatives, police frequently meet and work with select community members and groups i.e. civic associations, tenant organizations, businesses, churches and other issue-oriented groups. These groups tend to be politically organized, and their members and representatives more likely to attend forums organized by the police. Police therefore end up relying on self-appointed representatives to identify problems and concerns for the rest of the community. Even when police encourage wider participation, such invitations are rarely accepted partly because of traditional police–minority hostile relations and partly because of the historical disenfranchizement and marginalization of groups such as lower class young people. Groups that are disproportionately subjected to the aggressive enforcement of order-maintenance laws, such as the homeless or young minority males, often face social and political alienation from mainstream power, making them unlikely to participate in any effective way in the political process. In general, community policing tends to empower those who want more policing at the expense of others who may justifiably expect more control over the police.

COP in its conservative mode (Manning 1988) may involve marshalling more general community and state resources in a reaction that adversely affects others within the community. Indeed, if there is substantial conflict within communities about the community's problems and potential solutions, community policing may just perpetuate interventions by the dominant minority, imposing its standards on the community's majority. Further, community representation impact on police activities may be marginal over any other than peripheral matters. In some cases, police might limit community participation to the provision of crime surveillance information, which the police then use to focus their crime-fighting activities. Rather than empowering communities to advance their interests, community policing under this model simply enhances the police response to crime and disorder.

Implementing (potentially contestable) initiatives in the name of community policing heightens the risk of discriminatory law enforcement and police intrusions into private lives. Because certain order-maintenance strategies informally delegate the power to define community standards regarding prohibited conduct to only select community members and police officers themselves, community policing initiatives that endorse such tactics may facilitate the repression of political, cultural and sexual outsiders with the apparent imprimatur of the community. Discretionary police authority seems most problematic at that point. Allowing a select few, such as through the normally non-elected membership of the CPFs, to speak for the whole community seems problematic enough, but of even greater concern is the possibility that community consent to local policing might allow a majority of a

55

given community to legitimize police practices for everyone else when those practices could end up oppressing the minority. Majorities may dominate minorities in the policing of communities as elsewhere (Lea and Young 1984). Many community policing initiatives tend to credit institutions like business groups and churches as community representatives, when these institutions are likely to be heavily shaped by the distribution of power, wealth, and status within the domain and do not necessarily reflect the values and concerns of the broader community. For example, where a police officer regards the source of shoplifting in a shopping precinct to be a result of physical design and security factors, he or she may have a mandate to accept the shop-keepers' account and to dispute the property owners' account. Irrespective of who is right or wrong in such an argument, the police are non-accountably taking sides in civic matters. In such cases, who actually constrains the powers and rights of the police officer? To whom is the officer accountable in a case where the community is divided and the officers perceive more faults on one side rather than on the other (Albritton 1995)?

Bayley concedes that community policing materially legitimatizes the penetration of communities by powerful agents of government, while transforming the citizens into potential interest groups favourable to the police. Furthermore he notes it will most likely increase the relative power of the police among governmental agencies, and eventually weaken the 'democratic rule of law'. Nowhere is such a critique more evident than with regard to the koban and more obvious with regard to the Chinese household registration police[6]. From a civil and human rights perspective, community policing may be little more than a strategy for the police to obtain, by stealth, information for which they have no democratic mandate.

Further, COP has a clear political problem when it transcends the boundaries of criminal law intervention. While the degree of accountability of police officers to the criminal law and to the courts has long been open to critique, there is an even larger problem when police officers venture – with their problem-solving function – beyond that criminal law domain. When the officer transcends the legal mandate, he or she is subject to no obvious accountability.

In sum, there is a major problem of accountability with regard to community policing. Given the previous question marks over the political and legal accountability of the police, there is an evident search for new forms of accountability. With the arena of community policing, it seems that new opportunities for a more direct form of accountability are possible. But, in practice, such a relationship appears to be one-sided.

Influential minorities in communities may presume to speak for the whole community. Police agencies define the parameters of what matters are relevant to such community accountability and have the means to enforce their determination of the limits of that community influence. In doing so, community policing provides a chimera of accountability. It may legitimate police determination of community goals and priorities, bypassing conventional democratic channels with a more direct inter-actional relationship rather than opening up new avenues and opportunities for democratic accountability (Klockars 1988).

The myth of professional use of enhanced discretion in problem-solving

In Chapter 2 we considered the critical importance of the process of discretion in the development of community policing. Within the traditional crime-fighting model, the police frequently ignored minor, regulatory offences or left them underpoliced and, therefore, undetected. However, they were subject to limited organizational checks on discretion – for example, through the recorded criminal statistics. Discretion was relatively constrained. However, in several ways, COP and especially problem-solving policing, enhances police discretion to intervene in both criminal and civil matters without evident restraints.

Unavoidably there are critical choices to be made as in contexts where the police officer may have neither legal authority nor professional expertise. COP officers make decisions in an ambiguous, political, rather than legal, space. They deal regularly with uncertainty arising both from the nature of the laws that they are called upon to enforce and from a community's disparate interpretations regarding the level of order that officers should maintain, variables that render police work particularly difficult. In contrast to traditional crime-fighting policing, community policing, coupled with the enhancement of discretionary pubic order legislation, involves preventive problem-solving strategies that broaden the police mission, moving from enforcement of criminal laws in response to isolated incidents towards development of the most effective means for dealing with a multitude of troublesome situations – the cause rather than symptom of crime and disorder. Rather than constraining the police to the traditional relatively limited reactive crime-fighting role, COP may require the officer to be a political entrepreneur in attempting to change – sometimes in conjunction with other agencies, sometimes not – the underlying structures that might give rise to the various community problems of which crime is one symptom.

One way of conceptualizing that problem is to distinguish between liberal and conservative views of community policing (Manning 1988). The conservative approach allows considerable latitude to police intervention in problem-solving both legal and extra-legal. The liberal approach constrains police discretion to that of his/her legal powers, knowledge and skills. This conservative–liberal clash is central to the question of discretion in community oriented policing.

The conservative proponents of community policing (Kelling and Coles 1996) argue that police officers should go beyond the legal mandate of their behaviour, where appropriate and necessary, to use extra-legal powers as agents of informal social control to deal with local nuisances. The local public order problems with which police officers are faced are often multi-causal in character. If police officers are to deal with the causes of social problems, they must be enabled on some occasions to go beyond the legal mandate (like the mythological beat bobby of pre-war years) and intervene in matters which their immediate crime-fighting predecessors would have difficulty in recognising as their responsibility. Under the POP rubric especially, the police became all-purpose social intervention agents – but often in a rule-bound void, where discretion depended upon professional skills and ethics not upon law.

The liberal view takes issue with both the legal context of community policing discretion and also the non-legal context. Such critics point especially to the zero tolerance variation of community policing which suggests that maintaining public order serves an important police function because it reduces the social conditions that leads to the incidence of more serious crimes. The definition and enforcement of laws against low-level offences as part of order-maintenance strategies grants police officers authority that exacerbates the problematic nature of police discretion. Police officers develop extensive latitude in a manner that heightens the potential for arbitrariness and discrimination. Such discretion is largely invisible to the courts and to senior officers. Rank-and-file police officers autonomously enforce public order.

In addition, where community policing is coupled with recent legislation such as the British Crime and Disorder Act 1998, it enhances the freedom of the community officer to act independently of external constraints. That Act creates something called an 'anti-social behaviour' order which enhances discretion. Either the police or the local government can apply for such an order from a magistrates' court. The defendant does not have to be present at the proceedings, which are civil rather than criminal and operate under a preponderance of evidence rule. If the defendant cannot establish that his or her behaviour was reasonable in the circumstances, a variety of penal sanctions can be imposed. The defendant is guilty unless he/she can prove otherwise. The primary explanation for bypassing general requirements of the criminal law in this way is that there are courses of conduct that involve an accumulation of events, none of which is itself criminal but which together warrant severe measures. This totalizing structure increases the importance of police evidence and of police discretion in the public order context.

Secondly, there are major concerns about the way problem-solving in particular increases the non-expert and non-legal mandate of police intervention into social life. In such contexts, the development of COP means that the police are less likely to be bound by legal rules and law enforcement expertise – the law is no longer a source of authority or indeed, of professional policing skills for police officers who venture into the further reaches of problem-solving but simply an enabling device. As above, community police intervention may involve the police in essentially political processes in diverting scarce community resources – other groups lose out. In that process, police officers may engage in tasks for which they have neither a legal mandate nor the specialist expertise of, say, social work staff. Police discretion fed by sub-cultural and organizational biases, with neither minimal legal controls nor specific forms of professional expertise, may lead police officers to act and reinforce the predispositions of the wealthier, of the more articulate, or of the more bigoted.

Such discretion operates both at the general level – force tactics and strategies – and also at the rank-and-file level. Discretion problematizes the choice of enforcement priorities at the policy level. What community problems should be given priority: violent offences versus non-violent; serious crimes versus minor offences; violent crimes versus street disorder; serious drug use versus minor drug problems; the specific character of an offence versus the multi-causal social underlying factors? The police may also prioritize categories of crime according to whatever the police think that the majority of the citizens of the city want addressed, regardless of the views of the people in the immediate neighborhood where the problem exists and the policing is to occur – (using the Victorian parlance) that of the 'respectables' (where the definition of respectable may amount to police selection of acceptable behaviour) as opposed to those of the 'dangerous' classes.

Discretionary police policies are inevitably political. The norms – those of the police culture or of the civic representatives with whom the police commanders interact – are inevitably discriminatory. Many local people may wish to expel minorities, such as travellers or asylum seekers, or to exclude hostels for the handicapped and mentally ill. Are these norms the police should support in the notional community? In making these choices, the individual problem-solving police officer is accorded vast discretion. It is how this discretion is used, and how that discretion is controlled, however, not simply the extent of it, which is the key feature of COP. Attempts to check such police discretion or to address police discrimination and harassment have yielded only moderate success such as the controls over police stop-and-search powers in the British Police and Criminal Evidence Act 1984.

COP problem-solving policing allows two kinds of discretion in policing. It may mandate police officers to use considerable discretion in local quality of life issues, often independently of serious scrutiny, as in the case of zero tolerance policies. It encourages police officers to develop practices and encourage resource decisions in extra-legal areas. Some authorities, such as Wilson and Kelling (1982), encourage both of the practices, in the assumption that police officers will act correctly under the guidance of professional rules of behaviour. Others see problems in both contexts. Encouragement of police officers to operate low-level discretionary legal powers may often be subject to values and practices inimical to equitable policing. Proposing that officers transcend the legal context of enforcement to the extra-legal realm, where their legal powers are at best dubious, results in discretionary decision-making which is dangerous given the lack of formal rules and expertise. As with the critique of accountability, COP proposes that police officers enter civil domains under the banner of crime prevention where their decisions are often unmonitored and where they may be forced to choose sides in contentious community disputes. Rather than empowering communities to advance their interests, community policing under this model simply enhances the police discretion response to crime and disorder – in the sense of both reacting to the perceived problems and secondly 'dealing' with the problem. Implementing a variety of potentially contestable initiatives in the name of POP heightens the risk of discriminatory law enforcement and inappropriate police intrusions into private lives.

The myth of the universal relevance of community policing

In many of the earlier commentaries on community policing, and later in its export to transitional and to failed states, community policing is constructed as the panacea for community life, independently of context and of history. Community policing (especially where parented in highly decentralised United States policing) has come to develop a template for the application of community policing ideas to quite different communities – in terms of wealth, of cohesion, of stratification, and especially in terms of ethnicity and age. But bluntly, community policing works most effectively when it operates in a homogeneous community with little crime, and where support for the police is almost universal. It does not work where the opposite holds true. In particular, as we demonstrate in later chapters, community policing practices may have little relevance to societies where crime rates are rising and where, for good reasons, the police have been viewed as agents of oppression.

Some COP missionaries are committed to the notion that such policing is relevant to all contexts independently of the specificity of local needs – where, for example, there is often a strong resistance from community members to becoming involved in community policing efforts, partly for historical and partly for situational reasons. Antipathy may be interpreted as a failure to simply recognize the virtues of COP or to the general apathy and inactivity of the community. Community neighbourhoods chosen for the implementation of community policing are frequently the same neighbourhoods that have the poorest relationship with the police. It may be difficult to involve the citizens 'because community residents may not want to involve themselves in community policing' (Grinc 1994, p. 465). A community may simply be unable to participate in the community policing process because there may be no viable community to mobilise (Walker 1999). In many 'underclass' communities residents do not identify themselves with the neighbourhood or any of the local organizations within the community. COP fails to grapple with the social disorganisation characteristics of many inner cities. Divisions of age, of socio-economic class, and of ethnicity, militate against community unity. On others, historical oppositional experience to policing and perhaps greater reliance on local informal methods of social control may encourage a belief that the state police have little relevance to local affairs.

In communities epitomised by small-town 'Middletown, United States', or the wealthy walled suburbs, problems facing the police and community are few and relatively minor, and police support structures are paradoxically abundant – from watch schemes to Block Parents and so on. Community policing appears, from the available evidence, to be highly effective at mobilizing community resources as an add-on to crime prevention through problem-solving processes in white (?) undivided communities, with little crime. Such policing works best where it is least needed. Conversely, community policing works worse in heterogeneous or divided communities, where socio-economic deprivation is at it highest, measured support for the police is lowest, and crime rates are high. This is the paradox of community policing in that, 'the communities that need it most are least able to take advantage of it' (Walker 1999, p. 190). Such mixed communities are also characterized by the highest levels of public space crime. Residents in neighbourhoods at the low end of the economic spectrum may have a critical need for police services, but lack the kinds of organizational structures necessary to access these services.

Curiously, the problems of the universality of community policing appear not just in those other domains but actually in the locus of the apple pie source of American community policing itself. An interesting recent study of community policing in a small town in Maine – the prototype of wealthy homogeneous America – shows that the assumptions about the relevance of community policing in small towns may actually be misplaced. Not merely were there major disagreements between the police and the homogenous community over the priorities of law enforcement – police officers saw crime and disorder and child abuse as the priorities, local people regarded speeding as the major causes for concern – but there were also disagreements between different groups in that small community. Contrary to received wisdom, views were not unified even in the most favourable of circumstances. Citizen involvement in small communities in any case appears to be minimal. In a separate study of community policing in police departments located in small and medium sized cities and towns with populations between 15,000 and 170,000, most residents did little more than provide information to the departments. Collaborative strategies such as advisory councils and community forums seem to be generally the preserve of larger cities. It may be that in small communities, long-established social control mechanisms associated with community institutions and agencies mean there is little need for more formally structured strategies. Local police chiefs may view such forums of collaboration as infringing on their own long-standing semi-feudal authority (Cardarelli, McDevitt and Baum 1998).

This problem of the congruence between community policing and locality characteristics is most evident in our later discussion of policing in transitional and in failed societies. It is difficult to see the value or effectiveness of community policing in this instance from cities as varied as Nairobi and Delhi, in which the development of community liaison panels representing the business elite may simply exacerbate the division between rich and poor, between business people and those who occupy the city streets. The first street legislation in Victorian England was developed to enhance the commercial viability of the urban shopkeepers by criminalizing the hawking practices of the city itinerants (Brogden 1982). Street policing in that context had an economic imperative; similarly, in the 'third world' city. Community policing practices, which come to serve the most articulate business enterprises, simply effect a further social and economic division. This is the character of many of the models of community policing exported to alien domains, ones where demands for police reform are likely to be most evident.

The myths of police rhetoric – the legitimation function of local crime surveys

As much of the orthodox literature demonstrates, there is frequently a major difference between the rhetoric of senior police managers and the reality of community policing. Indeed, it may be that the community policing model narrative may say less about what is taking place in the community and policing and more about changes in police language and discourse (Kappeler and Kraska 1998) as part of a larger process of social change in the character of governance. The new local crime surveys often play a key part in manufacturing the new image of policing. They have become " ... a widely used means to determine what bothers the public and what goals it sees and seeks' (Marenin 1989, p. 75). Subtly, they contribute to the new community image of policing. Community policing may be better understood not as a reform movement, but rather as a realignment of the police institution's language and symbols to better fit changes in the larger society. Community policing may simply consist of an ideologically based rhetoric rather than of substantive practice, '... a series of ideological assumptions that link the police to the community and the community to the police in the minds of police administrators' (Manning 1988, p. 29).

Historically, the rhetoric of policing has allowed the police institution to develop autonomy from democratic and legal controls. Successive discourses have provided the rationales. Previous police rhetorics – legal, professional, and scientific justifications – demonstrate the importance of legitimizing discourses. Initially, police legitimation and the search for autonomy from democratic control was characterized by 'we do it because it is legally right' law as the key feature of police discourse and legitimation. This was succeeded by a professional discourse: as professionals we should be left to police according to professional values rather than according to political dictats'. In turn, this has been followed by a new scientific and technocratic discourse; rhetoric characterized by the emphasis upon fast response, upon computer data systems and upon more advanced technologies such as DNA 'footprints'[7]. Community policing needs to be understood as a further such self-justifying discourse with key rationales of community problem-solving, and of responsiveness to a community client. Now autonomy from political and legal accountability is constructed through a construction of the police institution as the signifier of community and neighbourliness, as a caring big brother who understands the needs of the local context (Murphy 1988). This has freed the police of burdensome constitutional constraints that previously limited their proactive authority. In the face of increasing social diversity, the rhetoric of expertise and autonomy is now based on rhetoric that signifies an intuitive understanding of essentially mythological community needs (Kappeler and Kraska 1998).

Community policing discourse, they argue, may have more to do with the change in the nature of governance and in the relationship between the police and the larger state than with the substance on the ground. Community policing may be better understood not as a process simply of making the police better at crime prevention but rather as a realignment of the police institution's language and symbols to the increasing diversification of society. As the nature of the post modern state changes, so must the police institution and its rationales. What was once the most visible form of state control – the police – now serves as a powerful mitigating medium for social and economic reordering through symbolic violence (Loader and Mulcahy 2003). Community policing rhetoric may thus provide a legitimacy gloss for non-accountable policing. The police might choose to publicize their work with a particularly cooperative private citizens' group as a police-community partnership, thus shielding themselves from more critical public scrutiny. By appropriating the community policing discourse in this way, police agencies employ a public relations facade that accommodates the needs of the police bureaucracy as a semi-autonomous corporate entity more than it serves as a democratic vehicle for police responsive to community concerns.

Community crime surveys (as encouraged by the British Crime and Disorder Act) are a key part of this new policing discourse. Discovering what the client wants directly, without going through the cumbersome democratic process, allows the police to determine community needs independently of the constitutional political apparatus of the state. Community police reformers repeatedly call for direct contact with the community's needs and concerns (as above). Local crime surveys have become popular devices for constructing – and confining – citizen involvement. The survey approach is packaged as a type of market analysis, by which the police ostensibly allow the citizenry to participate in setting police priorities. Advancing the community policing model is encoded into survey measures.

However, what seems superficially a positive measure contains fundamental problems. The survey instrument articulates for citizens the notion that the police are the providers of community solutions to police-identified problems. Specifically, they instruct citizens that fear of crime is a reality, that the easing of this fear is a measure of police productivity, and that solutions should be enforcement based (i.e. by the police not by other agencies). Other social ills such as unemployment and poverty are constructed by the survey rhetoric not as major problems in their own right but rather as factors whose importance lies in their contribution to the crime consequences (Brogden and Nijhar 2000). Elderly citizens, who share a range of social fears from poverty to ill-health to crime are, in effect, encouraged to believe that the crime problem is the supreme one, requiring appropriate safeguards and resourcing to the detriment of their other social fears.

The victim survey of community opinion functions as a police disseminated message which frames for the citizen the central tenets of the community policing model. Police forces administer these encoded messages to their consumers. These pre-framed categories are furnished to the same public as survey results. The community learns problems, causes and solutions from the police, but substance is absent. In this sense, therefore, the discourse of community policing has little to do with crime control itself. It has more to do – like previous and coincidental rhetorics – with distancing the police from political and legal processes of accountability and more to do with creating space for police independent from control. The police – unlike political representatives – know what the community wants from its crime surveys. Through the community rhetoric, the police determine the nature of the community, its problems, and how such problems should be responded to. Other community problems – unemployment, bad housing, poor health facilities, and so on – are now constructed as second order problems. Recognizing the latter as a greater priority than crime, or as the real cause of crime, would diminish the police autonomy and authority in determining communal social order and communal values. It precludes intervention by non-police agencies. Community policing allows the police to coordinate those other agencies under its own banner and leadership to solve its definition of the priority of community problems.

This is not a mistake, an error of understanding, but rather reflects that police construction of the social problematic. Together with partisan representation on community forums, the victim survey rhetoric is not an aberration but rather the way the COP discourse determines what is the community and what are its core values. The police (and criminal justice system) have become the premier problem-solvers for some of society's most complex difficulties. Politicians and the bulk of the public fall back on regulative measures from Anti-Social Behaviour Orders to target-hardening as a means to solve social problems rooted in gender, economic and racial inequality. It gives a new meaning to the older concept of the 'thin blue line'. Policing is now the central cohesive cement that provides coherence for an increasingly diverse society. The rhetoric of community policing is central to that process.

The myths of a Peelite history, of crime control and of the technological mistake

Box 3.2   *The 'English inheritance' of community policing*

If Sir Robert Peel were to look down upon the proposals, it is very likely that he would strongly approve of the return to his original concept of policing the community.

(Alpert and Dunham 1993, p. 450)

Community policing has a distinct British legacy. Until the industrial revolution maintenance of law and order in England was a collective local and social responsibility. Under the Frankpledge system in the early fourteenth century males above the age of 12 formed a group called a 'tithing' with nine neighbours. Ten tithings were grouped into a 'shire', which was supported by a reeve. In 1663 Charles II instituted a night watch in London, whereby 1,000 watchmen patrolled the streets from dawn to dusk. The 'London bobby' acted as a friend, philosopher and guide to Londoners.

(T. Mukherjee, *The* [Calcutta] *Telegraph*, 24 June 2003)

Community policing philosophy contains a nostalgic and unreal view of the past, an account that is embedded in official and scholarly discourse. That rhetoric assists the legitimation of COP practice. There are three elements to that historical construction. Community policing derives from principles first laid down by Sir Robert Peel in the early Metropolitan London Police. Secondly, in that golden past, the police were more effective at crime control, thanks mainly to the consensual relations to the community to which they were accountable. A third component is of more recent origin, suggesting that the 'police lost their way' in their relations with the community because of mistaken technological innovations.

Community policing is presented in police rhetoric either as the naturally evolutionary product of police history, or alternatively as an attempt to return to a fabled golden age of policing. It seeks to operationalize and reincarnate what was essentially a myth, an ideological golden past of policing a more consensual world. Like the rhetorics of accountability and community, the historical myth of community policing helps to justify present COP practice by suggesting that in some golden historical past, policing served the community, police officers were equals amongst equals, citizens policing citizens.

> Community policing is popular because it seems as American as apple pie. Community policing is characterized by 'Officer O'Leary' strolling down the avenue, holding an apple in one hand and twirling a nightstick in the other, shooing away pesky street urchins as he warmly greets passers-by. It's the quintessential village constable or the night watchman, who lives in the same community he serves. At a mythic level, community policing reminds us of a world we think we once had but have now lost. Police during that bygone era were often more brutal, lazy and corrupt than they are today, probably by a wide margin. But these myths have a power that derives not from their accuracy, but from the cultural understanding that they represent.
>
> (Skogan and Hartnett 1997, pp. 11–12)

The historical myth of the relationship between the police officer and the community is central to the orthodox literature. Typically, in the words of one of many North American textbooks on COP, Peak and Glensor (2002, p. 17) claim that 'Peel proved very farsighted and keenly aware of the needs of a community-oriented police as well as the needs of the public that would be asked to maintain it'. Champion and Rush (2001, p. 21) under the emblematic heading 'The Evolution (sic!) of Community Policing', claim two such sources for community policing – Robert Peel's construction of the Metropolitan Police in 1829, and the American experience from colonial times. They claim a community policing genesis in Peel's principles of policing which emphasised sober standards of police behaviour, including police commitment to observance of the law, seeking and preserving public favour, using minimum force to effect arrests of criminals, and always maintaining favourable relations with the public in the process of crime control.

Earlier, Braiden (1992, p. 7) in Canada locates the origins of COP in Peel's seventh principle 'the police are the public and the public are the police'[8]. In that context, the first police (despite substantial historical evidence to the contrary) spent their time securing the cooperation and respect of community residents.

Given Peel's aristocratic notion of the franchised 'public', the criticism of such a history needs little emphasis (Brogden 1982; Miller 1999; Walker 1999). It is bemusing to consider whether Peel recognized the interests of those outside the landowning and urban elites of early Victorian England. There was no recognition of the complexities of the compositions of social class, of gender and of ethnicity. Like others of his class, Peel inevitably had a paternalistic, partial and partisan conception of whom the police would serve and with whom they would seek cooperation. However, he certainly had a view of whom the police would not serve – the dangerous classes with their ethnic component of newly industrialized Britain.[9]

It is clearly absurd to legitimize community policing as a reincarnation of the policing of the early nineteenth century. Such cities were diverse and complex – they were not communities. The one key feature they shared was a notion of a dangerous class whom were commonly regarded by the police as outcast, beyond the rules of due process. A variety of permissive public order legislation gave the police an array of punitive powers to use selectively against the urban outsiders. In turn working-class people throughout the nineteenth century hardly supported the police but merely gave them an occasional grudging assent.

Assumptions about historical accountability are also mythological. Wilson and his colleagues are totally misleading to suggest that the police enjoyed substantial legitimacy in the pre-crime control era. There may have been a degree of accountability to the local Watch Committees outside London but talk about an accountable relationship with a cooperative general public of the period is plain nonsense in nineteenth and early twentieth century Britain and the United States (where many urban histories suggest that the police were primarily an adjunct of the local political machine). That historical legitimation is pure fantasy. In the United States, the police were always at the centre of political controversy (Harring 1983). The police did not even enjoy unquestioned legitimacy in the eyes of the people who were members of the same class and of the same ethnic group as police officers. As Miller's (1999) account of police brutality in London and New York makes clear, the latter was a direct response to the lack of legitimacy given to police, not an aberration. There is no substantive historical evidence that the police ever enjoyed majority support. Returning to a golden past is not an option for the advocates of community policing.

In addition to the Peelite myth, community policing is justified by a crime control myth – that at some previous time the police were effective at crime control. This past crime control function of police may be much exaggerated. The historical crime control function was often primarily a matter of police rhetoric and self-image. The revisionist evidence of routine beat patrolling in Britain and the United States is that it was always about maintaining social order and peacekeeping (Brogden 1991). The major aims (Walker 1999) of the police in the past were firstly to get and to hold a job; secondly to exploit the possibilities for graft that the job offered; thirdly to do as little patrol work as possible; fourthly to survive on the street by maintaining a degree of control over the locals which meant establishing challenges to authority by whatever means possible; and finally, occasionally they felt they had to go through the motions of 'real' police work by arresting occasional miscreants (the dangerous classes of Victorian and Edwardian England and, in the United States, the urban poor, recent immigrants and blacks). Police arrest patterns then were simply a giant trawling operation – people who were arrested were simply unlucky not criminal – and not different from those who were not arrested. The mythologized watchman system was inefficient and corrupt. It did not involve any conscious purpose to serve neighbourhood needs and hardly serves as a model for community policing today. In Edwardian society, policing the lower classes was often a largely moral operation – symbolically repressing the secondary economy of street activities such as street betting and prostitution, and lower class recreation – rather than dealing with crime. The police were alienated from the public, not because of the crime control activities, but their major function was to repress the economic and leisure activities of the lower classes (Brogden 1991).

Bound up with the Peelite and crime control myth is a technological claim. Crime fighting strategies (it is argued in the orthodox accounts) failed in the post-war years because of the way technological developments alienated the police from the public. Much has been made of the depersonalization of policing since the introduction of modern patrol cars, and the technological division between the police and the public[10]. But an equally strong argument could be made for the converse, that while the patrol car did isolate the police in some respects, the telephone brought about more contacts by encouraging and increasing police intervention in domestics and private disputes and problems. Telephone communications could summon police officers relatively immediately to intervene in the private space of street and household (Walker 1999).

In the days of foot patrol, police may have had extensive casual contacts with people in the street. But they did not obtain entry to private residences, simply because people had no way of contacting the police before the development of private telephones. The telephone has self-evidently increased demand for a different quality of intervention through police services. The recognition of such novel and immediate police-public communication does not deny that technological innovations such as reliance on vehicle patrols, replacing foot beats, contributed to the isolation of the police. But it does deny the strength of the argument about police isolation from the community.

The good old days never happened. The tradition of policing quoted in COP texts never existed. There is no viable older tradition to restore. Many community policing advocates have a highly romanticised view of nineteenth century urban life. These historical myths are important in understanding the ineffectiveness of COP. History – as in the Tythingman case – furnishes legitimacy for practices that may have more dubious purposes or may be problematic in delivery. Explanations of lack of progress in terms of technology distract attention from fundamental problems in police-public relations. The tradition of policing they quote never actually existed. There is no viable older tradition to restore. Alternative histories of the police to those presented in the supposedly evolutionary account of community policing are common[11]. Many community policing advocates have a highly romanticized view of the origins of the professional police.

The myth of public support for COP

In a recent evaluation of community policing programmes in eight cities, the Vera Institute found that all of them experienced great difficulty in establishing a firm relationship between the programme and neighbourhood residents. Efforts to do so floundered in part on decades of built-up hostility between residents of poor or minority communities and the police. Distrust and fear of police were rampant in many of the neighbourhoods where community policing was instituted. The evaluators concluded that the assumption that residents want closer contact with the police and want to work with them is 'untested' (Skogan and Hartnett 1997, p. 2).

The orthodox COP thesis assumes that citizens actually want to be involved in community policing, to which they will give their practical support. But there is minimal evidence for that case in respect of other state agencies: why should we expect people to act as unpaid public servants, as postal workers, schoolteachers, rubbish cleaners or what-ever? This inaction by communities in relation to community policing may be seen as apathy by police, which in turn reinforces existing schisms, distrust and police autonomy.

There are now numerous studies of COP in practice. But studies of two localities make exemplary critical points: in Chicago (Skogan and Hartnett 1997) and in Seattle (Lyons 1999; Reed and Reed 1999). The detailed analysis of a Chicago COP scheme represents one of the most effective of the genre. It constitutes a systematic evaluation of a relatively effective and well-resourced COP programme. Researchers, who have a long and reputable tradition of promoting COP, conducted it. It is also an exemplar critical study of the problems when COP is applied in social contexts other than that of small-town America. The second recent study starts from more critical bases, taking as given the racial and socio-economic divisions of North American cities. Miller analysed a specific COP variant – the implementation of the so-called Weed and Seed scheme in Seattle.

The Chicago scheme concentrated on the concept of 'neighbourhood capacity' – a key dimension in determining the responsiveness of the community to policing innovations. It focused on the local community police forums as core elements in the police strategy. The researchers concluded that the community capacity to be involved in that process was strongly rooted in the social and economic makeup of the study areas. For example, in the more homogeneous (as measured by racial composition and housing tenure) areas, wealthier residents turned out at a higher rate to community meetings. In high capacity beats, those who came to meetings were more representative of the community. In low-capacity areas, white homeowners and better-off residents played a disproportionate role – important because only a small fraction of the community attended meetings. In the latter context, it was consequently unlikely that major interests of all residents (stratified by race and by socio-economic class) were actually represented at the meetings. Similarly in the more middle class and homogenous areas, local residents were more likely to cooperate in joint problem-solving.

> There seemed to be two reasons for this. First, better-organized whites were posed to take advantage of the resources that the programme brought to their neighbourhoods. Second, the manage-ment of the programme, allowed officers to pick and choose their target populations. They naturally focused their efforts in places where they felt most welcome, and where their initial efforts seemed to be most effective.
>
> (Skogan and Hartnett 1997, p. 3)

Whether the majority of community residents agree about the community's problems and their potential solutions is unknown. If this silent majority is merely apathetic, it still may agree with the more active minority about the problems and potential solutions. Although the majority may not actively participate in community policing efforts, it is not likely to undermine them either; if it can be mobilized to participate, all the better. On the other hand, if the majority is alienated from the dominant community, or if it is supportive or actively involved in what the minority has defined as the area's social problems, then community policing efforts are likely to meet resistance. Even if a consensus were achieved, community policing efforts may still prove ineffective in reducing a community's social problems because community policing programmes do little to address the more fundamental problems of poverty, racism, illiteracy and unemployment.

Lyons, and Reed and Reed, came to similar conclusions from their Seattle studies. In the community policing project, local residents and a precinct police captain disagreed about which physical disorders were more important. The precinct commander's main priority was abandoned cars used for drug dealings. Residents were more concerned with the overall appearance of the neighbourhood. Unlike in Chicago, Weed and Seed represented a top-down scheme from the federal government to both respond to local crime (weed) and at the same time (seed) generic crime prevention development. She reminds us of a long standing criticism of police historical orthodoxy that the parish constable of Early Modern England was stranded between two different conceptions of social order, local and national – of attempts to graft federally concerned notions of social order onto communities that are far removed, geographically and often psychologically, from visions of national policymakers. Local social order and national social order are not necessarily the same things. The outright opposition in the locality to the Weed and Seed programme from the start was curious because the scheme appeared to bring two benefits – money and different styles of policing from what had been customary.

The local community defined crime prevention as social order in a quite different way from national policy makers. As elsewhere, communities define problems broadly and sought to identify if the police were willing to act within that mandate. But the police were more likely to identify problems that are convictable and measurable in their role as law enforcers (Boostrom 2000[12]). When invited to participate in the direction of crime prevention and control in collaboration with the new COP scheme, residents and local community leaders endeavoured to shift the new resources away from the emphasis on preventative law enforcement and crime avoidance strategies (such as situational crime prevention and 'hot-spots' policing) towards employment opportunities and broad economic, educational and social development. Members of the local community were far more interested in community development for its own sake with crime prevention simply as one aspect of that concern.

Secondly, where the new crime prevention policy had the dysfunction of increasing police authority over marginal groups, community leaders found the police unresponsive to community concerns about harassment and abuse. In particular in a historically sanctified way, the police used 'race' as a proxy for dangerousness in determining which community crime concerns were legitimate[13]. Indeed, most such crime prevention community policing initiatives are in minority locations where crime control is the primary example of state authority. Such plans frequently do not address the problem of fear of police harassment and abuse. The promotion of police discretion in such contexts turns residents' attention away from basic community development to achieve narrow law enforcement, resulting in greater discrimination against minorities – the police officers may in any case have a lower tolerance of ethnic diversity than do the locals. Such crime prevention strategies under the rubric of COP contain specific assumptions about the nature of the genesis of crime and its resolution. Elected officials do not simply respond to the generic demands of the community, they help create that will by catalysing on the fear of crime and of the anxieties of social order that lie beneath the surface of crime control debates. Crime control in this formulation is driven not just by a fear of crime but also by value judgements about moral decline, family dysfunction, and constructed relations of the connection between increasing diversity and social disorder and crime (Lyons 1999).

In the Seattle case, as elsewhere, the Weed and Seed approach used crime control, through COP, as a justification for other funded programmes such as economic development, recreation, urban planning and so on. The degree of the success for the programme was therefore measured not through generic benefits to the communities of such widening opportunities but through quantitative indices such as the recorded criminal statistics. The previous crime control rhetoric had persuaded the public to judge the police by such statistical indices. If they were to discard that measure, they would be unable to meet political demands for some measure of effectiveness. Social and economic programmes were judged as a success or failure not in their own terms but insofar as they contributed to crime reduction – a federal government focus but not necessarily a community one.

Generally, inner cities that become the focus for COP crime control strategies emphasize government authority and national rather than local determination of the problem. The police are the ones who both implement and interpret – according to their own culture – that programme. Lyons concludes that the police, through monopolizing the decision-making process in the community, limit the range of possible responses to perceived disorder, exclude not only the unrealistic and the illegal, but also the ones most amenable to community support. If community members want the police to engage in an activity that is not on the police agenda (because it is not cost effective, because it does not strengthen police organization, because it limits police discretion, under-utilizes police manpower and so on) they may have little potential to challenge the practical decision-makers.[14] Support for the police and willingness to engage in consultation processes is for many people a non-starter beyond a minimum level. In practice, there is a major gap between both formal state aims of such programmes, police organizational definitions of the nature, source and resolution of the problem, and general community social priorities. It is not a gap that is readily bridged[15].

The myth of linking with informal networks of control

One contribution to the development of COP thinking has been the legacy of social disorganization theory in the United States. In those downtown areas, high rates of recorded delinquency are correlated with conditions of social disorganization (ineffective informal social controls). As long as these conditions exist, no matter which individuals or groups move into the neighbourhood, high rates of crime and delinquency will continue. One outcome of the critique of that fulsome body of theory and research has been the recognition of the existence even in those socio-economically deprived areas of informal structures of normative control.

Hence a more recent addition to community policing ideas is the realization that for COP to be successful it has to link with latent informal mechanisms of social control embedded within communities. The logic of COP assumes communities to be a form of association capable of informal social control, of a degree of self-help independent of external intervention and support. A central strategy of COP is to link with existing informal networks of social control. Social order is maintained in communities not by the presence of some visible or threatened coercion but by an implicit consensus over certain practices. These norms may be legal associations or voluntary groups, schools, families and the like. But in the inner cities (and indeed in the squatter camps and townships of transitional societies) they may include some forms of tolerated deviance. The importance of quasi-legal social control practices in lower class communities raises a further problem for COP.

But advocates have not worked out the full implications of that perception. For example, many of the earlier criminological ethnographic studies emphasized the street as the location for public recreation. Historically (Brogden 1991), such public space was the arena for much working leisure, such as street betting and gambling. Police action against it was designed to enforce statutes rather than local social order. Similarly, at a starker level, some lower class communities may tolerate the users of drugs, prostitution and various forms of deviance that ease the pressures of community life. Informal community controls may be overtly illegal and in conflict with police duty to enforce legal norms. Some members of crime-ridden communities may not see marginally criminal behaviour as all that important. Indeed, they may, in part, depend upon marginal criminal activities as the basis for community cohesion and a source of employment through a secondary economy of the street[16]. Segments of the local community may actually cohere around such deviant activities. The core legal mandate of the police does not allow them to cooperate with formally illegal practices, despite their contribution to social cohesion and the local economy. Further, the police sub-culture may in any case regard such boundary-crossing as intolerable. Such problems loom even greater when a degree of self-policing occurs outside a legal mandate. In the absence of an effective state police, street level justice and the encouragement of vigilantism by citizens may flow from connection to informal networks which have a degree of local legitimacy (Brogden and Shearing 1993).

As Jane Jacob says in her pathbreaking 1961 text on urban America:

> The first thing to understand is that the public peace – the sidewalk and the street peace – of cities is not kept primarily by the police, necessary as the police are. It is kept primarily by an intricate, almost unconscious network of voluntary controls and standards among the people themselves, and enforced by the people themselves.
>
> (pp. 31–32)

It is these networks that police are most likely to find to be illegal and therefore, if not to be tolerated, then to be repressed. COP comes up hard against aspects of communal social solidarity.

The recognition of the informal networks represents a major advance on previous COP thinking. But – as is especially highlighted in the successive chapters on policing in transitional society – it poses major problems for the police mandate. In transitional societies especially, where the police themselves may often be viewed as law breakers, repressing lower class street deviance with severe violence, as in parts of Brazil, informal justice networks together with activities that (illegally) sustain the local economy may be the basis of local networks. For the new COP missionary, such contact constitutes a formidable dilemma.

The myth of organizational change in COP

An often-forgotten legacy of Sir Robert Peel is that he constructed a policing agency based on paramilitary lines – command structures, ranks, forms of discipline and measures of efficiency. While clearly there are variants of that model in present-day policing, that organizational structure remains evident throughout Anglo-American policing. How can community policing, especially given *inter alia* the diversity of skills, the degree of discretion required of community problem-solving officers, and the commitment to consensual citizen consultation, relate to that inherited organizational model? The Anglo-American highly centralized, militaristic, bureaucratic and professionally oriented model of policing from Peel onwards, designed for technical efficiency, has remained largely unchanged for nearly 200 years.

At the organizational level, few proponents of community policing accept any easy answer to the changes required in organizational structure by the requirements of COP. Problems have been raised in terms of the rank and file resistance, of the gap between the management culture of policing and that of the other ranks, and of the need to develop COP as a wholesale rather than a piecemeal change. Both police managers and rank and file frequently recognize contradictions between official statements to the media and in official police reports, and what actually happens on the ground. Some of these problems may simply be organizational. For example, long-serving rank and file officers may need considerable persuasion before they can adopt quite different approaches – in the words of one commentator 'the new community police officers must realize that the one-way street of policing the community must now take two-way traffic'[17]. Police officers who have long been used to informing residents of the 'facts' of crime, a form of vertical communication, have difficulty in developing a lateral encounter, learning to take citizens' views seriously. The blunt reality is that if you were to construct a community policing structure on the basis of what has gone before, you would not design it with a paramilitary organizational structure.

As Weisburd and McElroy (1988) noted 20 years ago in early evaluation of a CPO programme in New York city, the new roles assigned to police officers were quite incompatible with their location in a military mode of organization. Similarly, in the UK community policing programmes continually encounter organizational buffers, committed to preserving the *status quo*. The pressures in such a para-military organization against change and innovation are intensive. A British Home Office Report, for instance, on the introduction of problem oriented policing in Britain, revealed that implementation was patchy, had little local police backing, was poorly understood, was often used as a label to conceal other activities and rarely enjoyed a long run, with most projects being prematurely abandoned (Leigh, Read and Tilley 1996) primarily because of factors relating to the organizational model of policing. There are many examples of organizational resistance preventing the development of COP. In Houston, for example, the project for neighbourhood oriented policing was known as 'No-one on Patrol!'[18] and eventually discontinued the programme because the organizational culture was deemed not to be ready for community policing (Zhao, Lovrich and Thurman 1995). Until recently the police were not usually renowned for their managerial sophistication and institutional finesse in adapting to change, while die-hards within the occupational culture would continually insist that the core business of policing was 'catching crooks' (Punch, Van der Vijver and Zoomer 2002).

Organizational change is always problematic but it is too easy to blame the organization for resistance. One of most serious COP fallacies are that police organization can be effectively decentralized, both organizationally and managerially by adopting community policing strategies alone. While this is hardly a new criticism, it is not one that has yet been adequately answered. Whatever the nuances of concern with crime against citizens, the police are a state agency committed to internal security and ordering (Albritton 1995). Officers are recruited, trained, promoted, and socialized, in terms of that primary function of public ordering and security on behalf of the state. It does not help police performance in expecting specialist-trained officers to be jacks-of-all trades committed to a variety of interventionist welfare and inter-agency relationships. It inevitably diminishes both specific law enforcement skills, and the professional and disciplinary controls. In practice, COP may leave the existing competencies and practices of the average police officer untouched while giving a new professional legitimation to them.

Further, there is a tendency of many police specialists to focus on 'police reforms' or 'innovations' like COP as if they occurred in a self-contained social vacuum – without reference to, or recognition of, the larger social forces and determinants of modern policing. Police models of organization designed in the nineteenth century now inhabit a post-modern society (Kappeler and Kraska 1998) with new forms of differentiation and control. Police organizations have demonstrably been remarkably resilient to modernization apart from in developing new techniques of autonomy. Many orthodox police specialists focus on 'police reforms' or 'innovations' like COP without reference to or recognition of the larger social forces and determinants of modern policing.

As Zhao (1996) has demonstrated, in a comparative study of over 200 municipal community policing agencies between 1993 and 1996, police priorities have remained unchanged in this period. Rather than representing a systematic adaptation to a changing environment, COP would seem to represent for many police agencies a method of strategic buffering of a core police mandate reflective of the existing model, unaffected by the external exigencies. COP may simply be a part of internal police reform. Policing is reconstructed to reflect the police technological mandate and organization. The search for the most efficient means to achieve both the organizational demands of contemporary policing and the demands for ever more effective crime fighting technologies from both police and public create a technical imperative that has led the police to pursue the widest autonomy in their functions and operations in modern history. The problem with change in policing towards COP is not an aberrational problem of initial resistance but rather a structural one of the police mandate and of the way the police agency relates to the wider state. The reality is that it is much easier to persuade the community that COP is in operation – to change the community's view – than it is to actually change the police organization in order to practice COP. Cosmetic practices are inevitable. COP is an excellent public relations tool for an organization that cannot 'solve crime' but which seeks to ensure the community that it is 'doing something'. Conversely, it can create unreal expectations of the ability to solve community problems – increasing public complacency that 'something can be done if only the community supports the police more and allows more resources', while diverting public attention from non-police processes that might actually reduce both crime and the fear of crime.

Other problems may relate simply to restrictions on organizational resources. With a crime-defined mandate, the relative division between what constituted a police task and what does not is relatively clear-cut.

But the new community policing approach provides little guidance as to when the work of problem-solving is no longer police business. Community policing can become an infinite black hole into which resources are sucked, unless clear limitations on the parameters of policing are specified.

Of course, while community policing appears to be directly related to a history of police decentralization, especially in the United States[19], there are exceptions to the rule. In a few countries ranging from the Netherlands to Sweden and Australia, which have traditional central-ized structures (albeit often alleviated by policing tiers), community policing has reached the level of orthodoxy. But the latter are exceptions. Generally, community policing requires an organisational structure which emphasizes local policing and considerable local discretion.

Police cultural and organizational mandates are resilient to change. Irrespective of the new schemes, the reality is that policing for minorities continues much as before. The same 'miscreants' are 'moved on' on the streets, the same groups of youths end up in custody, and the same middle class citizens have the views of law and order reaffirmed. As Manning claimed some years ago, it may be that 'community policing is no different from other police strategies aimed at shaping and manipulating public opinion' (1988 p. 400.) Organizational problems are one thing, but there are other more structural criticisms of the differences between the official picture and the reality of practice.

The myth of the Anglo-American model – the failure to recognize alternatives

A rather different objection to the development of community policing relates to the common assumption that, at the end of the day, there is only one model of policing in historical trajectory – that of Anglo-American trajectory. A unilinear development is assumed, an insular model of policing regarded as the universal orthodoxy. At best, a degree of con-vergence is assumed in which other models eventually adopt the Anglo-American path.

Crudely, there are two generic models of crime-fighting policing in the West. One is the Peelian model, much adapted according to local national and cultural circumstances. It began locally and grew outwards from small towns and cities (as in the golden age mythology above). The result historically was a patchwork of different police organizations concerned to enforce social order in communities from a local source. Latterly, they were accompanied in North America especially by the development of a higher, separate, tier of policing (such as the RCMP and the FBI) in the form of a national or federal police with a limited mandate. Such police depend on common law *citizen rights* rather on than the statutes of the central state.

An alternative model that derives from societies as different as eighteenth and nineteenth century mainland Western Europe and the Ottoman Empire, is the *gendarmerie*[20]. That model was originally constructed by the central government or ruler (Liang 1992) as a kind of internal army, and operates within *powers delegated by the central government*. Many of the police forces developed as a legacy of the Napoleonic period in Europe – in France itself, in Spain, in what later became modern Germany, in Italy and so on. They were gendarmeries consisting of state functionaries, an arm of the central government – in effect, policing the internal boundaries of the state in the same way that the army policed the external boundaries. In such countries today (Austria is an obvious example), community problem-solving may be perceived to be outside the police mandate. Policing is conceived within much narrower directives and mandates.

An influential variation on the European gendarmeries was the *colonial model* first appearing within the then British Empire, in Ireland in the early nineteenth century (Brogden 1987; Waddington 1999). The nineteenth century Irish Constabulary was an armed police service centrally-organized, committed to maintain the rule of the British Empire over the native Irish. In turn, the Irish Constabulary spawned some 140 colonial police forces across the world – ranging from the North West Mounted Police (later the Royal Canadian Mounted Police), the South African Constabulary and, *inter alia*, the Hong Kong Police. Hong Kong, through the early years, was policed by former British colonial levies such as Sikhs and Ghurkhas, with a predominantly British officer class. Their primary function was to maintain the rule of Empire and in particular to safeguard trade and mercantile connections. They were the opposite of a community police.

The key difference between the Peelite structure on one hand, and the Napoleonic and colonial on the other, is summed up in the phrase 'Peelite policing was a case of locals policing locals, Napoleonic and colonial police was one of strangers policing strangers'[21]. The Peelite model also granted much more discretion to local municipal authorities about the nature and practices of 'their' police force. That model appears – despite its paramilitary structure – much more conducive to the development of community policing than the gendarmerie and colonial police model(s) because it emphasises the *local* source of powers and responsibilities.

For example, while many changes have occurred in former colonial policing organizations such as that of the Hong Kong police since those early days, its structures, traditions and practices derive from that colonial, gendarmerie, model not from the Peelian tradition. Many ex-colonial territories have recognized that the evolution within a colonial policing tradition and structure to a community policing model is too formidable a problem. Complete force reorganization has sometimes been the alternative. In the early part of the century the establishment of the Garda Siochana in the newly independent Republic of Ireland was the first attempt to completely reorganize an ex-colonial police structure along community and non-colonial lines. Much more recently, such changes have occurred in Singapore with a version of the koban system, to a lesser extent in Malaysia and the Philippines, and in Indian states such as Kerala, Goa and Uttar Pradesh[22]. A key to this reconstruction of national and local state policing has been a recognition that a semi-militarized ex-colonial force, originally established for the purpose of maintaining external rule, is quite incompatible with the construction of a democratic community police agency. From this perspective, the question for a former colonial police force such as that of Hong Kong wishing to develop community policing (Lau 2004) is whether it follows the Singapore example, or if it can – optimistically – transform the old colonial structure to one with a quite different mandate and practices. One solution within larger territories – such as in Canada (as above) – has been to allow for the development of local community and urban forces (tiered levels of policing, in which different police agencies deal with different tasks) which can be community-oriented while allowing the maintenance of a federal policing institution with more evident coercive powers and practices.

As we shall argue in the succeeding chapters, COP is essentially an Anglo-American invention. Within a long history of such legal colonialism (Brogden 2005), COP is sold overseas as the 'only' model of policing. In doing so, those salespeople deny obliquely the legitimacy of alternatives, both from the West and from Asia and from indigenous communities elsewhere.

Overview

As noted in the introduction to this chapter, what is intended here is a positive critique. Not all aspects of community policing have eventually been negatively experienced. In Anglo-American societies, a central core of community policing programmes has begun to emerge. Crime prevention programmes such as education about home security have been accepted virtually universally. In addition, programmes such as foot/bike patrol, the maintenance of crime prevention units, and the permanent assignment of officers to fixed neighbourhood-level geographic areas have been widely adopted by police agencies in the Anglo-American context. Conversely, some police organizations have abandoned their pretensions to be community policing organizations, suggesting that the reality of those programmes is dawning in some quarters. Several consequences are evident.

In the first place, COP appears to have been frequently discarded in favour of the euphemism of neighbourhood policing which has actually been brought about by financial cuts in all local state services[23]. A second resolution has been to use an alternative and sometime weasel rubric of community problem-solving. For example, in Pittsburgh[24], the police chief abolished the formal COP title and replaced COP on the ground with 'Community Problem Solvers'. In Britain especially, COP as a total organizing philosophy has largely been discarded from internal police discussion and replaced as appropriate by the narrower intent of problem-solving policing, often reinforced by variation on the community safety contract theme (see Chapter 5). Indeed, the major thrust of local policing in Britain is now devoted to specific problem-solving realities for the most part with only *ad hoc* and public commitment to the wider intent of COP. Finally, many police departments have abandoned COP entirely. For example, the Houston Police Department discontinued some of its community policing programmes in favour of traditional police work during the early 1990s because the organizational culture was deemed not to be ready for community policing. Elsewhere, in Poland (Chapter 8) and in particular in South Africa (Chapter 6), community policing has been effectively abandoned and a crime-fighting mission installed (itself a major change in both those countries from an internal security policing function). It is a long way from Houston to the initial experiences of community policing in the transitional and failed states but the debunking of the mythologies in this chapter does not augur well for the implementation of community policing overseas.

Notes

1 For example in Bucqueroux and Diamond's claim that 'Community policing is our best bet against terrorism' (www.policing.com/op-ed.)

2 Manning's devastating and all-encompassing critique of COP was initially made in 1988. Mastrofski has made similar contributions. Few of the criticisms appear to have been answered.

3 For a clear delineation of these issues see Manning 1993, pp. 122 3.

4 The obvious examples are in Belfast, in Northern Ireland, where a motorway neatly bisects the Unionist and National communities and in the apartheid South African townships.

5 See Chapter 7 for 'a useful' Nairobi example.

6 See Chapter 4.

7 Erickson and Shearing (1986) – what they call the 'scientification of police work'.

8 While ironically on p. 8 noting that 'There is a tendency to romanticize our past. ...'(!).

9 In Latin America, ironically, a different conception of Peelite history has been used to defend the military structure of the Brazilian police (Clark 2003). Critchley writes that 'the idea of the police as developed by Sir Robert Peel and applied subsequently owes a considerable amount to the military model of organization and discipline ...' (1978, p. 120) (although one Brazilian military police officer claims that the origin of Brazilian community policing lies in the Scottish city of Aberdeen! – Silva Tatigiba 2004).

10 As illustrated in England and Wales by Unit Beat Policing (Holdaway 1994).

11 See, amongst others, Brogden, Jefferson and Walklate (1988).

12 R. Boostrom (2000) The Community-Oriented Policing and Problem-solving Paradigm – What Have We Learned? http://oregonstate.edu/dept/IIFET/2000/papers/boostrom.pdf

13 See also Skogan and Harnett's comment on race and community policing in Houston (1997, p. 14).

14 Boostrom (2000) in a national survey of COP schemes in the United States notes further that COP may simply increase historical tension by excluding minorities from involvement.

15 See the study of a different COP programme, Crime Stoppers, in Canada by Carriere and Ericson (1989) which comes to similar conclusions.

16 See Chapters 6 and 7.

17 See Chapter 9 on Northern Ireland.

18 Quoted in Punch, van der Vijver and Zoomer (2002).

19 With some 20,000 police forces ranging in size from one-person departments to the New York City Police Department with some 32,000 personnel.

20 See Chapter 6.

21 Although as Miller (1999) and Brogden (1991) have shown, in practice from the outset British police often encompassed stranger policing.

22 Some US cities, such as Columbia in South Carolina, have adopted a version of the koban programme – see Chapter 1.

23 For example, the Report by the Virginia-based Public Administration Service Associates [July 2002] claimed 'This all out effort to become "community oriented" and the resources it required, significantly reduced the time and assets available to the (Seattle Police Department) to maintain proficiency in fundamental policing skills'.

24 indypgh.org Andy Mulkien, 13 November 2002.

Chapter 4

Community policing on the Pacific Rim

... the underlying factors for the success of the Japanese police's ability to combat crime can be seen to be their ability to gather a range of information, the general compliance and law abidingness of the population, and a legal environment which furnishes them with every advantage in the pursuit of suspects.

(Finch 1999, p. 509)

Introduction

In this chapter we explore the variations in community policing in three Asian countries, where quite different agencies of community policing have developed. Such policing structures represent legitimate alternatives to the Anglo-American model. Some forms of community policing are indigenous to South and South East Asia – the development of the koban system in Japan and its reconstruction as Neighbourhood Police Post in Singapore is the best known example. The koban system has spread in various forms to other Asian countries and (as noted in Chapter 1) to cities in the United States. The Singapore adaptation of the koban has developed its own history and been adopted in neighbouring countries. But the major contrast with the Anglo-American model – not merely structure but especially in the policing agencies' relationship to local communities as well as to the central state – is that of the Chinese People's Republic.

As with the COP structures in the West, there are alternative views of the function and efficiency of these structures. Different sources furnish different accounts. In all three cases, Japan, Singapore, and China, criminal justice is characterized by four principles:

- Close cooperation between police, state prosecution and the penal system.

- Citizens are encouraged to assist in maintaining public order, and they reportedly participate extensively in crime prevention campaigns, apprehension of suspects and offender rehabilitation programmes.

- The police are granted considerable discretion in dealing with offenders.

- The community police have wider functions than in the West – generally summarized by the notion of their right to keep a 'household register'.

However, as elsewhere, behind these principles in practice there are major caveats about the efficacy of such community policing structures.

Community policing in Japan

By far the most well known of the alternative models to the Anglo-American is the koban structure of community policing in Japan. However, it contains a similar mythology of historical roots, of police integration with homogeneous communities of citizens, and of effectiveness. The Western source of this community policing myth is David Bayley's eulogistic account (Bayley 1976). Bayley argued that the Japanese system has inherent advantages over other systems and that the United States could learn much from that model.[1]

Bayley concluded that American police have much to learn from Japan about programmes of community involvement. Before critically dealing with Bayley's early account, this chapter lays out the orthodox view of the koban system of community policing.

Box 4.1 *Bayley's summary of the koban system*

---

decentralized, allowing them to be accepted as an integral part of the community;
routinely engage in counselling, advising and mediating functions;
engage in problem oriented policing;
recognize the 'permeability' of the boundary between police and citizen.

An orthodox history

The koban system developed indigenously from Japan's history. Until the Meiji Restoration in 1868, the criminal justice system was controlled mainly by state functionaries, *daimyo*. Public officials, not laws, guided and constrained people to conform to moral norms. In accordance with the Confucian ideal, officials were to serve as models of behaviour. The population, who lacked rights and had only obligations, were expected to obey. Such laws as did exist were transmitted through military officials in the form of local legislation. Justice was communal – kin and neighbours could share blame for an offender's guilt – whole families and villages could be flogged or put to death for one member's transgression.

After 1868 the justice system underwent rapid transformation. Reforms drew heavily on the post-Napoleonic French system of policing, specifically the highly centralized character of that model, and because of the range of administrative functions including both preventive policing and preventive surveillance – both deemed necessary to social and economic modernization. The first publicly promulgated legal codes, the Penal Code of 1880 and the Code of Criminal Instruction of 1880, were based on French models with detailed specifications of offences and punishments. Both codes were innovative in that they treated all citizens as equals, provided for centralized administration of criminal justice. Traditional notions of collective guilt and guilt by association were abolished. In keeping with the French influence, under a semi-inquisitorial system, primary responsibility for questioning witnesses lay with the judge and defence counsel rather than with the police. Innocence before trial was contested rather than assumed.

Later (in 1881) the police structure was strengthened on a Prussian model (Aldous and Leishman 2000) including a more effective surveillance system and wider diffusion of police powers. The construction of a new two-tier system of police stations, branches and koban/chuzaisho enabled the spread of government access to the smallest communities, laying the foundations for the later koban system[2]. Administrative centralization was continued up to the late 1930s with the local koban increasingly representing an extension of the state's presence in the locality – one conducting crime and administrative functions but also committed to a political role of surveillance on behalf of the central state. The police were supported by a variety of neighbourhood associations who assisted the police in documenting local incursions, disturbances and incivilities.

After World War II, occupation authorities initiated wide ranging legal changes. The gauleiter, General MacArthur, hoped to cause a permanent political reorientation of the Japanese population and made police reform a priority. The police were to serve as his demonstration project in democracy (Bayley 1976). He stripped the Japanese police of their intrusive neighbourhood function. The neighbourhood associations, which had allowed neighbours to spy on each other for the benefit of the police, were eliminated. The police system was purged – all police personnel who were members of 'anti-democratic' paramilitary associations (the vast majority in some jurisdictions) were replaced. Criminal procedure adopted many common law characteristics, with accusatorial safeguards against arbitrary police actions in relation to arrest and forced confessions.

Police powers and functions were limited to maintaining the peace, investigating crimes, and protecting life and property, specifically excluding functions of the central state. More importantly, the orientation of the police officer was changed. Stating that it was his intent to 'see the Japanese police force patterned on that of New York City', the American adviser (New York) Commissioner Valentine insisted that the Japanese police officer think of himself not as an object of control, but as a 'real friend of the people' – ironically heralding the reincarnation of the koban, in the interest of democratization[3].

However, immediately on the departure of occupation forces, Japan (like West Germany) reverted to versions of its own historically-legitimised structure. Policing reverted to Japanese tradition. Key features of the Meiji system were restored – especially central control. The Japanese police became an administrative organ of the state under the control of the Ministry of Home Affairs, with police*men* as state servants. Local municipal authorities employed the police but under central direction. Police officers were expected to work only within their municipalities – the latter employing all but a minute proportion of the police establishment. Legislation limited police work to passive involvement such as maintaining social order, keeping harmonious relations, and crime prevention. Local prefectures financed, and directed the patrol officer on the beat, in traffic control, in criminal investigations, and in other daily operations, but under central supervision.

Most arrests and investigations are performed by prefectural police officials (and, in large jurisdictions, by police assigned to substations) who are assigned to central locations within the prefecture. Experienced officers are organized into functional bureaus and handle all but the most mundane problems. Crime control is perceived to be 'everybody's business', a community affair, i.e. not a function allotted solely to the local or state authorities[4]. For example, many civic associations and lay volunteers take an active part in policing duties. Thus the Japanese equivalent of the Neighbourhood Watch system arose spontaneously and historically from the community rather than – as in the West – prompted by police agencies. Locals may often report the presence of strangers. The *chonakai* system – community structures that deal with leisure facilities and wider community concerns – incorporate crime prevention functions. This community crime prevention role may be supported by police ancillary schemes, most of whose members are retired police officers – as in crime prevention associations, traffic safety associations and so on.

Two caveats are important before proceeding to develop the notion of the koban. Police officers have less power to intervene in domestic or private matters than in Anglo-American policing. Secondly, ethnic conflict with the police, endemic to Western societies, is reportedly minute in Japan due to the lack of such recognizable ethnic minorities. Japan represents a relatively homogenous society with few ethnic divisions[5].

The centrality of the koban as a community policing structure

The Japanese koban offers a legitimate alternative to present day community policing in Western accounts. The key feature is the fixed community police post, koban (where community police officers work shifts around the clock), in the cities and chuzaisho (essentially, a residential police box where an officer may live with his family in attached quarters), in the rural areas. The koban can be any physical structure accommodating between two and 12 officers, featuring a symbolic red light and serving districts of some 12,000 people. The orthodox accounts describe them in comfortable terms. 'All day, policemen at the koban (police boxes) keep watch on the neighbourhood, answer questions, and help those who are in need of assistance"[6]. Kobans form the first line of police response to the public. Both koban and chuzaisho play the role of community safety centres for local residents. New police officers spend much of their training period attached to police boxes. Citizens may go to these boxes not only for street directions, but to complain about noisy neighbours, or to ask advice about how to bring up their children.

About one-fifth of the total establishment force is assigned to the koban. Working in eight hour shifts, they serve as a base for foot patrols and usually have both sleeping and eating facilities for officers. These officers endeavour to become a part of the community, and their families often assist in performing official tasks.

Police officers exercise inquisitorial legal powers functions to obtain intimate knowledge of their jurisdictions – for example, conducting twice-yearly house-by-house district surveys on residents' names, ages, occupations, business addresses, vehicle registration numbers and availability for emergency response. Formally, participation in such surveys by the population was voluntary and apparently rarely challenged. Survey information is stored in the kobans as the basis for crime investigations and for other duties such as checks for missing persons.

In Bayley's words, comparing Japanese policing to the earlier reactive crime-fighting Western tradition:

> The American policeman is a fireman whereas the Japanese policeman is a postman, because a postman goes round the community every day even where there is no mail to deliver, watching and asking questions. The successful koban officer cultivates the ability to listen patiently, allowing people to 'sound off' about their problems.

Koban officers are formally mandated to deal with affairs unrelated to crime. Patrol officers rarely discover genuine emergencies but are there to demonstrate the existence of authority, monitor suspected persons, correct minor inconveniences – such as illegally parked cars – and generate trust through the establishment of familiar personal relations with a neighbourhood's inhabitants. Like the police community forums in the West, Koban Liaison Councils (consisting of a mix of local citizens) provide a more formal contact between police and the community.

The koban itself may function in varied ways, apart from its crime role – acting as a telephone centre, providing a postal address for transients, and advising over lost property. Its crime control function is limited to the first line of reaction and investigation. Any serious matters are passed to more specialist departments. The koban officer's function is to document crime scenes and to 'round up witnesses'. But he (and the rare 'she') plays only a very small part in the processing of suspects. Decisions to arrest are normally made in the central police station. Suspects may be questioned briefly in the koban but most serious matters are referred centrally.

Like his counterpart in Goldstein's outline of problem oriented policing, the koban officer exercises substantial discretion in attempting to sort out local minor problems, normally without resort to the full force of the law. Professionally informed common-sense and local knowledge and status is the key to the koban officer's community role.

A revisionist view of the koban

More sceptical considerations of the koban illustrate some of the tensions that also characterize Western community policing. In approaching that critique, a general appraisal of the Japanese police must be considered – not one limited to the koban – because of the centrality of the latter to Japanese policing style.

Under the pre-war Meiji regime, the policing system had been intended to conduct two crucial roles. It was intended to project the image of Japan as a modern civilised nation in the Western mould (hence the importation of advisers on policing from France, Germany and copying the English beat system), and assist Japan's attempt to join the ranks of the great powers. Secondly, through the three tiers of policing – district HQ, stations, and police boxes – it guaranteed internal security. The dispersion of police personnel and importance of neighbourhood police box were critical to this centralized direction of local control and surveillance (Aldous and Leishman 2000). By the 1930s, the koban system was perceived as the state's key grass roots agency of control. The networks of kobans and chuzaisho served as crucial local agencies for surveillance and control, swiftly alerting such elite groups as the Special Higher Police ('thought police') to sources of political opposition and resistance. The police became ever more intrusive, more repressive, and more determined to ensure order and compliance in the face of Japan's increasing international isolation.[7]

More recent criticisms centre on the Japanese police's notional success as a crime-fighting agency and on its relationship with the local community. In practice, far from being indigenous, both the beat system and the koban police box may have Western origins (Aldous and Leishman 2000). The idea of the police box (the old static Watch) came from England and like the beat system drew both on London and Parisian innovations[8]. One of the claimed utilities of the koban structure is that it leads to a high 'clear-up' rate for criminal offences – a rate well above that of most other industrial countries. With respect to the recorded criminal statistics, koban officers are indeed remarkably successful. But major scepticism has been expressed in several commentaries on that figure. For example, the Japanese police have minimal restrictions on their powers in detaining suspects. There are few legal rights to prevent the suspects being maintained in custody until a 'confession' is obtained and there may be no access to legal advice during that period. An apparent 'confession culture' exists in which suspects may be wrongly cajoled to admit offences. The formal checks on police powers are considerably weaker than in other countries (Finch

1999). There is little – unlike in the West – media interest in highlighting abuse of the powers.

Investigations may not be as straightforward as supposed. For example, many Japanese police neglect to note victim details in their crime reports[9]. It also means that victims' rights are more neglected than under COP. As those local researchers note 'Japan's crime data base is beyond salvage, law enforcement concepts are decades out of date…' Until recently, there has been no use of that key COP device – victim surveys – for assessing police effectiveness and providing more accurate data. Further, academic researchers have little access to officially produced data (Finch 1999). This lack of access is especially problematic given the almost total reliance on the artificial police clear-up rate as the measure of efficiency. Crimes of the household (as above), the major area of inter-personal violence in the West, have largely been ignored as outside police jurisdiction. The murder rate is higher than that of the UK and 1999 saw a 25 per cent rise in recorded sexual crimes (although this figure is subject to reporting caveats). A '… police force once seen as the industrial world's model is failing to catch some of these new predators'[10]. Indeed, taking these various factors into account and drawing on earlier data, Finch (1999) claims that United States' officers are more than twice as productive in dealing with homicides. While Japan is a relatively homogeneous society, there is little evidence of the Japanese police recruiting officers from the local ethnic minorities such as the million or so citizens of Korean origin. It is the latter that may be targeted by police officers' stereotyping of 'suspicious strangers'. There is – compared to the West – still a gross under-recruitment of women officers.

The mythology of the koban itself is increasingly being scrutinized. Several reports (as with some community policing practices in Western societies) suggest that they may become a repository for police officers who are not very competent at other policing tasks and of young officers who have little experience and little choice over the career location. Both in Japan and elsewhere, the practice of community policing on the ground may not readily relate to the rhetoric from the senior command.

Despite the public relations gloss, Japanese policing does not encompass the decentralization expected of community policing elsewhere. As the elite of a centralized organization, '… some 500 senior administrators call the shots … below nearly 250,000 provincial officers serve like enlisted men in an army … because Japanese force is a class-based society, nobody below can stop them'[11]. As a model reflective of a static conservative society, the koban system has failed to keep pace with the urbanization process. Muryama's (1990) study of police patrolling suggests that the system has failed to adjust to changing family and work patterns, and to social mobility. Urban anonymity has made it difficult for koban officers to maintain local contacts[12]. The basis for communities to be served by the koban system in the urban metropolis no longer exists. If the koban system ever was a community based organizational response to local people, the foundation of that system – the community of citizens – is absent.

Aldous and Leishman (2000), drawing on a detailed survey of the Japanese academic literature, furnish a potentially devastating account of the koban's legitimation. They argue that Western accounts on the koban are a-historical – treating the koban like the Tythingman of Saxon England as a part of a golden past that community policing can re-construct. Once placed in its proper historical context, the koban can be seen more clearly as an agency of surveillance, rather than one concerned with social service. The rose-tinted readings have more to do with nostalgia and a golden isles view than with critical evaluation of the evidence. The koban in its reinvention, as in the West, has come to be associated with a golden age of policing.

A key theme in recent critical writings is that the major function of the *Chuzai-san* (the resident beat officer – community bobby) is to gather information from local residents (Finch 1999). The kobans act as clearing-houses for much non-crime data. There are three aspects to this intelligence gathering process: the household visits of the chuzai-san, the koban's network of informers, and the six-monthly household documentation – restoring pre-war practices. A card is held for each family or business, and official information on family members is collated, as well as other information and gossip '… only "Communists" refuse to participate' (Finch 1999, p. 493).

Historically the Japanese police were regarded as a repressive arm of state. The post-Occupation reconstruction replaced that surveillance function of the modernizing state with a gloss of service to the community. The contemporary Japanese state requires an active political role for the police in development of the centralized authority needed for effective national government. The community policing function of the koban cannot be separated from its resurrection as a means of surveillance of the private lives of individuals.

This critical view of Japanese policing has of course a cultural base, a point that is made more seriously in the succeeding accounts of community policing in China. What is intrusive and oppressive in one culture may not be seen in the same way in the second. While recognizing the importance of the koban as an alternative to Anglo-American COP, it is important to appreciate its downside. As we have suggested, in terms of effect in relation to crime, there are considerable reasons to be sceptical about the Japanese police achievement. In particular, the forms of legal control over suspects held by the Japanese police are substantially more inquisitorial than in many Western forces. The koban itself may serve for some as an information centre and clearing house for relevant state materials. But it is also a repository of a variety of personal information regarding individuals and families that would not be regarded as akin to that of the community constable or the local police stations in the West. The type of community policing practiced in Japan would constitute a major breach of civil liberties in the West. There is a further more general lesson on the export of Anglo-American police strategies. Local practices are often resistant to fashions from elsewhere. Japan represents a key example of where the attempt to implant an alien policing structure failed dismally. Attempts to transplant community policing to other jurisdictions face the same obstacles.

Community policing in Singapore

It is tempting to consider community policing in Singapore as simply an extension of the koban model. But the legitimacy and autonomy of the Singapore system requires treatment of it as an indigenous structure. Further, in its commitment to problem-solving, it significantly varies from the koban. The Singapore system is almost as important as the koban as the basis for export to parts of Asia[13]. A critical account of the Singapore model of community policing is subject to several important caveats. All the available material of the Singapore Neighbourhood Police Centres (and its Neighbourhood Police Post predecessor) derives from official (or semi-official) sources as well as Bayley (1989). There has been no academic appraisal of its function and relations to the local communities. Secondly, Singapore is a small and relatively unitary state with a semi-authoritarian government. Internal critiques of policing, indeed of the state itself, have been discouraged. Finally, it is also – according to the recorded criminal statistics – a low-crime society. It does not appear in any way comparable with its Asian neighbours, nor indeed with COP practices in the urban metropolises of the West. In the absence of a wider literature, the following material should be viewed with the same scepticism as has been applied to the Anglo-American and Japanese models.

Singapore adopted the koban system in 1983, replacing the previous British colonial policing inheritance, under the rubric of the

Neighbourhood Police Post (NPP). Japanese koban experts supervised the innovation. The rationales given for that development were a substantial increase in recorded (and arguably preventable) property crime, changes in the spatial distribution of the population from the city to the new suburban estates, and increased expectations of the police from a better educated (and more demanding) population. Within ten years, the system had been adopted throughout the territory.

The NPP were to have two primary features. They were to represent a decentralized model of policing with increased discretion for local officers and they were to emphasize proactive as opposed to reactive policing. The new NPPs were based on where demand was greatest and on the numbers of local households and the needs of the local population. They focused on four key practices: foot and bicycle patrols to enhance visibility and community contact, regular household visits, proactive crime prevention functions such as equipment-marking, and community initiatives such as the establishment of neighbourhood watches. Problem-solving practices were later added to these functions.

Box 4.2 *An example of problem-solving in Singapore*

The NPP used to receive many complaints about coffee shop patrons consuming beer after midnight, even when the coffee shops were closed. Residents complained about the consequent noise, litter, vandalism and other public order problems. The NPP resolved the problem in several ways: by cooperating with the coffee-shops owners to stop the sale of beer and to control the supply of refreshments prior to evening closure. For example, coffee-shop furniture was to be secured against vandalism and potential weapons such as empty bottles removed. Underlying this local strategy was the encouragement of peer influence amongst the coffee-shop owners to encourage the support of good crime prevention practice (Singh 2002).

The NPP system has recently been reformed, replacing those units with Neighbourhood Policing Centres (NPCs), in an attempt to change the system from one that was 'community based' to one that was 'community focused'. The central purpose of the change was however to make the Singapore police more proactive in the community and more committed to wider problem-solving. Community involvement was to be enhanced and policing was to become more sensitive to the peculiarities of the local context. It had been argued that there were several drawbacks to the NPPs. An officer received little job satisfaction, dealing with only a small section of a particular case. Giving them more involvement in the overall process would presumably enhance their sense of ownership of the case and increase their effectiveness. It would also increase the contribution to case resolution by making more use of their local knowledge. It would ensure that crime victims had one primary contact with the case progress and avoid him or her being dealt with by potentially competing and confusing policing agencies. Each new NPC consists of some 100-120 officers, serving a population of some 5,000 households. This development was accompanied by significant changes in the functions of the new NPCs and of the police organization as a whole.

Box 4.3   *Changes from the NPP system to the NPC system*

NPP system	NPC system
Community policing post with limited services	One-stop policing providing the full range of policing services
General services to contact residents and establish points of contact	Focused on services that are critical to safety and security
Low value tasks and narrow job scope	High value case involvement and better quality officers
Compartmentalization of services with many officers each performing a separate task	Integrated service process with one NPC officer handling the entire service process
Lower priority on proactive work	Dedicated resources for proactive work
Community based policing	Community focused policing

Generally the objective has been to increase officer involvement in individual cases and to ensure that the policing system narrows its focus – proactively – to more directly safety and security issues, thus removing more peripheral and time consuming non-crime functions. Critically, like the Japanese and Chinese policing system, the Singapore system is directed at the notion of the household responsibility for crime and social affairs rather than as in the West at individual citizens.

As we note at the outset, it is difficult to critically appraise the Singapore system without access to independent materials. Bayley (1989), as with Japan, had earlier provided a euphoric account of the new policing system. Singapore sells policing to much of Asia and its model is widely admired in neighbouring countries. But it is a peculiar case in a South Asian context. Essentially, a city state, it enjoys Western standards of development and socio-economically is ranged with so-called 'first-world' states. Singapore has a relatively unitary population with little international migration, suggesting that whatever the values and potential failings of the Singapore NPC, it is not a system that is easily imitated in other domains.

Community policing in China: mobilizing the masses

The Chinese are desperate to change and want to change to our model of community policing officer. But they realise they have to change their whole infrastructure.[14]

Interpreting community policing in China requires several changes of gear from the understanding of Anglo-American community policing. Like the koban (and indeed the Singapore Neighbourhood Policing Centre), it emphasizes collective rather than an individual aproach to policing. The household and the community are core concepts, not the citizen. Secondly, it reflects indigenous tradition – it flows from Chinese history and especially from early Confucian ideology (as reinterpreted during the Maoist period). Thirdly, of course, it may embody a different notion of policing – one that emphasizes social responsibilities to the state rather than individual rights of the consumer of policing services. Like the Japanese system, it is also much more intrusive into social affairs than policing in the West. China represents a society in which community policing as state spying from one perspective may be regarded as community safeguarding on the other. Finally, while sources are limited on its character and effectiveness, there has been some critical comment by (mainly) Chinese scholars. However, sources as elsewhere are still susceptible to the problems of official production.

In China there is a very low police to population ratio, signifying that policing is perceived not simply as an official function but also as the responsibility of a variety of local civil agencies – from local 'struggle' committees to the collectivity of the household. As in the rosy-tinted accounts of Japanese policing, in China policing is 'everyone's business'. This is not merely an empirical, if complicated, fact. It touches on a much larger debate about the state police/private police continuum[15]. It raises questions about both the nature of policing in China – and indeed in the Anglo-American societies – and also the relation between the state and local communities in terms of responsibilities for policing matters. On one hand, reading the several accounts of community policing in today's China as through the official discourse and orthodox presentations of

COP in the West, one can find little difference in glossy presentation. However, in China serious recent academic studies, such as that of Wong (2001) claims that the Chinese experience of community policing until recently has been a positive one, bolstered by communal solidarity and responsibilities, and a low crime rate. Wong acknowledges however that he furnishes an account of the formal intent of policing advocates in China, while practice on the street may be different. That academic account contrasts favourably with Western experience of community fragmentation, apathy and a high fear of crime.

The Chinese police's wide powers have been a subject of controversy and criticism. This largely stems from the fact that the Chinese police are not only granted regular police powers such as to arrest and detain, but are also given considerable discretion to impose various administrative sanctions. These latter may result in an individual's loss of freedom for months or even years. The police have the authority to impose such sanctions on their own initiative and discretion without any court approval and supervision.

Historically, social control in China was decentralized and organized around natural communal and intimate groups. As Leishman has noted elsewhere such local policing was infused by Confucian teachings. Remarkably, this system still influences Chinese society.

Box 4.4   *Influence of Confucianism on the Chinese policing system*

---

1. Crime control is a local, indigenous and family affair.
2. Crime control starts with prevention. Prevention addresses early symptoms and manifestations of personal problems. Successful crime control addresses the root cause, and not the outward symptoms of crime.
3. To be effective, crime prevention must be a multi-faceted, comprehensive, and integrated enterprise, involving the individual, the clan, neighbours, community and the state.
4. Crime control and prevention measures should be variegated. Confucius observed 'inspire them with justice, correct them with administration, guide them with rites, keep them straight with honesty, appeal to them with benevolence, reward them with benefits, and persuade them to follow'. More simply, crime control can be best achieved through moral education as supplemented by fast, severe and speedy punishments.

(adapted from Wong 2001)

Integration of civil and state structures

Central to Chinese community policing is the parallel and collaborative existence of civil and state structures. Central to the former is the *baojia* system of household security. It was a system of local control, instituted in several forms during the imperial period, a system based on mutual responsibility of households. Local populations were divided into units, usually composed of ten households each. Members would have the mutual responsibility of seeing that everyone in the baojia unit maintained good order. If a violation occurred and caught the attention of officials, everyone in the baojia unit would be punished for the crime of one of its members (Chen 2002). With Western intrusions in the nineteenth century, the system disintegrated but retained its ideological significance with regard to the collective nature of civil policing.

By the latter part of the nineteenth century, local functionaries who had originally played no part in the baojia were all that was effectively left of the policing. From the time of the '100 days' reform (1898-1899), the baojia system was administered under the newly constituted and Western-influenced police department. The essence of baojia changed. The administration of public security and the baojia administrations which had previously been separated were now integrated. These changes to baojia administration were only a part of a major reform of the police institution. Policing, in the modern Western sense, thus came into being. This reform was designed to remodel the force along the lines of Japanese and Western police practices. By 1902, the baojia structure was largely a thing of the past, being replaced by local neighbourhood police on the one hand and a centralised police bureau on the other, although the spirit of the baojia remains.

Wong (2001) offers several justifications for this continuing commitment:

- People have a right to their own governance. As expressed most clearly in Shearing 'policing is everybody's business'.
- The people have the responsibility to fight crime – the Tythingman theme from the West.
- People are in the best position to see that 'people's justice is done, including making decisions as what to police, who to police, and how to police.'[16]
- The people are deemed to be more in contact with misdemeanours and thus more vigilant – they 'own' justice and will consequently take responsibility for it.

- The people are in the best position, being more able and efficient in conducting their own business to be, in Western terms, the 'eyes and ears of the police'. It is unrealistic to expect the police to provide security without cooperation from the people. The state police are not omnipresent nor are they omnipotent.

It would be difficult to find a more exemplary version of community policing philosophy than Wong interprets from Chinese society. Traditional views on social regulation and crime control were informed by the following premises: crime control is a local, indigenous and, above all, family affair:

- Crime control starts with prevention. Prevention addresses early symptoms and manifestations of personal problems. Successful crime control addresses the root causes, and not the outward symptoms of crime, e.g. the moral degeneration of the individual, the cultural pollution of the people, and criminogenic social conditions of the community. Crime prevention must be a multi-faceted, comprehensive, and integrated enterprise, involving the individual, family, clan, neighbour, community and the state.
- Crime control can be best achieved through moral education and supplemented by fast, severe and instant punishment.
- Crime control is part of a wider system of regulating and creating community solidarity, irrespective of the nature of the formal state.
- The community is geographically defined and has to cope with the misdemeanors of all, whether local or transient (Chen 2002).

The strong emphasis on a communal existence, with powerful neighborhood committees, produces throughout the country a social control net that is very different from that present in Western countries. While more formal systems are emerging, especially in urban areas, the organization of local policing is grounded in mass participation through a network of committees. These popular justice institutions are both proactive and reactive in identifying potentially troublesome social situations, preventing crime, resolving conflicts and dealing with offensive behaviour (Wong 2001).

The first function reflects the collective as opposed to individual notions of justice in Chinese society. In particular, as in the West in terms of problem-solving, it seeks to deal with the cause of social misbehaviour. Like the newly reconstituted restorative justice system in some Western cities, it aims to resolve problems and deviance informally, rather than involving officialdom. The second function of crime prevention has its nearest Western proximity in the symbol of the Norman Tythingman[17]. Crime prevention is placed firmly in the hands of the local Self Defence Committee (SDC) who are themselves responsible for infractions and subject to compensation claims. Titles of units vary and may not have direct Anglo-American equivalents. But China does in practice appear to operate a legitimate variant on the community policing model. For example, one of the key police agencies under the control of the Ministry of Public Security is a 'patrol police' according to Xiancui[18]. In China the Police Patrol conduct street policing as a deterrent and as '... well as helping victims of various offences, providing help to anyone who needs it on the street like giving direction to tourists, helping children and aged persons who may have lost their way home and so forth'. Practice, as elsewhere under the community policing rubric, may be different. But it is easy to see how such a formula could extend to community problem-solving and community partnerships.

Communities are endowed with far greater rights and responsibilities than in the West. This view is not just a reflection of the political ideologies of different Chinese regimes, but also reflects continuing different cultural perceptions. Consequently, local community policing revolves around three local structures: the Public Security Committee (PSC), the Mediation Committee (MC), and in the household registration process.

Under the Security Defence Act 1952, PSCs were established in local areas and (after new legislation in 1978) were to be mainly concerned with providing for local public order through crime prevention – community crime watch and mutual surveillance, and order maintenance such as mediation and supervision over offenders (Wong 2001). In practice, the PSCs are delegated three policing functions: conflict resolution; crime prevention; and household registration. Under Maoism, the primary role of the PSC was one of securing communal support through rising class-consciousness. Now it attempts to achieve law and order by educating the people to the spirit and letter of the law, and organizing people to provide for mutual security defence against crime. The PSCs exert two policing functions. Firstly, to resolve local conflicts and disputes by reference to law, regulations, custom and village agreement before they become unmanageable. A successful mediation resolves disputes without disrupting existing relationships. Secondly, they act as generic problem-solving structures.

The PSCs constitute the basis of community policing and are vehicles of self-policing which de-emphasize bureaucratic features and the professionalization of policing. They are composed of local cadres and interested persons of the neighbourhood, including retired people.

Originally regarded as informal controls, they are now increasingly incorporated into the local state apparatus[19]. Membership depends upon ideological correctness, experience to handle public affairs and commitment to local harmony. Their task is to assist police in matters of social order, under the leadership of the local police. They act as the first response agency for local misdemeanours, domestic disputes and potential problems of social order. Locally the PSCs act as a kind of citizen watch scheme. They bring suspicious people or activities to the attention of the local police (it is for those individuals to justify their actions rather than the other way round). Unlike Western values, the commitment is to restore community harmony rather than to recognize individual rights – informers, for example are not disdained as in the West, but are regarded as necessary to communal solidarity. The actual mode of policing is reliant upon the time honoured system of mutual surveillance – peers, friends and immediate neighbours reportedly have little compunction about taking action when deviance is suspected (Chen 2002).

The Mediation Committee is a critical feature of local policing in its widest sense, aiming to solve disputes without resort to heavy handed intervention by an alien legal process. Mediators dispose of local disputes through the use of help-education and victim-reparations, thus avoiding criminal stigmatization and legal labelling. (However, mediation is optional and people are notionally free to use the formal court system instead.) The state police are ancillary to this process and have no formal involvement. MCs are critical because of the Chinese commitment to the principle that law is not an ideal vehicle for solving local problems. Behaviour which is directed by moral values is superior to behaviour that is directed by fear of legal sanction (Chen 2002).

Thirdly, the system of household registration provides a key local element of local policing, although functions go far beyond ordinary public security and control of criminal deviance. Each neighbourhood police station has to have a household registration section. The register is administered by the registration police, who are a subdivision of the ordinary local police and whose specialized task it is to carry out registration work. The household registration police also have subsidiary roles in other domains of policing, and these include the maintenance of public order, the prevention of thefts, aiding and supporting all criminal investigations, and the work of the neighbourhood committees. Without registration, one cannot enter school, obtain and hold employment, participate in elections, serve in the armed forces or marry. It is a citizen's passport into direct relations with the welfare state. Annual checks on population and households include such minute details as the correlation of house numbers with household population figures. The police station may sign a contract with local groups, such as businesses, factories and schools. In rural areas, a responsible person in each village is designated as an official household agent in charge of registration matters. The person works closely with the household police officer at the police post. Several types of record are maintained to deal with local problems – a book is kept on the distribution of all persons without a registered household and any registered households without some or all of its registered residents; a chart is kept containing the name, residence, and household address of all the residents in the area; a photo album of all the youth and able-bodied in the area between 16 and 50 years of age; and a map showing the distribution of households. This system allows both community structures and the police to keep track of the potential disrupters of both communal norms and of state laws (Dutton 1992).

Community policing in the small Chinese community has much in common with the Japanese koban system, especially with regard to record-keeping. Like the koban officer, the household registration system allows the SDC and the police to keep track of the movement of suspected criminals and of local disruptive characters (Wong 2001). Like the Japanese system, that information gathering process can also be used for central state surveillance processes. The process of policing essentially means that traditional, classical methods of surveillance are pressed into the service of the contemporary regime.

Social change – the rejection of community policing

Paradoxically, such local policing is moving in the opposite direction from that of the West and away from notions of community policing. While in the West different forms of community policing are the dominant policing ideology, the Chinese police seem to be moving to a more professional and bureaucratic model of policing. The rationale is simple. The changes occurring in the Chinese police must be understood in the context of China's economic reforms which have dislocated local social structures, destroying the local *Gemeinschaft* in favour of a *Gesellschaft*. Wong recognises several conundrums in these relationships, ones mirrored in English history with the conflict over the role of the village constable – between local social norms and state decrees, between state ideology and instrumental local needs, and the exigencies of local democracy and state administration direction (Wong 2001). Whether it is pragmatic policing or scientific policing the result is the same. Policing in

Box 4.5   *An offical Chinese version of community policing*[20]

Beef Street station has 51 officers. Since 1985, the station officers have been collectively cited for meritorious conduct. Because the station's financial situation is precarious it received offers of bits and pieces from units outside the precinct and from the masses who are keen to help resolve some of their needs. But station leaders have always refused such good intentions. 'Love the police, love the profession and love Beef Street' is the shared understanding of police officers at the Beef Street Station. Because the predominant residential population of Beef Street are of the Hui nationality, the people's police officers in this precinct all study the Party's policy on national minorities and take classes so that they can cultivate an understanding of the customs and habits of the Hui. Most of the officers on the staff of the station are Han Chinese, but they all believe that 'when in Rome, one must do as the Romans do' and the station persists with opening only a Hui nationality kitchen and respecting Hui customs. At Beef Street Station, the household registration office is the station's 'civilised window' , and on the wall hangs the opinion box, the comments book, a road and rail map, a map of the streets of the area, as well as household registration rules and a place for public notices. Above the entrance, 19 officers who patrol have also set aside a time to aid the 56 people in the area who are old and lonely. They help them wash their clothes and clean the house. They get coal for their stoves and, at festive times, they come to greet them. They take them to the hospital to see sick friends, and they ensure that the old are taken out to have a good time and, at the same time, make sure they are warm. For the rest of the masses, the station also helps to resolve disputes.

China is becoming more instrumental than 'ideological'[21] . Secondly, the urbanization process has broken up those local structures of control with especially dislocated youth. Geographical mobility, especially the flight from the rural areas to the cities, has undermined those agencies.

Finally, as the police become more and more professionalized and specialized, they become more isolated and alienated from the people they serve. For example, the police are less interested in establishing a rapport with the people and more and more interested in catching criminals and fighting crimes. In pursuing aggressive crime fighting strategies, e.g. indiscriminate fight crime (*yanda*) campaigns and stop and search operations, the police alienate local residents they are supposed to serve, depend on and be accountable to. Increasingly the police officers are seen as dictating to the people rather than engaging and involving them. In adopting scientific crime fighting methods, the investigation and detection of crime is made the responsibility of specialized units. This alienates crime victims and ignores local community sentiments and input. The specialization and bureaucratization of investigation have the net effect of reducing the participation and involvement of the community structures (Wong 2001).

The problems with Chinese community policing are similar to those noted elsewhere. Critically, the distinction between community policing and community spying is a distinction that is subjective and waits further discussion elsewhere. Secondly, the local community policing often reflects the tension between the local society and the central state. What comes first: social order in the community according to local norms, or the rule of the law imposed centrally? Like the village constable of early industrial England, the incompetence of the local policing system may not be pathological but because it is stranded between two quite different conceptions of social order. Finally, community policing necessarily reflects the degree of social stability and integrated communities. Many communities in China, rural and urban, are the subject as elsewhere of larger social, political and economic change, especially the urbanization process. Social order – community policing – works best during static periods. China is in the midst of a long and complicated process of social and political change, and intact communities are rare.

Overview

This chapter has several implications for the study of the development of community policing. First of all, Asian Pacific Rim community policing strategies have legitimate, different, origins from those of the Anglo-American model. While there may often be coincidence in practice, some of the core assumptions – as in the concern with households rather than individual responsibility and in the relationship of the people to the state – may be quite different[22].

Secondly, a critical analysis of such structures must start from a different basis. In particular, what might be perceived as state intrusion into personal life and into community affairs has a radically different meaning when viewed through other cultural lenses. Models may be similar but the assumptions on which they are based are different. Thirdly, especially in China, the notion that policing is delegated to an official state functionary rather than to the community is an alien concept. The continuum between police and people is – relatively – unbroken as compared with the division between civil communities and official police functionaries in the West. Finally, the critique of such structures and practices remains only tentative, especially given the problem of access to appropriate alternative sources of data on the effectiveness of community policing.

Notes

1 Similarly, in Northern Ireland as part of the Peace Process, the Milton Eisenhower Foundation sponsored visits by local politicians to koban structures in the United States.
2 The metaphor of 'snail's feeders', alert and sensitive to danger, signifying the neighbourhood police – noted by Aldous and Leishman (2000).
3 Quoted in Aldous and Leishman (2000).
4 Although problem-solving as such it is not formally perceived to be part of the police mandate.
5 Conveniently ignoring the reported two million or so citizens of Korean origin.
6 Yano (1989, p. 127) quoted in Aldous and Leishman (2000).
7 Given that degree of local control, a different reading might suggest that it is unsurprising that it later became the basis for Singapore's adoption under the 'elected dictatorship' of Lee Kuan Yew.
8 Finch (1999) makes the point that the orthodox accounts of the koban in the academic literature are primarily from Americans attempting to find ways of improving their own system. The latter take policing in the United States as the starting point, and view models such as the koban as the basis for home improvement. See Brogden (1991) for the importance of the beat as a system of local control.
9 Wehrfritz and Takayama quoted in *Newsweek International*, 21 February 2000.
10 Ibid.
11 Quoted in *Newsweek International*, 21 February 2001.
12 Cited in Aldous and Leishman (2000).
13 See Chapter 7.
14 Bramshill course tutor, commenting on the exchange of 20 British police officers with their Chinese counterparts and the studies of the latter at Bramshill Police College (*The Independent*, 19 March 2000).
15 See Shearing (2003).
16 Wong equates this theme to Wilson's (1968) principle that community notions of justice must prevail over the rule of law.
17 The local officer held responsible for crime prevention during his tour of duty and himself would be liable for damages if any crime or loss was committed in the community during his term. Indeed, in the early 1900s, the British depicted these as being 'a superior sort of constable'. Quoted in Wong (2001, p. 191).
18 Quoted in Wong (2001).
19 Chen (2002) notes that in the West the PDC would be regarded as informal

structures whereas in China they are recognized as official structures within the state.

20 Quoted in Dutton (1992).

21 Feng (1994) quoted in Wong (2001).

22 There is one major exception to the Chinese experience – that of Hong Kong, where attempts have been made unsuccessfully to change a colonial style police force to a community policing agency – see Lau (2004).

Chapter 5

Aspects of community policing in the European Union

... le community policing est-il une simple manière d'accompagne un processus spontane de ressuirannce sociale de ceux qui s'inscrivent dans le rêve americain au prix de l'exclusion de ceux qui y derogent, trop pauvres, trop deviant?

(Donzelot and Wyvekens 2000)

Introduction

Asking Western European countries if they are in favour of community policing is a little like asking them if they are in favour of Christmas. Without exception, within the official discourses, the member states of the European Union from France to Finland are in favour of, and practice, community policing. Official discourse provides no basis for doubt about intent and practice[1]. All member states support more direct police involvement in communities. But the devil is in the detail. Practice and understanding of the concept seems a long way from the material discussed in Chapter 2.

In the European Union, perception and attitudes to community policing vary according to primary – historically, politically and culturally informed – definitions of the police function. The police systems of continental Europe have more centralized police systems than in Anglo-American societies. Such systems (Mawby 1999) are

- structurally more centralized and militaristic;
- functionally inclusive of many political and administrative tasks;

- not dependent on the ideological notion of public consent but are much more tied to the central government and less accountable to the public.

In practice, of course, there are marked variations within such general parameters. For example, Switzerland has a canton-based system. On the other hand, the Netherlands (1993) reorganized its policing into 25 regionally based forces. Sweden moved from a local system to a national policing structure in 1965. What is most common is a structure where one centralized military police force is counterbalanced either by a second central policing agency or by a medley of local urban forces. Continental police systems are also distinctive in terms of roles and responsibilities. Welfare and community orientation are rarely evident. They have traditionally conducted a wide range of administrative functions (such as responsibilities for passport control and tax collection). Where, as France, Spain, and Italy, the core function of policing has generally been regarded as defending the central state, considerations of community involvement in that practice are not regarded as of critical relevance. In countries which have transcended the Napoleonic inheritance to develop decentralized policing structures, as in the Netherlands, community policing initiatives relate to the larger political transformations. Further, where schemes have been developed with a community policing aspect, crime prevention rather than the elevation of community-police relations has normally been the major objective.

Schematically three different models of policing are visible in Western Europe (Tupman and Tupman 1999): Napoleonic, national and decentralized. Thus a country which has retained the principles of the Napoleonic inheritance, such as France and Italy, maintain a policing system (gendarmerie responsible to the Ministry of Defence, or its equivalent) and a civilian organization (national police) responsible to the Ministry of the Interior or Justice. There may also be a judicial arm of the police which deals with investigatory and prosecution functions. In national police forces such as Finland, Greece, and Ireland, members of a unitary police service can be posted anywhere in the country and are responsible to a single centralized authority with a designated senior police commander. In decentralized police structures, as in Germany and Great Britain (and of course in the United States) there is no central unitary body or commissioner. However, such countries have almost as many variations between them as with regard to the other models. Thus Germany has some 12 different police forces dealing with different functions. In Great Britain (that is excluding Northern Ireland[2]) 51 different police forces deal with the same issues, but in different geographical locations.

Box 5.1 *Models of Western European policing*[3]

Napoleonic	National	Decentralized
Austria		
Belgium		
	Denmark	
	Finland since 1997	Finland before 1997
France		
Greece until 1984	Greece post-1984	
		Germany
	Ireland	
Italy		
Luxembourg		
Netherlands until 1990		Netherlands after 1990
Portugal		
Spain		Spain
	Sweden after 1965	Sweden before 1965
		UK

There are several implications of these models for the critique of Anglo-American style community policing. First of all countries which have retained the original Napoleonic model contain legal structures which have traditionally regarded the priority of policing as defending the social order of the state not the local, communal, quality of life issues, presumed central to community policing. Culturally, organizationally, and politically, policing is perceived in considerably different ways than within the decentralized structures of Anglo-American countries. However, national policing structures, as in the case of the Netherlands, have broken with the Napoleonic past to develop much more local influence and sensitivity, although retaining certain other Napoleonic features. However, complexly, just because a state supports decentralized policing does not of itself provide an atmosphere conducive to community policing – as in Germany with its functionally differentiated forces.[4]

However key historical practices and structure suggest, in practice, major variations in the interpretations of the practice of community policing. The evidential material on community policing in the European Union varies in quality. In part, this problem relates to the lack of importance given to the concept.

This chapter makes several points. Judging by the experience of Western Europe, there is no 'inevitable progress' towards community policing. Secondly, as in the previous chapters, police strategies reflect national and cultural histories. Even if there was some substance to the claim that Anglo-American policing once had community consent, that consent is not perceived as a necessary imperative in large parts of Western Europe where alternative forms of *proximity policing* have been developed.

Box 5.2 *Key features of the Napoleonic system*

- Police function is traditionally to defend the social order of the central state.
- Policing may include a range of administrative duties.
- There are often two national policing agencies, one counterbalancing the other.
- Relatively restricted public accountability and rarely any local accountability.
- Often structured on militaristic lines with minimal local discretion.
- Few welfare functions.

Centralized policing systems – adaptation of the Napoleonic inheritance

France – proximity policing and community safety contracts

The quotation from Donzelot and Wyvekens demonstrates again the ethnocentric assumptions that Anglo-American policing has set an inexorable path for the rest of the world to follow. Community policing is the future. There are indications that Western European countries are now trying to catch up. The French example demonstrates clearly that legitimacy in police development is not an Anglo-Saxon prerogative. However three factors in France have prompted calls for a form of community policing – rising recorded crime rates, similar rises in the fear of crime, and riots in the (largely) ethnic minority estates (Dupont 2002).

France has inherited a policing structure which is at major variance from the norm of Anglo-American countries. Compared to other democratic countries, France has a relatively large state police with 90,000 gendarmerie and 135,000 national police, nearly twice that of Britain's. In such a model of Napoleonic policing, the police are merely part of a centralized administrative apparatus in constructing a public order, which includes notions of social tranquillity, citizen safety, public health and state security. In France, policing has three markedly different elements: as an instrument of the state, as an organization with its own history and as a centralized bureaucracy. These dimensions imply that the police act under authority of the government, in accordance with the social demand for policing, and also in their own professional interest. Consequently, interest in community policing has been peripheral. Local community social order – and concern with communal crime and welfare – has been secondary to other priorities (Monjardet 1996). Local police organizations have historically been rare.[5] From 1941 to the early 1980s there were almost no municipal forces. However some 3,000 municipalities now enjoy a local policing system totalling some 13,000 officers – only some ten cities have more than 100 such municipal officers (2,000 in Paris) – the nearest form to a community police. They represent a kind of auxiliary police and relieve the state police of matters regarded as 'foreign' to real policing. But they were designed to avoid direct competition with the powers of the centrally organized policing institutions.

There is some dispute over whether in fact the gendarmeries may actually be nearer to neighbourhood contact than the Police Nationale. Because the gendarmerie covers most suburbs, small towns and countryside, contrary to a PN officer, a gendarmerie agent (despite living in barracks) may in the course of the day investigate a crime, regulate the traffic, register citizen's complaints or patrol the district – an approximation of community policing (Monjardet 1996). Further, the local gendarme may deal with the totality of a case – processing is under a single officer – from complaint through investigation through to report to prosecutor. The Police Nationale is only separately involved at each stage of processing. In any case the gendarme's work time is about twice that of a Police Nationale officer.

But the most evident community policing structure in France are the new public safety policies under the banner of 'proximity policing'. Local agencies are required to adopt a partnership approach to co-produce public safety, aiming to bring these institutions closer to their users. However, the proximity they are intended to install does not substantially change police work and any ancillary staff hired especially for that purpose, to convey this *proximity* approach, are functionnaires with ill defined roles, entailing the risk that they become barriers instead of bridges between the institutions and their users (Donzelot and Wyvekens 2000).

Proximity policing

The French version of community policing, *policing de proximité* (neighbourhood policing) was introduced in 1999 as the basis for a comprehensive training for some ten per cent of the police establishment. While some accounts regard policing de proximité as a British invention[6] others maintain it is a recent native development, as implicit in the Bonnemaison strategy from the early 1980s. The latter was a local initiative, essentially an inter-agency crime prevention strategy, with the police coordinating its central organization (Dupont 2002). After electoral losses in 1981, the political Left recognized rising public concerns with crime and delinquency. It therefore turned to socialist mayors who had had to deal with community safety and security problems because of the vacuum left by the central state's neglect of such matters – hence the development of local crime prevention initiatives. These new crime prevention structures involved all interested public and private agencies, including the police, the gendarmerie and the judicial authorities. The police role in this inter-agency development became the basis for proximity policing. The key features of proximity policing are as bland and as open to interpretation as much of the COP rhetoric:

- police action is structured around specific localities and districts;

- permanent and continuing contact with the local population is required, within the framework of the local security contract;

- the police role is to be versatile – from coercive to social service functions;

- substantive responsibility and discretion is to be delegated to the police;

- qualities of interpersonal service are required of police officers, especially in relation to vulnerable people.

The notion of proximity itself is to cover all relevant local agencies and ensures a continuing local dialogue with the public. It is not simply an enabling device, bringing the two parties together but rather a mode of action with continuing collaboration sensitive to local needs[7].

The central aims of the police de proximité are to adapt the functioning of the police to local needs, to give priority to the population's security expectations and to integrate policing into a local policy of safety which is to be decided with local authorities and other agencies interested in safety matters (justice, social services, schools etc) and representatives of the local population (municipality, residents' association). Such community initiatives suffer from major handicaps however; police officers are deliberately not posted to their own locality because loyalty to the central authorities is preferred to loyalty to the place of origin and to local affiliations. Thus urban police departments have become detachments of the state police with very little social and functional ties with the place in which they work. Most constables will spend the major part of their career changing localities every few years to move closer to their region of origin, where they will finish their career and retire. Such an occupational priority does not foster local involvement and interest in local problems.

Secondly, the implementation of the police de proximité plans was due to take place during the three years from early 1999, in five police districts, and then in another 62. This was however a voluntary schedule and progress nationally has not been smooth. The piety of commitment to community policing is illustrated by the national police response to the European Union consultation process:

> No special community policing statute has been created as the sort of the community policing mission encompasses all officers posted to the National Public Security Headquarters...
> (Council of the European Union 2003, p. 39)

Proximity policing and the local security contract

The practice of proximity policing must be based on an evaluation of local crime problems and then outlined in a formal Local Safety Contract (CLS)[8]. This contract, initiated in 1997, applies to both the national police force and to the gendarmerie alike. The police must now share its expertise with other partners and must take into account the latter's expertise and expectations and conversely, prevent the police from being held responsible for everything, since objectives and means have been decided in common. The central state has encouraged this initiative by financially rewarding municipalities that effectively adopt the scheme (Dupont 2002).

This contract has historical origins. The French administrative approach to social crime prevention has always included the police and other parts of the criminal justice system, social housing agencies, health and social work agencies, public transport authorities, managers of private rented accommodation, and the city administration in relation to cleaning and lighting.

The CLS is negotiated for a given area (associations of towns, town, neighbourhoods, transport networks and so on). Like watch schemes elsewhere, the contract may be either territory-based or interest-based (as in transport systems). It constitutes a written undertaking which outlines local priorities for security maintenance and a description of the methods to which each party is committed. The proximity police are required to be familiar with these priorities. To achieve them, the police are expected to use a variety of local methods: protocols of agreement (local joint action statements and the techniques to be utilized), regular exchanges of information with institutional partner agencies (such as those dealing with delinquency, neighbourhood committees and so on), and local victim surveys on perceptions of crime priorities and police effectiveness.

However there are no local legal structures such as community forums to formalize police-citizen coordination. Indeed, the only response by the national police organization with regard to such statutory structures is simply to state that citizens are entitled legally to arrest the perpetrators of crime and take him or her to court – a long way from even the relatively pious functions of the Anglo-American community forums. As the gendarmerie describes it 'There are no privileged channels between the gendarmerie and the population, apart from dialling (to the) gendarmerie operations centre' (Council of the European Union 2003, p. 36).

In a way not dissimilar in intent to those of the household police (although less complete and systematic[9]), the police keep three data sets on local communities. The Sector File records information on community expectations of policing, delinquency records, and a variety of general data. The Neighbourhood File records data on crime-prone sites (crime-mapping) ranging from location and identity of partners to child and youth entertainment sites, and data on transport, traffic and road safety. The Sector-Based Operational Instrument Panel (TBOS) is intended to track local incidents and includes reports on delinquency and insecurity, the status of police action towards resolving local problems, variety of quality service measures on public perceptions and reaction (such as records of complaints), local crime data and general outcome indicators.

In Paris, where proximity policing involves some 10,000 officers, the local safety contract contains six sections: to develop community response to crime, to prevent and respond to juvenile delinquency, to prevent and control drug crime, to control the fear of crime and to help vulnerable factions of the population to develop victim support schemes, and to reinforce community partnerships (Body-Gendrot 2004).

In the Paris security contract signed between the state, the Police Prefect designated 209 sites of 5,000 to 15,000 residents to benefit from community police officers. In the most problematic area, 100 'night mediators' work with public housing managers and public transportation agents to reinforce public safety. However, this scheme has little value in practice with minimal overall coordination and often utilises civilians with little motivation for the work; agents may be unfamiliar with one another and with the overall purpose of the scheme, relying in part on students who do not want to be on suburban patrols but prefer to work in urban centres. As elsewhere, much of the new community policing, whether proximity policing or tiered civilian municipal safety work, is performed by young inexperienced auxiliaries hired to supplement other demands on police establishments[10].

A critical Paris study suggests major problems in the implementation of the scheme (Body-Gendrot 2004). The development of community policing in Paris is riven (it is claimed) by conflicts between local and central state authorities – between the Paris Prefect and the Paris Mayor. Paris policing is under the control of the former and of the central state, not the elected local Mayor. Faced with a lack of local policing, the Mayor created a Bureau of Prevention with a corps of auxiliaries 'Inspectors of security of the City of Paris'. The new socialist mayor (in 2001) wished to develop police de proximité by deploying 1,000 police on streets – re-defining the police function from order maintenance to fighting crime. Hence he constructed an informal bargain with the Police Prefect to provide 500 municipal agents (AMIS) in each of 2001 and 2002 to conduct a variety of local proximity policing functions – such as supervising street crossings to safeguarding children, and 400 agents of security for traffic duties and 'quality of life' offences (dogs, garbage, alcohol etc). While these new tiered community officers were paid by the city, the latter required formal permission from the state to deploy them. The state/city conflict impeded any local 'community' policing development.

In any case, the limited safety contract (the nearest to the notion of community policing) has not been an evident success. It has not met with universal approval across the country. Further, the very notion of a contract is a problem – obligations to it are voluntary not binding. It is a one way process. As a contract, it is exceptionally vague in terms of the commitments to it by the various parties. As with many such schemes in Anglo-American societies, it has experienced little in the way of evaluation. More generally, national police structures and practices remain intact and local policing remains an 'add-on'.

> Here is the real challenge of the gendarmerie: as the centre of gravity shifts from the countryside to suburb, it faces the same problems as the PN and appears less and less able to preserve its own mode of neighbourhood/community policing.
>
> (Levy and Zauberman 2002)

This limited critical analysis of the development of proximity policing and of the Local Safety Contract suggests many obstacles to the French development, some peculiar to France and some which reflect more universal problems in the concept of community policing. Apart from the unchanging central organizational characteristics of the national police and of the gendarmerie, police unions fear that national bargains are being undermined by local initiatives. As elsewhere, the police culture perceives preventative policing as a digression from real police work. Limited audits show that street level police do not adhere to community policing policy (Levy and Zauberman 2002). Policy research in Paris shows that beat officers tend to redefine their proactive tasks in traditional ways. Instead of concentrating on problem-solving and assistance to citizens, officers individually, and the police organization in general, may use their position to gather criminal intelligence thus jeopardizing their relationship with local people. As far as Paris itself is concerned, given a 30 per cent a year turnover in manpower, there is a major problem of continuity in local relationships. Victim surveys have been criticized by the Minister of Interior for apparently challenging the 'official' truths in the recorded crime reports – traditions of police secrecy are apparently being violated.

In any case, post-September 11, much may have changed in French policing, with old habits being reinforced, *inter alia* the Minister of the Interior assuming responsibility for both the police and the gendarmerie with a general expansion of the more coercive features of the French policing structures. But there are other problems – the dependence of local initiatives on a few motivated officers, the disjunctions in training, the extent to which such developments paradoxically increase public expectations of the police, and the fact – as noted elsewhere – that in the inter-agency partnerships required by the CLS, the police tend to dominate (Dupont 2002). Whether that reaction is transient or permanent history will decide, but the omens are not good for a more locally oriented, democratic community policing.

Belgium – policing facing two masters, central state and locality

Belgian policing is in a process of transition – with many hiccups (Van den Broeck 2002). Belgium reflects a state in which the Napoleonic legal and policing inheritance looms large. But the traditional commitment to a centralized structure has recently shown signs of disintegration with episodic movements towards the decentralized structures critical to the development of community policing. As in France, the Belgian police are not independent of the political, judicial and administrative structures of the central state. Before the 1990s generic crime prevention and detection, and public order policing, were carried out by a three-tier structure: the national gendarmerie, provincial police and local municipal forces. The primary feature of all three agencies was reactive crime control.

Several national scandals encouraged the development of community forums rather than proximity policing[11]. The malpractices which came to light in 1998 in police and judicial circles gave a major impetus to a development of a community policing model with some movement towards a more decentralized community-sensitive model. This intention was embodied in two pieces of legislation – the Police Functions Act (1992) and the Integrated Policing Act (1998). Under the auspices of the Ministry of the Interior, the Office of the Commissioner-General for Local Police Relations (CGL) was instructed to develop a community policing programme. The new structure emphasises agent de proximité – community police include auxiliaries (as in France) who work in a given district and do not conduct administrative tasks. Unlike Japan in particular, Belgium's movement towards community policing is based on the recognition of cultural diversity and of ethnic mix.

What started initially as the incorporation of community policing into the existing structure, became later a comprehensive multi-agency policy which envisaged cooperation and coordination between the police, the totality of the prevention projects and other local authority services – a 'local governance of crime' (Crawford 1998). Den Broeck argues that community policing in Belgium is essentially about policing unsafe areas. In addition, there are now attempts to integrate COP into neighbourhood crime prevention. For example a system of NWS is adapted to Belgian norms, hinging around a coordinator who facilitates a two-way flow of information between police and local networks of people (*Buurtinsformatienetwerks*). Within that structure, Civic Wardens like Dutch City Guards (see later) are employed in most cities in tasks such as unemployment registering, conducting problem-solving, observing and reporting functions.

Community policing in Belgium is committed to the notion of a local inter-agency coordination 'safety and crime prevention contracts'. These contracts specify three partners with the police, the 'public', the various local state structures which have connections to crime and general quality of life issues, and specific local organizations from Social Services to schools and local business interests.

As elsewhere there are problems. Firstly, much of the political rhetoric in Belgium calling for local community policing as an interactional partnership has lacked practical expression (Goris and Walters 1999). Increased participation in these contracts may tell us more about the politics of local communities and the fragility of local agencies than the success of government crime policies. The contracts are often reduced to a rather crude model of recruiting local agency support within a framework of political rhetoric. Secondly, den Broeck surveyed local opinion on the development of the new safety contracts and community policing generally. Citizens questioned the organizational and cultural readiness of their local police forces for the full-scale development of community policing practice. Most people agreed that the genuine implementation of community policing required a massive organizational and cultural change, one for which Belgian police tradition was unprepared. The legacy of geographical centralization is regarded as the key historical impediment in the transition to a more local form of policing. In any case, decentralization of the police organization and the decision making process does not automatically result in more community participation. The public complained about the lack of transparency and recognition of citizen inputs into local police decision making. Local *ad hoc* projects prompted by both police and local and central authorities have created considerable confusion. Thirdly, the dominant national crime fighting culture does not regard problems between people as real police work but as social work. Most senior officers managing the new neighbourhood teams come from the emergency Intervention Department and are bred and tested in the traditional crime fighting culture.

For all these reasons an exclusively crime-centred approach continues to dominate the present policy as also within the neighbourhood policing teams. Similar legacies prevent a major shift in police cultural relations from the traditional para-military orientation to one of dealing with local interest groups (especially when different socio-economic interests are involved) and interpersonal conflicts. In group disputes, social schisms may simply be reinforced. Belgian police culture has no history of mediation in problems of neighbourhood nuisance and incivilities. Traditions of reactive policing are a further handicap to the development of proactive problem-solving. In Belgium, the support for a movement towards a measure of community policing is clear. But pragmatism and history appear to outweigh any serious development.

Italy and Spain

Italy also inherited the centralized Napoleonic traditions. It has adopted localized community policing with difficulty. Official commentary (Council of the European Union 2003) provides little more than a statement of intent, with community policing being grafted on to a largely unchanging central policing structure. Both the two central police forces, the Polizia di Stato and the Arma dei Carabinieri, claim community policing developments in recent years. A variety of essential unilateral and central directed initiatives are noted – a call centre service to collect crime reports, services to collate crime reports from less able groups such as the elderly and from institutions, a centralized information service on police activities, proposals for mini police stations, new problem-solving training and local police patrols in designated problem areas.

A measure of COP was adopted in early 1990s and was a limited experiment of community liaison officers. Local Senior Lead Officers exercised a virtual monopoly of COP, resulting in more recent years in a brief training in inter-agency collaboration and techniques, producing a new inter-disciplinary approach aiming to integrate beat officers in a comprehensive training and deployment system. But reportedly there was an absence of central policy commitment direction, resulting in a variety of uncoordinated experiments across the country. The major problem in creating the new *Polizia di Prossimata* (as opposed to *Polizia di Stato*) was the difficulty in organizational transformation from a 'situational response' to emergency calls to a system of proactive crime prevention and community engagement. It also recognized that the senior lead officers and beat officers could not work in isolation and required not just intra-organizational sensitivities and commitment but also integrated agency work such as joint police-civilian street teams, and developments such as close liaison between police and psychiatric service over referral processes.[12]

As with other centralized policing systems in countries of the European Union, Spanish reaction to community policing is confused by the division between the semi-militarized Civil Guard and the National Police Corps. There are local municipal police forces but they are limited essentially to the implementation of city ordinances. There is little local accountability, with the provincial Civil Governors acting as the major regional source of police direction.

Like its neighbours, the Spanish police introduced a Policia de Proximidad (in 1997) emphasizing a fixed police station as a constant point of reference for the local populations. In 2002, the Cortes called for a reorganization of local structures including policing with regard to a greater emphasis on citizens' security needs. There have been limited local developments – again as additions to rather than alterations to the centralized structures locally. Three community policing elements are discernible – Integrated Community Modules (self-sufficient and multi-functional police units attached to local police stations, intended to be responsive to local crime fears), a Preventive Community Police (essentially foot and bicycle beat patrols), and Technical Community Police (responsible for detailed checks on offences committed in the districts). On their own initiative, these bodies can initiate dialogue with local groups and individuals and develop local security contracts. Generally, Spanish policing is similar to the other countries inheriting the Napoleonic centralized model with substantial formal discourse and intent – but little discernible change on the ground.

A similar prognosis is apparent in Portugal where an Integrated Community Policing Programme started in 1998. Nationally, the Portuguese police are committed to a new preventative approach to local security in its widest sense but, like Spain, development remains minor, given the national policing structure[13].

Decentralized systems – the example of the Netherlands

The Dutch experience shows how traditional centralized para-military policing on the Code Napoleonic model may not be an obstacle to local community policing in the long term. Holland represents a major deviation from the normal Western European problem of attempting to develop neighbourhood policing in the context of a traditional state centred policing tradition. The Dutch police have experimented with COP for some 30 years and over some three generations of police officers. This has been reinforced in recent years by the importation of concepts and practices from the USA, the UK and elsewhere (including the koban concept of local police kiosks from Japan), by renewed innovation at the local level, and by the resurrection of the community beat constable. Consequently, present community policing in Holland should be understood as developing from a long process of experimentation, trial and error, and major social and economic contextual changes. It reflects independent conceptions and experience and also limited 'borrowing' of ideas from Anglo-American policing. Recent Dutch history has demonstrated an indigenous approach to local policing.

Police reform reflected wider changes in the political and social environment of Holland. Political changes helped to usher in a welfarist and tolerant society with considerable repercussions for the police. From the early 1970s onwards Dutch policing became socially conscious and engaged in a range of experiments. Many police forces were structured on a three-tiered model of reactive patrol, preventive patrol (comparable to a problem oriented approach) and of beat constables. The latter had, at that time, a widely defined task. Their main duty was to keep their neighborhood quiet and safe, to 'restore contacts' with citizens, and to gather information for the Criminal Investigation Branch (CID). They worked only in their beat area: they solved problems; communicated with other public agencies; and their task was primarily defined in terms of crime prevention (Punch, van der Vijver and Zoomer 2002).

In the late 1970s, the Dutch police began a programme of decentralization and increased police-community interaction. Police in The Hague established a system of permanent beat officers who made sure that local people recognized them and could approach them. Several related community policing practices were adopted.

Box 5.3   *Initial Dutch developments in community policing*

- Informal contact groups comprised of precinct residents and local officers meet on a regular basis and discuss issues of concern to both the police and communities. Communications reportedly flourished and the police improved their understanding of what was actually going on at the street level.
- Precinct books provide comprehensive descriptive and statistical information (i.e. demographic, crime statistics, socio-economic problems) for each precinct. Officers use the books to familiarize themselves with the communities they patrol.
- In order to make sure that police are aware of the needs of the public, the police conducted local crime and victim surveys to ascertain, in systematic fashion, what those needs are and to make sure that they are reflected when police policies are set, ensuring the highest possible public satisfaction.

(adapted from Neild 2000)

At the end of the 1970s several studies, reflecting both an internal police critique and a wider public perception, seriously questioned the legitimacy and credibility of the police in relation to citizens. This brought about a fundamental shift in thinking based on two main causes. One criticism concerned specifically the system of the beat-constable; often caricatured by the public as 'Boners', and denigrated by their colleagues for being more like social workers than police officers (Punch 1977), and conducting allegedly time wasting practices. This criticism stimulated the start of the 'neighborhood teams' movement. The beat constables should disappear and neighbourhood teams be installed to promote integration at local level. External integration with local representative structures would be complemented by internal integration and task integration (each constable being multifunctional, sharing in most facets of daily police work). The teams would deal with nearly all routine police affairs and this externally problem oriented approach would improve legitimacy and effectiveness at the local level. These changes in several police forces often proved to be very difficult in implementation. There were, however, as in the city of Haarlem from the early 1980s, measurably positive changes in perceived levels of victimization and a decrease in the fear of victimization, and a positive change in community views and contacts with the police (Punch *et al* 2002).

The most recent step in the development of community oriented policing in the Netherlands has been the introduction of the new style community beat officer during the 1990s. This has been coupled with – as in France – Local Security Contracts, a commitment by civic officials to sign a community safety contract with local agencies[14]. The new community police project encompassed citizen involvement in dealing with crime and safety problems, and coordination with local public and private agencies. Citizens were to be formally involved in determining local police priorities. There was a major shift in the responsibilities of the new community constable and his or her role in the overall police organization. Whereas the former beat constable was just an ordinary police officer, the community officer was to be held responsible for organizing security in the area in a much wider sense. If he, or she, needs assistance from colleagues in specialized departments then they are formally obliged to help (although practice may differ). The new officer was to be at the centre rather than at the periphery of the organization with enhanced discretion – in effect decentralizing the traditional policing structure. Community policing is, then – Punch argues – no less than the pivot around which the rest of the force is organized, quite differently from many such schemes in other countries, despite the rhetoric. Ideologically, what is most characteristic in the new relationship between the police and the community is the acknowledgement that the police are no longer the sole guardians of public safety as they used to be in the Dutch towns and cities.

Punch provides critical case studies of the cities of Amsterdam and of Utrecht. Inner city Amsterdam was perceived as a major test case for the development of community policing, given its diverse ethnical and socio-economic context. In Amsterdam, a 20-year policy of leniency towards small-scale misdemeanours faced a reaction in relation to an apparent increase in the recorded crime rates and in terms of visible signs of social deviancy, such as in public drug use. The public wished to re-emphasize the traditional normative boundaries[15]. There had been a government sponsored move to bring back traditional control agents in public areas such as tram conductors, school caretakers, the concièrge in apartments, and an autonomous patrol, *Stadswacht*, of uniformed officials geared to cooling down minor offences. The new structure maximized police discretionary decision making. The formation of an Inner City Support Team (with about 75 officers but designed to grow to 120) was intended to increase police visibility on the street. Although one of the objects of the Inner City Support Team was to make the police more visible (to 'blue on the streets'), it is the community police officers who really give the police a personal face. They are the ones who get involved in consultation meetings between residents and traders in the inner city. They are also the ones whose task it is to work with other agencies and the local government in dealing with social problems that are more complex than just crime. Police management has the task to make sure that these different ways of policing do not interfere with one another.

But as a COP exercise, it was heavily influenced by the controversial zero tolerance of New York's broken windows policy, although represented to the public as a return to traditional Amsterdam policing. As a broken windows variant, its COP character is controversial, implying a return to a heavy-handed policing of the city's residuum. In that sense, at least, the Amsterdam version of COP relates to the original Peelite formulation of policing morality, the 'nuisances' and the street economy of the lower social orders. The police should take strong action against those who do not comply with social norms and 'public morality'. The pressures of a major conurbation, the diversity of different socio-economic interests, the presence of a complex ethnic (as well as Dutch) under-class, under a media spotlight, ensured that the new community policing of inner city Amsterdam was a long way from the more Utopian view of COP operating in a homogenous society with little crime and disorder. In Amsterdam, community policing was not of a model that would be recognized in small-town United States.

Changes in Utrecht followed a similar pattern, albeit with considerably more preparation for officers in terms of the broad COP philosophy. The impetus was the same kind of moral panic about street 'nuisances', together with a business interest to enhance the commercial character of the inner city at a time of major investment in that sector. Past tolerance (especially of drug abuse) was deemed to have gone too far. The underclass was considered to have broken the boundaries of tolerance. A dedicated team of officers within each area was tasked to deal with the problems of the street, establishing clear, tighter rules of conduct and enhancing the physical environment to reduce opportunities for crime. However, it extended the broken windows theme to include problem-solving policing (such as finding accommodation for a young runaway), cooperating with and instructing shopkeepers and negotiating at the multi-agency level. The policy also recognized that a total zero tolerance practice was impractical – it was broken windows with a pragmatic 'human face' (Punch *et al* 2002).

There were however continuing problems. Other police units with a more generic role were critical of the apparent autonomy and lead role of the new specialist team of community officers. Problem-solving, dependent as it is on inter-agency cooperation, was inhibited by the unwillingness of other agencies, themselves not attuned to the new policing tactics, to dispose of what they saw as police constructed problems, under a policing imprimatur.

Dutch experience needs to be placed in context. In particular, the policing development cannot be divorced from wider societal and administrative change. For example, the so-called 'polder model' requires that Dutch agencies and local citizens are expected to attempt to reach agreement over common problems. Such concerns are innate in the commitment by local mayors (formally the supervizing officers of the local police) to ensure that contact with citizens over security issues are accepted by all relevant agencies. Inter-agency cooperation is embodied in Dutch custom and law. To ensure consultation over local safety matters, there is regular consultation between the senior crime prosecutor (the main overseer of police investigations and prosecutions), the local mayor and the commissioner of police. City council internal affairs committees regularly discuss matters relating to police policy with the mayor and the police commissioner. Secondly, it is inappropriate to discuss community policing in Holland without reference to the presence of the *Stadswacht* scheme, a second tier of functionaries who possess neither police authority nor armaments, but are present in neighbourhoods to assure members of the public. One of the functions of their presence is to give to the public a more secure feeling by acting as a kind of trouble-shooting patrol functionary. Finally, Punch argues that significant changes in Dutch society ushered in a period of considerable experiment and innovation. In a sense this development has continued almost unabated.

Nevertheless, certain problems in community policing seem to have remained constant over the years: the conservative police culture which has been a major obstacle in implementing community policing, and the extent to which modes of community policing are subject to wider social pressures regarding the limits of tolerance. Independently of organizational innovations and intent, community policing is at the mercy of external forces regarding the nature of the police role in a divided society.

National police systems and community policing
– the Scandinavian countries

The new wave of community policing came to Finland in the briefcase of a police officer who visited San Diego and imported the ideas of more systematic, proactive and holistic approach to policing – and Goldstein's book *Problem-Oriented Policing*.

(Virta 2002, p. 124)

Anglo-American community policing has been implemented in Finland since 1996 (Virta 2002). Unlike in countries such as Belgium, the development of community policing did not reflect a sudden social conjunction. Finnish welfare society is relatively stable. There are few significant social divisions. Recorded crime rates are low. There was no urgent pressure for policing reform. Both the adoption and the implementation of the community policing strategy has been a part of wider public sector modernization – in the Finnish case, community policing was regarded as part of a natural process of police evolution.

One source was the traditional trickle of policemen and policing ideas from abroad. Secondly, community policing was seen also as a response to the demands on and expectations for improved police services. But there had been a long tradition of the community policing style (called the 'village police') since the 1960s. A policeman lived in his or her own district and was familiar with the residents and local social norms. Community policing of foreign origin was not initiated until 1978, and in 1981 the Ministry of Interior issued directives. In 1987 there were 160 community officers in 40 different police districts (two per cent of the entire police force).

Community policing has been implemented in Finland systematically since 1996. A few area-based neighbourhood policing initiatives and experimental projects were adopted since 1978, but they were not very successful. The model was based on the problem oriented approach, and the main principles were crime prevention, proactive policing and multi-agency cooperation.

In 1996 the three main techniques for implementation of community policing were a local security management model (in the cities a strategic, holistic approach, based on multi-agency cooperation), a problem oriented programme and a neighbourhood policing model (contacts with the public made easier by mobile phones, foot and bicycle patrols). A specialist community policing strategy was adopted in 1998 with the main focus on problem oriented policing, directed at local security and quality of life matters, in cooperation with local authorities, businesses, residents and other partners. In this process, victim surveys and surveys of police satisfaction play a major part. There were *ad hoc* innovations, for example in the development of bicycle police in 1998 as a response to the demand for beat policing. By the end of 1998, there was an evident bifurcation between community policing and conventional policing in practice.

A shift in thinking and practice occurred in 1999 when community policing became understood more as a dynamic development process, rather than as a static model or objective, as before. In 1999 the government passed a resolution on a national crime prevention programme, imposing a duty to ensure that the community-policing model was adopted throughout the country, establishing local security plans for all municipalities. Community policing in effect became a local security partnership. The new policy represented a relatively new recognition that the primary function of police was to be coordinated prevention rather than event based reaction. At the beginning of 2000 the Finnish Ministry of the Interior sought to combine traditional measurements of efficiency with the new local victim survey evidence of police effectiveness.

The problems in implementation are similar to those noted elsewhere: resistance from older officers and from the police culture, community policing being regarded as not real police work. External factors created barriers to implementation – such as demographic shifts, racial conflict and high levels of unemployment. Inter-agency collaboration remained complicated. In practice, many of the proposals with regard to community policing have remained euphemisms. Some police districts contain statements in their annual reports and strategies 'everything we do is community policing') but practice remains largely traditional.

Neighbourhood policing efforts have been rare – no mini-stations or cop-shops and very few community constables.

Generally, the most effective changes in Finland were seen at the philosophical level, in new thinking about police, community orientation and customer orientation. There were changes also in operational strategies and tactics, and a strong emphasis on the development of crime analysis, problem-solving, and proactive crime prevention, and reliance on local victim surveys on satisfaction with the local police. However, changes in organizational structure are less evident (Virta 2002).

The Norwegians have developed their own local community policing experiments. Most recently, a Report to Stortag on Police Reform (2000) recommended a more service minded and community oriented police organization. Typical in that Scandinavian policing – as in Sweden – is that crime prevention is based on strategic problem-solving, while policing remains primarily reactive.

In Denmark, ideas about community/proximity policing gained momentum in the early 1990s (Holmberg 2003). Before that time, the police in many larger towns and cities employed a number of designated 'local officers'. But such units often led an isolated life. Their responsibilities were limited to local patrolling, contact with citizens, and routine local administrative tasks – serving subpoenas, checking motor vehicle registrations and so on. Conducting a local administrative function, such units became an organizational repository for older officers[16].

Local policing was gradually replaced by the new concept of proximity policing – small police units often stationed in proximity police stations (Neighbourhood Police Posts – NPP). Some ten per cent of the Danish police fulfil functions in relation to these posts. These neighbourhood or proximity police conduct a variety of outreach functions within general problem-solving ideology – Operation Neighbourhood Watch, counselling on safety installations to prevent crime, revisiting the victims of crime. However, apart from the Watch Schemes, the Danish police do not contribute to the establishment of citizen groups or involve any citizens directly in policing activities. As in other Scandinavian countries private citizen groups such as that of the 'Night Ravens' may conduct patrol activities during asocial hours and at places of entertainment. Community forums have been institutionalized via representatives of local councils rather than informally as in Anglo-American societies. All 54 police districts in Denmark have a statutory board consisting of elected representatives such as local mayors or city council members. The local board or forum must by statute convey information of police activities to local inhabitants and propose policing priorities to the local chief constables and to the Copenhagen Commissioner.

In some police districts, this change has been only superficial. The new units had the same duties, and were manned by the same officers as before, but in others, the officers were given new tasks in addition to the old ones. The most important of these was participation in a local crime prevention network (cooperation between schools, social authorities, and the police, focusing on crime prevention among children and juveniles under the age of 18).

Holmberg (2003) notes a number of positive consequences of the drive towards proximity policing: a better relationship between the police and other agency personnel, and improved relationships between the police and certain citizen groups. It allowed more police innovation, use of discretion, more reliance on social skills and knowledge rather than on legal powers leading to non-legal outcomes. The new proximity police units were intended to reach out to local citizens with a focus on crime prevention, but in practice they had limited success. These units were often alienated from the rest of the police, and they also found it difficult to define their role towards citizens. Culturally, they were often derided as 'social workers' and not doing 'real police work'. Such proximity police appeared to spend some two-thirds of their duty involved in administrative duties. Proximity policing had in any case developed because of organizational pressure not because of any public demand for such a policing transformation.

There were problems in this enhanced discretion. Patrol officers have been shown to use their discretionary freedom in a way that relies heavily on 'social profiling'. Citizens fitting the police stereotype of 'typical perpetrator' were subject to extensive control and were in some instances denied the leniency granted other citizens. Some officers found the goal of establishing ties and providing services to local citizens incompatible with general enforcement of the law. Others found it important to uphold their role foremost as law enforcers. Supervision became very difficult. Tasks developed had no clear goals leading to infinite possibilities of resource requirements. Continuity of such individual project work was difficult given the normal rotation requirements of personnel. In districts where a single officer serves each neighbourhood, Holmberg notes major differences in the general level of enforcement. Role relationships with other professionals and the public were often confused by the development of wider policing duties.

Community policing in Scandinavia, as elsewhere, relates to local traditions and context. A liberal democratic movement towards community policing reflects a larger public expectation of public consultation. In such relatively unitary societies, police officers generally face fewer schismatic relationships than do many officers in more diverse societies. Nevertheless, in most cases, community policing remains a Utopian ideal superimposed on, and resisted by, traditional policing structures and cultures.

Overview

> Community policing as it exists in Germany is seen therefore particularly in terms of crime prevention and less in terms of prosecuting criminals or structuring operations ... None of Germany's police forces has implemented community policing in ... its operations and equipment.[17]

These illustrations of the development of community policing in the European Union are subject to necessary caveats. The critical and academic literature is sparse. Official discourse dominates the accounts. Euphemisms of intent abound, but the essence is that considerations of community policing are very much secondary to a local crime prevention function.

However the more serious reasons preventing the development of COP in these contexts reflects often quite different conceptions of the notions of policing. Specifically, within those countries that have inherited directly Napoleonic (and indeed, Roman) structures of policing in which that function is critically a central administrative practice of the central state, devoted to the preservation of the larger social order, considering the development of community policing is not comparing like with like. These alternatives to Anglo-American policing models suggest that comparative community policing is not merely about creating 'add-ons' to central structures and functions, but also represents a systemic divergence from the essence of police work. That divergence is not just an aberration – an accident of history – but reflects quite different assumptions about the police function. There are other local factors that inhibit the growth of community policing – most evidently in Germany in the context of a *Rechtsstaat*, or law-centred state, as opposed to the relative pluralism of local values in the United States. That commitment in Germany to a 'principle of legality' leaves very little discretionary powers in the hands of the patrolling police officer. While regarded as a key part of German police professionalism,

> ... this lack of discretion may also negatively affect the flexibility of the police-citizen relationship. In contrast, the American police enjoy significant discretionary power, which tends to lead to abuses when misused, but also may create good feelings between the police and the citizens when properly applied.
>
> (Cao 2001, p. 178)

Of course, such countries are not immune to both external and internal pressure to copy practices from elsewhere. Externally, professional bodies from other countries exert pressure for change towards their own models. International state agencies such as the European Union and NGOs provide an institutional pressure for change. Internally, citizen groups, media, and professional bodies, faced with reported rising crime rates and local fears of insecurity, problematize traditional models of police public relations. Police scandals such as the Dutroux case in Belgium also create demands for a new model of policing.

However there are reverse pressures, not just the conservatism of historical legacy. As we noted in the Paris case, the rise of international terrorism (as in 9-11) allows the reaffirmation of traditional paramilitary gendarmerie policing. Similarly, moral panics about asylum seekers in Western Europe, together with the relative diminution of state borders in the European Union, encourages forms of policing antipathetic to the ideology of COP. The only substantive context in which there is a convergence is that of the development of local security contracts – which involves not just change within the Napoleonic models but also within Anglo-American societies and policing traditions. Community policing can coexist with a Napoleonic legacy, but in the key illustration in this chapter, larger contextual factors have forced community policing advocates to retreat to the most divisive form of that practice – variations on the zero tolerance approach. Attempts to modify traditional structures are at the mercy of larger contextual factors of which history is only one. It is not difficult to retreat into an established pattern of public order policing when the expression of public mood calls for more rather than less social control.

Notes

1 Council of the European Union. Presidency. Police Cooperation Working Group, 7521/03.
2 See Chapter 9.

3 Adapted from Tupman and Tupman (1999). Spain appears in two columns because of the co-existence of two provincial forces, Catalan and Basque, with the national police.

4 The best conceptualisation of these issues is in J. Ferret, The state, policing and "old Continental" Europe, *Policing and Society*, 2004, 14, 1, 49–65.

5 On the central local tensions under the Napoleonic policing models, see Ferret (2004). A recent article which clarifies the conceptual problems and emphasises the political context of proximity policing is in J. Ferret "I order you to adapt": Evaluating the Community Policing, French-Style, *European Journal of Crime, Criminal Law and Criminal Justice*, 2004, 12, 3, 192–211.

6 Hence the 1999 newspaper headline in Rouen on the introduction of proximity policing: *Rouennaise travaille à Anglais*.

7 One commentator has described proximite policing from the point of view of the under-class: 'The policing, despite its fancy name, is a mixture of community work and "zero tolerance" for "small crimes"... (Crescent International, 1–15 May 2000) in commenting on the killing of a Muslim youth by the police.

8 For a fuller account of the CLS, see Dupont 2002.

9 See Chapter 5.

10 Dupont gives a more positive account of such auxiliaries, especially in their effect in opening up lower policing ranks to ethnic minorities. That tiered argument is similar to that of Brogden on Catholic recruits to the new police service of Northern Ireland (Brogden 1998).

11 Such as the Dutroux affair – see Punch (2004).

12 Italian commentators have repeated the claim that the introduction of COP in Sicily has led to an immediate reduction of gang-related murders in Palermo from 200 per year in the mid-1990s to nine in the year 2000 (with other curious claims that in particular districts significant reductions in burglary and theft rates had been achieved). Despite its repeated assertion, it is difficult to find any evidence that would validate this startling claim (Jones and Wiseman 2001). In that report, the authors claim that in various ways community policing is more advanced in Western Europe than in the USA with *inter alia* more interagency cooperation with social workers etc than in the US, more effective evaluation, more serious attempts to modify para-military structures. It would be difficult to substantiate that claim.

13 Indeed, Portugal is now exporting it '... community policing programmes to Croatia' OSCE press release, 1 July 2003. On Greek development of a similar policing organization with Local Safety Contracts, see the excellent Rigakos and Papanicolaou (2003). A recent article furnishes empirical evidence on attempts to develop community policing in Spain – see A. Rabor, The implementation and evaluation of community policing in Spain: results and future prospect, *European Journal of Crime, Criminal Law and Community Justice*, 2004, 1, 3, 212–231; and

14 Mayors retain a post-Napoleonic function in, 'nominally' at least, providing a civilian support role for the local police.

15 For instance, urinating in public became public 'enemy number one' and was even held to be undermining the foundations of the historic sixteenth century buildings in the centre; at weekends portable urinals are placed at hotspots.

16 With a retirement age of 63, and few possibilities for officers to leave the force before the age of 60, the Danish police force needed less demanding functions.

17 http://europa.eu.int/comm/justice_home/eucpn/docs/crimepreventiongermany.pdf p.3 EUCPN, Crime Prevention in Germany.

Part 2

Community policing
in transitional and failed societies

> The desire to adopt community policing … can be understood as a
> new and more democratic paradigm of law enforcement. It is
> attractive, perhaps rhetorically compelling. However the practice
> of community policing is the result of a long institutional, legal, and
> cultural history which in the last analysis may be very peculiar to
> Western European and North American society, and which may not
> be replicable in any other country…
>
> (del Buono 2003, p. 22)

Locating all the disparate schemes that utilize the rubric of community
policing in transitional and failed societies is subject to immediate
disclaimers. As elsewhere, COP is used as a generic term rather than as a
specific concept. Extreme examples from the South Pacific demonstrate
the breadth of that rubric. The Fijian community police warn locals about
the new green shoots of marijuana plantations. The Australian Federal
Police in the Christmas and Cocos Islands include hurricane watching
and myriads of unique ancillary services under that heading. In the
Solomon Islands, community policing is equated with peacekeeping as
one (temporary) resolution to internal schism. In East Timor, after the
destruction left by the Indonesian-sponsored militia, community
policing is being constructed under a UN (CIVPOL) mandate.

However in practice, COP in that export process is often reduced to
four easily recognized procedures – watch schemes, police community
forums, problem-solving policing and local (foot) patrols. That basic
model is fashioned in the West for implant in failed and transitional
societies in response to problems of rising crime, public expectations of a
response, and the collapse and delegitimation of local policing
structures.

Chapter 6

South Africa: the failure of community policing

South Africa's past, racial division, and citizen suspicion will prove to be great obstacles to overcome ... South Africa may be the best test case of community oriented policing in the world. If the South African Police can successfully implement community-oriented policing under these conditions, then it may be possible to do so in any democratic country in the world.

(Oliver 2001, p. 422)

... strengthen the Community Police Force to improve their capacity to mobilise the people against crime and to improve cooperation between the people and the law enforcement agencies.
(Inaugural address of President Thabo Mbeki, 25 June 1999)

Introduction

South Africa represents a test case of community policing in transitional societies[1]. It furnishes a unique case study in which the community oriented policing model (COP) has been regarded both by Western donor countries and agencies and by many local recipients as the solution for a range of social and political ills. Reacting against the authoritarian centralization of the apartheid state and its coercive agencies, COP, with its emphasis on consensual relationships between the police and the public and in its commitment to police decentralization, seemed apposite to aid agencies and NGOs, prompted by powerful allies in the donor states. Promoting COP ventures was regarded as the ideal form of policing for the New South Africa, as part of the larger democratization process. But in civil society, COP was a solution to a problem of political rule rather than a resolution to a policing crisis.

With the advent of democratic rule, South Africa enjoyed new access to a wide variety of foreign donor packages. Development of technical experts to assist in crime prevention and criminal justice reform became an almost routine feature of the exchange relations cemented under both bilateral and multilateral agreements (van der Spuy 2000).

The imperative for police reform

Since the Union of South Africa was formed in 1910, the South African Police (SAP) had the primary task of repressing the indigenous peoples, like any other colonial police force. The SAP was constructed to contain and control black South Africans by keeping them in their place as a subject population. This 'colonial' role in subjugating the majority of the population led to an emphasis on militarism within the force, the adoption of universal riot control training and later the deployment of ubiquitous armoured vehicles. Although not well funded, the SAP did this relatively efficiently, by virtue of the political and technological capacity to use maximum force as a first resort within the context of permissive legal rules (Brogden and Shearing 1993).

Throughout, the SAP took its orders directly from the government of the day, and from 1948 onwards, became the enforcement arm of the infamous apartheid regime. This regime also created a number of nominally independent 'homelands' and autonomous territories that were authorized to raise and direct police forces, under the 'umbrella' of the SAP. The police in territories such as Lebowa and Qwa Qwa were established in the image of the SAP, with senior officers being recruited from and/or trained by the SAP. By definition, such a policing system was not based on consent. In fact, by the time that the political transition to democracy began in 1990, the SAP had become

> ... totally committed to the fight against those organizations and people who were committed to ending apartheid ... it was an inefficient and ineffective police force, which had lost the confidence of the South African public.
>
> (van der Spuy, 2000)

Thus, while the 'new' South Africa inherited a functioning police force of considerable size, this had been geared to the repressive needs of the apartheid order. The police were agents of a state that created crimes through its efforts to erect moral, economic, and political boundaries between the races and to ensure the continuation of socio-economic inequality. It was these crimes that received the most attention[2].

The Transition to Democracy
Prior to April 1994 there had been much pressure from local communities, and from potential international donors – and indeed, from the SAP itself – for the development of a policing system that would be accountable and transparent. The consensus was that South Africa should develop a model or style of community policing much like that found in developed democracies. Community policing became the dominant theme underlying the process of police transformation initiated by the new government (Shaw 2002). Consequently a fundamental part of the transformation has been the demilitarization and civilianization of the new police service and the attempt to introduce an ethos of community policing.

Policies promoting community policing structures and practices consequently dominated the first period of transition. They were promoted by two general factors – the collective idealism in the transformation process and the perception of a cosmopolitan group of donors that police reform was the key to the new mode of governance.

> Community policing ... the prevailing buzzword in the international policing debate ... became the dominant theme underlying the process of police transformation that was initiated by the new government.
>
> (Malan 2001, p. 181)

Notions of community policing, gleaned from contact with the international police fraternity, had gained currency in enlightened South African police circles in the late 1980s. The potential influence of international policing models on both the SAP and local academics led to the introduction of the first community policing structures in the early 1990s (Marais 1992). Bilaterally, institutional community policing developments had origins in the National Peace Accord of 1991, which provided a vision for a fundamental transformation of South African policing. The Accord emphasized two new policing themes – accountability and local cooperation with the public.

The SAP instituted a Division for Community Policing in late 1992 and (with some lethargy) set about establishing tentative Police-Community

Forums at local level. Ironically, the Community Policing Division was created coincidentally as the Security Police Division was reduced to a third of its original size – nearly two-thirds of the new community policing division, and almost all of the senior staff were drawn from the security police, leading to immediate suspicions from black communities. From a police point of view, community policing assumed an intelligence gathering character in which the community would hopefully become a police resource. But communities had a different view of it – the police had always been the most tangible form of state oppression in poor communities, and also the most hated and distrusted face of the state. The agenda of these communities was therefore to reverse the imbalance of power, and bring the police to be accountable to their needs. Community policing was about the control of the police – and much less about preventing crime.

The fact that community policing was introduced almost simultaneously with democratic rule in 1994 gave it an added significance. Local communities regarded that style of policing to represent the same kind of liberation that it expected in the political and economic arenas. Inevitably, control of the police through community policing was a major feature of the election platform of the liberation movements (Scharf 2000). The campaign for community policing became a major part of the political struggle. The call for community policing was articulated as a political device for improving police legitimacy and for enhancing accountability (Shaw 2002). Not merely was community policing seen as important in making the SAP more legitimate in the eyes of the previously disenfranchised – it was also perceived as a lever of political change in policing. These two functions, however, were often contradictory.

The Interim Constitution for the Republic of South Africa came into force on 27 April 1994, providing the major set of guidelines for the transformation of all state departments. It conceived of progress toward community policing as crucial to democratic civilian control over the police. A key part in this process was played by the Canadian-based South African academic Clifford Shearing. The latter used the opportunity to influence the development of a particular model of policing, an approach embodying a number of community intentions. The first was the uncontentious one of changing the definition of the police from a 'force' to a 'service'. Secondly, in Shearing's optimistic approach was the reconception of the police as people who enable communities to solve their own problems rather than as people who solve problems on their own. Policing for the state police was to become 'everybody's business' rather than simply 'police business'. Thirdly, Shearing encouraged the conception of a private police – state police continuum in which the division between policing as a community affair conducted by non-uniformed locals and by state functionaries mandated for the purpose was to be diminished. The key anvil of this development (merging Shearing's vision with the more orthodox COP approach) was through the development of 'consultative forums' designed to permit communities to make their policing concerns known to the police and to provide a vehicle for holding the police accountable. Police-community forums were to become the most visible form of COP in South Africa and a major focus on which the struggle for democratic policing would succeed or fail.

The first pillar of COP – active partnership between the police and the community – was to be supported by a second strategy, that of problem-solving. Local police officers were to be encouraged to use consensual extra-legal strategies, and where appropriate, to avoid clumsy reliance on the instruments of criminal law and procedure to solve local policing problems.

Community policing – the first steps

The first formal step was an Act of Parliament to '... provide for the establishment of community-police forums in respect of police stations' and a variety of related community oriented structures. Under the new government, these principles were formalized within the South African Police Service Act (1995). Key provisions bolstered civilian influence over policing at local and national levels: the creation of National and Provincial Secretariats for Safety and Security which could advise political executives on police policy and monitor adherence of police to those policies; the requirement on the National Commissioner of Police to publish yearly his future plans, priorities and objectives (to enhance transparency and police monitoring); and critically, the creation of statutory Community Police Forums where local police commissioners could liaise with and account to the local community.

Within the government's major national policy framework, the Reconstruction and Development Programme (RDP), there was also a significant influence on the goals of police transformation. The RDP determined that the police must be made more representative of the people, more responsive to human rights, and more answerable to the communities which they serve. Community policing development was to play a major *political* function in the transformation of South African society. In this initial phase of transition, a variety of community schemes were developed such as in Box 6.2.

Box 6.1 *Defining the core principles of community policing*

The Community Policing Framework 1997 defined the core principles for community policing in South Africa as:

Service orientation – the provision of a professional policing service, responsive to community needs and accountable for addressing these needs.

Partnership – the facilitation of a cooperative, consultative process of problem-solving.

Problem-solving – the joint identification and analysis of the causes of crime and conflict and the development of innovative measures to address these.

Empowerment – the creation of joint responsibility and capacity for addressing crime.

Accountability – the creation of a culture of accountability through the needs of communities.

Box 6.2 *Examples of community policing schemes*

- Youth and police in Orlando in Soweto established a youth subforum to address the high crime rates in the area.

- In Gallo Manor workers formed a sub-forum to work in partnership with the police to counter the problem of burglaries.

- In Benoni the SAPS, in partnership with local Chambers of Commerce, created a Business Watch with a kiosk in the town to encourage the reporting of crime and action against crime in the Central Business District.

- In the Adopt-a-Cop project of the SAPS partnership between police and schools each school 'adopts' a policeman/woman from their local police station. The 'cop' attends events at school, talks to the children about their safety, listens to children's problems and allows reports on child abuse.

- McKinsey, the international management consultancy under Project Lifeline, used its expertise to assist in local logistical planning so that police stations might focus on problem solving and service delivery.

- Business Against Crime encouraged local businesses to adopt a police station in order to use their expertise in police training, resources, maintenance and fleet management.

Community Police Forums – contradictory goals

The Interim Constitution contained a detailed requirement that the new police service should establish a 'Community Police Forum' at every police station. However, the old SAP had taken the view at the outset that community policing was a communications strategy only. Consequently only the station commander felt bound by it. Other units – public order, drugs and so on – carried on as before, considering that they were not bound by community policing procedures and responsibilities. Nothing was detailed about what station commissioners should do apart from 'hold meetings'. Many issues were left to interpretation.

Many of the local politically based, transitional Peace Committees formed the core of the new CPFs (Scharf 2000) (although membership of the CPFs was not limited to political parties but intended to include any community group)[3]. Confusion over politics rather than over policing pragmatics was evident from the outset. The role and function of the CPFs was not laid down in any official policy (other than the SAPS Act, which basically reiterated the wording of the interim Constitution – until April 1997)[4]. The purposes of the forums were unclear. The impetus behind them seemed to be more concerned with local police accountability than in increasing police effectiveness (Malan 2001). The two aims did not always coincide. For communities long barred from the 'secret' world of policing under apartheid, the practicalities of policing and the duties of members of the new forums were confused.

This gap in the community policing knowledge was partly filled by international donor assistance. Community policing underwent considerable promotion from Western societies who evidently believed that such a police model was a primary prerequisite of a new democracy[5]. However, not until 1997 did the Ministry of Safety and Security publish detailed guidelines as to the practice of community policing on the ground[6]. Community policing was *ad hoc*, improvised and the work of bodies such as the CPFs subject to local power struggles to determine the practical rules. Donor-sponsored policing had some effect on community understanding of the forums. However, the police remained untrained in the consultative function.

Failure of the Community Police Forums

Community policing only had an impact at station level. It did not affect the higher levels of the SAPS. The most evident local consequence was the creation of many community forums, essentially unelected local structures consisting of nominated individuals who wished to see improvement in police operations on the ground. However, throughout their existence, most officers seemed to regard them as a necessary evil required to bring citizens in contact with the police but as having little impact on police themselves. Disputes arose between forum members and the local SAPS over the operational independence of the police (Shaw 2002). At first the police were determined to control the whole CPF process. Each side saw the CPFs differently. Local communities often wanted the police to be held accountable for past misdeeds. Conversely, the police wished those problems to be forgotten. Communities on the other hand were determined to let the police know about their past failings.

> In practice this meant that the community was essentially seeking to use the CPFs to penetrate the hated police agency, to tame and shame them and make them accountable to the community for both the past, the present and the future.
>
> (Scharf, 2000)

There was major conflict over policing priorities. Communities expressed their crime priorities to the police, creating immediate quandaries for police officers who saw their priorities unexpectedly challenged. The SAPS had expected that its own objectives – such as responding to murder, armed robbery and the like – would be also the community priorities. But when some CPFs expressed the view that rape was the crime that worried them most, the police were confused and lethargic because they regarded sexual or domestic assailants as being peripheral to police concerns. Conflict over priorities dominated many of the urban CPFs (Scharf 2000). The CPFs became a battleground for community infighting and arguments over what constitutes good community representation. Some were taken over by gangs. One consequence therefore was the marginalizing of those groups that were least organized and politically articulate, particularly women and children.

In other, often rural communities, the old power imbalance remained – the CPFs were little other than places where the farmers complained about loss of stock. From his Manenberg (Western Cape) study, Scharf lists the problems of the Community Police Forums.

- Who should chair the meeting?
- Who sets the agenda?
- Who takes the minutes?

- Where are the meetings held?

- What say does the community have in staff appointments (especially in relation to the station commissioner who may be represented on the forum)?

- What members of the community had the right to take part in the forum (political parties, individuals, or organizations only)?

- What constitutes representation of all interest groups in the community?

- What level of participation was the community to be afforded in the weekly management meetings?

- What are the powers and duties of the community visitors to police stations (checks on custody procedures)?

- What were the Security Policemen now doing wearing different labels in the sheep's clothing of community policemen (Scharf 2000)?

There was some prompting from the central state such as the National Secretariat (consisting of civilians and academics). The latter was charged with advising the Minster and overseeing police operations and policies, and monitoring police performance. A civilian who was ranked in uneasy equal status headed the Secretariat with the SAPS Commissioner to emphasize the accountable and transparent aspects of policing. However, its policing expertise was limited and commonly disdained by the 'professional' police. Its impact on forum practice appears to have been negligible.

In that minority of CPFs that manage to survive beyond the first phase of community policing, Scharf noted a degree of cooperation between the local police and communities – for example (with external support) training both police and community members generally about CPF procedures and specifically with regard to processing sexual assaults – thus establishing low levels of trust between community and police and consequent incremental low level mutual support. However, many other CPFs never actually reached that limited stage. Community Forum members demanded that the police act on behalf of community instructions. But the police – taking a legal standpoint – declined, making the forums look like in Shaw's words 'toy telephones' (Shaw 2002). In most cases, the police appeared to believe that COP generally was too soft for the tough conditions in townships. The fact that only a fraction of the police was trained in COP by 1998 resulted in it being more a public relations strategy than a new policing style.

Box 6.3   *Example of a successful CPF*

CPFs have been successful in some places and unsuccessful in others. At a workshop in July 1997 hosted by the Diakonia Council of Churches, obstacles hampering effective community policing were raised. These included lack of knowledge and training about CPFs in the community, poor representation by civil society, police involvement in crime, the involvement of known criminals on some forums, a lack of transparency and a lack of resources to carry out CPF-sponsored projects. In addition, members of CPFs from the community were often labelled as 'spies' for the police. A deep mistrust between communities and police was fostered under apartheid. Last year the KwaMakhuta CPF won a competition for the community most effective in dealing with crime. KwaMakhuta is a peri-urban area about 35 minutes outside of the Durban city centre. When the CPF was first started in 1995, the police were only able to investigate about 13 per cent of crimes in the area effectively. Now police are able to investigate about 60 per cent effectively. This is largely due to a relationship of trust that has been built between the community and police. The chair of the KwaMakhuta CPF is a representative of the church who has been able to shape the CPF's proceedings to include an opening and closing prayer. The chair has also been able to involve other clergy in the community to take part in the CPF. This in turn has helped to strengthen community trust in the entire process.

(Rev. Mbonambi Khuzwayo, *Working for Solutions in Community Policing Forums*, July 1998 http://www.durbanpeace.org.zajul98.html)

Evaluating the Community Forums

Thanks to a variety of South African agencies and to international donors, evaluation of policing in South Africa has been more effective than most. Most prominent is the recent Pelser and Louw (2002) study[7]. The latter found that most local police officers were often quite unfamiliar with the policy on COP. More than a third of SAPS station managers (36 per cent) and 37 per cent of the station CPF respondents interviewed in the research indicated that they knew little of recent state policy on the issue. Most critically, there was deep divergence over what all respondents – police officers and community members – saw as the key feature of community policing – the Community Forums (implementation of the community policing policy has focused almost wholly on the establishment and activities of the CPFs). For police respondents, CPF partnerships were mainly concerned to provide assistance in dealing with particular issues, and in acquiring additional resources for general policing purposes or, in some instances, crime prevention activities. CPF partnerships are associated with activities intended to address particular problems, often police-defined, and commonly concerned with acquiring resources to solve those problems.

Citizen members of the CPF saw them in a different way. Such partnerships were most likely to be interpreted as a means to enable greater access to the police, acceptance of community representatives by the police and positive working relations with the police. Very few members saw their function as being about joint problem-solving. The issue for the CPF respondents is therefore primarily a means of enhancing relationships between the police and those they serve. Practical issues raised in the interaction between the police and CPF representatives have superseded the original policy goals. Thus, the representation of community priorities and needs, enhancing police responsiveness to these priorities through monitoring and evaluation, and helping to improve police service delivery, are not prioritised by practitioners at the area and local levels. Indeed, local level practitioners were clear that community structures, like local youth groups, women's groups, religious groups, and other interest groups like farmer and taxi associations were rarely involved. Rather, the CPFs appeared to target government and the stronger, more organized sections of civil society in their activities.

However Pelser and Louw acknowledge that despite different understandings of the purpose of the partnership between the police and the CPFs, there appears to be a real shift in the thinking of the primary practitioners towards understanding local level crime prevention as the key role for the CPFs. This correlates with the policy shift advocated in the 1998 White Paper on Safety and Security. Views also differed about the ownership of the policing process. SAPS respondents stated that community policing was the function only of the Community Police Officer not of other officers of the SAPS. Respondents claimed that confusion included the lack of dedicated resources, of systematic support from their supervisory structures, and the hierarchical command structure of the SAPS – resulting in a dispersal of limited police resources (i.e. too much bureaucracy and too little decision making at the local level). However, most of the SAPS respondents were clear that the policy had a positive effect on the manner in which they performed their functions.

Public scepticism was however high. Community respondents, many of whom had been victims of crime, believed either that crime in their areas of residence had increased over the past four years, or that the policing initiatives have had little significant impact. They also believed that the quality of policing had not changed significantly or that it had become worse (partly due to perceptions of police corruption and lack of motivation), and therefore they remained ambivalent regarding confidence in the police. However, this was partly counterbalanced by a willingness to report crime and increased satisfaction with the police response to that reporting.

More generally, at the end of the day, the community respondents said that there was little need for engagement with the police as long as they did their job and did not harm the public. In effect, the CPFs served little purpose as long as the police did the job expected of them by the community. It is clear that in their present form and functioning and without meaningful government support, CPF structures are poorly placed to engage meaningfully in the roles outlined for them (Pelser and Louw 2001). Therefore, implementation of the community policing policy through the establishment of the CPFs has not been effective in relation to the core goals of the policy of ensuring wide-ranging input on community needs and priorities, improving police responsiveness to community needs, developing a joint responsibility and a wider capacity for addressing crime (Pelser and Louw 2001).

The latter argue that this failure is mostly attributable to the continuing lack of meaningful and systematic support from the state (although required by legislation). Thus, in their current form and functioning, the CPFs are poorly placed to draw participation and support from community based organizations or other local role players, and to mobilize participatory community crime action initiatives. Public safety security and policing in the SAPS priority areas therefore remain a long way away from being seen as a common responsibility, or everybody's business. They remain in the perception of the general public still very much 'police business'.

The problem of crime

Since 1999 crime-fighting has been reinstated as the official discourse. Little remains of community policing apart from occasional rhetoric, the remnants of a few – mainly white – Community Forums and training procedures. Ministerial discourse increasingly emphasizes the crime fighting role of the police and has encouraged a more coercive approach to crime with far less emphasis on internal problems of police reform. This discourse connects with the majority South African public, increasingly concerned about crime, and unsettled in relation to policies over which the majority had felt disempowered by the period of police transformation following the 1994 election.

Early optimism on the part of the recipients had envisaged a speedy donor-led transition from the paramilitary SAP to a new community oriented South African Police Service (SAPS). This Utopianism was soon dashed by realism, especially vocally expressed by the black majority whose views on the country's level of crime and social order had long been suppressed (van der Spuy 2000). The negative reaction to COP was due to three criminogenic factors – the social disorganization left by the collapse of apartheid; the political vacuum as old politics, structures, and state agencies were dismantled without new ones with adequate viability, effectiveness, and political legitimacy being constructed at adequate speed; and the township crime problem, newly confronting the wealthy inhabitants of South Africa's white suburbs. The latter, previously immune from crime, became relatively integrated into the New South Africa, crime and all. The problem of crime became the major reason for the failure of community policing. Political democratization of the police was perceived as obstructing that crime function.

As COP failed to gain any substantive support, given the larger material problems and social and economic inequalities, a new focus on crime developed. The level of crime was simply too great an obstacle to harmonious community policing and problem-solving. Since 1994, high levels of crime have accompanied the process of political liberalization as social controls were loosened and new opportunities arose for criminal activities. Initially, the new South African state had to depend on the same instruments of governance, such as the police, that had been used to enforce authoritarian rule — while under immense pressure to ensure more equitable policing and criminal justice for all in the face of rising crime levels. Rising reported crime was related to political, economic and social trends which began before the political transition, but which were accentuated by rapid political reform. The transitional period – as elsewhere – had created a vacuum in the instruments of social control allowing more opportunities for crime. A culture of violence remained endemic – families had suffered from institutional violence for decades during apartheid due to the policies of mass removals and migrant labour of apartheid. Primary social controls had been grossly affected. The liberation movements had encouraged violence by young people against the apartheid state to make the latter ungovernable – one impact being that many South Africans had become used to the notion of physical violence as a means of solving conflicts in the home, in social life and in the work environment. Firearms were frequently available[8].

On the increase of organized crime, there are no adequate figures, but there appears to have been a major rise in armed robberies (especially of cash in transit and banks), burglaries in upper class areas, commercial crimes, vehicle thefts and car-jacking, suggesting the prevalence of illegal syndicates. Organized crime is exacerbated in South Africa by an efficient transport system, ready markets for contraband such as endangered species and dagga, a good banking system and a ready supply of trained recruits. A criminogenic youth population – nearly a third of the population were under 15 years and 44 per cent under 20 years in 1996 – was a further impediment to normalization. Social disorganization resulting from rapid urbanization and consequent overcrowding, unemployment, and increased consumer demands and expectations all contributed to a high crime rate.

None of this was helped by the breakdown of a larger criminal justice system[9]. In this crime wave, some were more likely to be victimized than others with little criminal justice reaction – the poor being most likely to be victims of intra-class violent crime with almost a third of victims aged between 16 and 25 years[10]. An inadequate economic infrastructure contributed to crime, for example, women in rural areas supported electrification as high priority because it reduced their vulnerability to sexual assault (Schonteich and Louw 2001). Continued political violence in certain areas of the country (such as rural KwaZulu-Natal), and the emergence of gang-warfare and vigilantism in the Cape peninsula, suggested that community policing strategies would not easily take root where more robust law enforcement methods were needed to diminish the conflict (Shaw 2002).

Legal changes have not helped. The Bill of Rights, desirably giving more rights to the accused and to victims, also extended key due process safeguards to suspects. It became a popular scapegoat for police inadequacy. Former Human Rights advocates in the Cabinet began to harden as they started to talk about a 'war on crime'. Similar legal changes were perceived as obstructive – for example, the change from a confession based system to an evidenced based one, as well as the various artificial rectifications required by necessary affirmative measures. The development and processes of the Truth and Reconciliation Commission, no matter how desirable in themselves, also had the contrary effect of polarizing community and policing over the crimes in particular localities. The police themselves felt uncertain and paralyzed – let down by a new regime which had introduced so much uncertainty into their lives. A new and conscious nationalism did not help – a rising xenophobia resulting from the notion that 'foreigners' are responsible for South Africa's growing crime problems (Shaw 2002).

Even the new Police Commissioner, who had been one of the apostles of the change process, now used crime fighting as a metaphor to describe community policing (Shaw 2002). The police – as elsewhere – opposed civilian oversight of the criminal justice process.

> The South African Police Union has put out the word to its members to arrest officials of the new Independent Complaint Directorate who appear to be interfering in police work ... the union said that the directorate's main task seemed to be to disgrace and humiliate police by continually harassing them while they were trying to do their work.
>
> (*Independent on Sunday*, 5 June 1999)

The policing impediment to reform

The new South Africa inherited a dysfunctional police force of considerable size and resources, primarily committed to public order regime maintenance rather than to bandit catching. By Western standards, the South African police lack adequately trained personnel. This situation is exacerbated by a youthful population; an immense geographical area; and the problems relating both to a rapidly urbanizing society and to the expanding informal settlements. A quarter of all police officers were recently described as functionally illiterate, on average some 235 police officers are killed in any one year. Of these, one-third are killed on duty and while that number is actually declining, it is matched by a corresponding increase in those killed off duty.

Police officers are three and a half times as likely to be killed on duty, as are members of the general population.[11] During 1998 1,283 police members were convicted of criminal charges (one per cent of the total establishment). In the year 2000 approximately 14,000 police members (ten per cent) were being charged or had appeared in court on criminal charges – these figures perhaps only being the tip of the abuse iceberg (Newham 2000). There is a major problem with police misconduct – possibly artificially exacerbated by enhanced reporting procedures (Marks 1995). Police officers are some three times as likely to be involved as suspected perpetrators of crime as are members of the general public. While this internal policing problem may not be unique, they reflect in part the quality of South African police morale, organization, training and remuneration. Recruitment of alternative personnel from the liberation forces was minimal due in part to the low status and oppositional character that the state police held in the eyes of former ANC combatants (Laufer 2001). During the first phase of the post-apartheid experience, senior personnel of the old SAP ensured a continuing coercive legacy.

The reorganization of the SAP had encountered massive internal policing problems – the merger of the ten 'homeland' policing institutions with the old South African Police; inconsistencies of language, of quality of personnel, of affirmative action processes and of technology. Organizational chaos replaced a relatively disciplined unitary coercive structure (Shaw 2002), a process not assisted by the way bureaucratic inertia seems to have been as common in the post-conflict stage as it was under the apartheid state (Malan 2001). The composition of the police remained monopolized by minority Afrikaners at the command level (Scharf 2000). A few members of the former township self-defence units remain integrated into a 'community constable' role and there has been a degree of lateral entry in to mid-managerial posts but not into frontline policing positions. In effect, the structure and practices of the SAPS have remained largely unchanged.

In an early study, most police respondents claimed that community policing was not working (Prinsloo 1996). One-fifth of them were totally unfamiliar with the existence and objectives of the CPFs although the latter had been statutorily enforced. Legalism – the old ideology of the SAP – was the only legitimate basis for policing – not community consent. The police were characterized by low morale. More than half were disillusioned with community policing. Two thirds said the forums were only there to restrain their functioning and 90 per cent said that politicians were forcing them to adopt a soft approach to criminals. A further two-thirds claimed that the community did not cooperate and disdained them. An entrenched cop culture has been impossible to transform (Marks 1995).

A survey of Gauteng police officers revealed that the introduction of community policing simply meant that the community should help them in combating crime. Very few officers recognized that COP should also encompass problem-solving, transparency and accountability (Mistry 1997). The Pretoria Police College evaluated new training based on community policing and concluded that the idea and practice had not yet taken shape. As a consequence, there was no agreed understanding about how to implement the principles learnt in college. In many serious-crime stations, trainees believed that community policing was not applicable in those areas, as the lives of policeman and women were constantly in danger. Trainees were not resistant to community policing personally, but they felt that once they were introduced to the realities of policework, they would be intimidated by senior officers and told to 'forget what they had learned'. Problems were exacerbated by a lack of official clarity about what exactly community policing actually meant[12]. A sample of police officers revealed that the legalistic disposition remains dominant in the South African police – positive extra-legal problem-solving was beyond their imagination. Under the apartheid government, policing was rule-based – determined by rules, regulations, and hierarchies rather than by initiative, consultation and discretion (Mistry 1997).

According to one senior commentator, community policing failed because despite investment in training and retraining, many rank and file officers have little idea of what is expected of them. Officers at supervisory level also lack training. There is major doubt about their commitment to community policing (Marks 1995). The police enjoy poor conditions of service. High levels of danger mean much demoralization of police and consequently little personal commitment to transformation. The police institution in South Africa has neither the capacity not the organization to adjust to a community policing ideology (Pelser and Louw 2002).

Box 6.4 *Policing in South Africa in relation to social class (Louw and Shaw 1997)*

> - The poor ... are more likely to be policed by the public police in a reactive manner than are the wealthier classes who, in South Africa, are increasingly more likely to be policed preventively by private security.
> - The problems of criminality in poor communities can often be traced to socio-economic circumstances, which can be altered by interventions quite apart from policing. Yet the response of state institutions is more likely to be reactive in such cases than seeking innovative and preventive policy interventions.
> - Preventive strategies, given the poor's limited ability to cushion themselves from the costs of crime, are also more appealing. No matter how efficient the system of criminal justice, it will do little in the forms of restitution for victims of crime and those they support.
> (Louw and Shaw 1997, p. 1)

As early as 1992 (p. 6) a key policing innovator, Etienne Marais, questioned delphically,

> ... is community policing practical, indeed possible in the present South African context, characterized by deep divisions, and a militarized policing philosophy? Is community policing such a good idea considering its inherent sophistication as a means of social control ... Can community policing be pursued indeed promoted separate from concern for and reality of the absence of real community empowerment in SA?

The continuing problems of the SAPS are numerous. Policing in Cape townships such as Gugelutu is often characterized by violence against suspects and old habits appeared to have been inherited. 'Eighty per cent of the police in Gugelutu are virtually illiterate and believe the best way of solving problems is to apply force in the most barbaric way' (*Cape Argus*, 3 July 1998). Policing in townships may be by second-rate police just like the kitsconstables of the apartheid era (Brogden and Shearing 1993). Police methods are unchanged on the ground, with officers drawn from the local communities given superficial training as police before being deployed at police stations and given less demanding duties so that their more experienced, and better trained, colleagues could be released for active policing duties (Kilpin 1999).

Most police stations operate at a capacity of 70 per cent or lower (Kilpin 1999). Skilled personnel have often moved to higher salaries in the private sector. The Employment Equity Act and other human rights legislation created uncertainty about the future of policing staff and removed the relative simplicity from their work with consequent loss of commitment and morale. The Constitution of 1996 required human rights-based approaches to policing, involving substantial organizational changes in the style of policing, consequently making many members feel disempowered. The police, like other state agencies, are suffering from what has become known as 'transformation fatigue' – change is continuing all the time. Finally, while the police role in the community may have been arguably enhanced, international donors have paid little attention to other parts of the system such as the courts, the prosecution and the prisons – logjams occur[13].

The elevation of crime fighting

Crime fighting has become the focus of both external pressure and internal demand (as epitomized by the development of the high profile Scorpion unit, a specialized newly recruited squad of graduates to combat serious crime). As early as 1995, the ANC supported the formation of a highly centralized Public Order Police Unit (POPU). One example of this serious crime focus has been Operation Crackdown.

> Every couple of weeks the police, often with the help of the South African National Defence Force (SANDF) targets a high crime area and moves into it commando-style or over the weekend. The result is mass arrests of illegal immigrants and suspected drug dealers. These processes appear to have little effect on the rate of serious crime – certainly not social crime prevention insofar as they are

aimed at achieving indiscriminatory mass arrests. Many of the illegal immigrants soon find their way back again, making problems of the overloaded court system and overcrowded prisons even worse.

(Kilpin 2002)

While some observers have claimed that 'service delivery' and 'crime reduction' were simply added to the community policing aims, the latter eventually proving the cuckoo-in-the nest in determining future policing priorities (Pelser 1999). The second Police Act (1997) reflected a return to a more law and order bandit-catching process, with an apparent revival of a more centralized policing structure. The pressures of rising crime and the internal upheavals experienced by the police during the transition forced the police back into a more traditional crime fighting mode, in which the community was seen simply as an aid to intelligence gathering (Scharf 2000).

South Africa's internal crime problem has become intermeshed with larger international concerns over cross-border and global crime. Domestic insecurity has been perceived as a threat to international stability and community policing notions are downgraded as secondary to bandit-catching functions across borders. International assistance is now geared to different policing tasks such as combating organized drugs crime, illegal migration, and precious metal smuggling, as part of a larger international concern with the globalization of crime. Criminal investigations are to be improved by proportionately increasing the number of detectives and better detective training programmes. Within that context, donor commitments changed from COP to prioritizing police training and reorganization.

The National Crime Prevention Strategy (NCPS) had been adopted by the Cabinet during May 1996 as an 'overarching vehicle of police reform'. The NCPS was intended to address the lack of coordination and interdepartmental linkages in the fight against crime through a '... comprehensive multi-agency approach to crime prevention'. Like many 'expert' treatises on transformation in South Africa, however, the document was long on analysis, but very short on practical solutions (Nina 2000). The strategy aimed to draw together key role players in government in an attempt to provide the basis for the restructuring of the criminal justice system, and in the longer term, more effective crime prevention programmes. By the end of 1997, the government realized that such reforms were no panacea for success. Resistance in the different justice departments – sins of omission and well as of commission – meant that there had been little impact.

Not surprisingly, Nina argues, despite major investments in the NCPS and in community policing projects, crime rates have continued to increase, as has public concern about safety and security. Concomitantly, there has been a decrease in public confidence in the police and a strong outcry for government to 'do something' about crime. Electoral considerations spurred the ANC government to shift its emphasis to a search for policies that will lead to better crime prevention and the more effective combating of crime. Hence the new White Paper on policing (1998) strongly emphasized the need for effective law enforcement and '... an investment in, and focus on, the institutions which are essential to show that the state can, and will, act against criminals'. The drafters of this policy document clearly did not have CPFs in mind.

> Recent government policy papers, while not discarding community policing, focus on the need for more effective detective work, improvement of the criminal justice system, and efforts to address the socio-economic causes of crime.
>
> (Cawthra, 1997)

Private policing for the business class

The development of community policing has also been hampered by what may be in Africa a major of feature of community policing schemes elsewhere – the development of alternative police for profit for those who can afford it. Given the historical economic inequalities in South Africa and the divisive lifestyle and housing location inherited from apartheid, such a private police development is perhaps inevitable.

The South African private security industry is one of the fastest growing economic sectors and continues to grow in response to the prevalence of crime, lack of sufficient police coverage and insurance requirements (Carrier 1999). Since 1970 the industry has expanded at an average rate of 30 per cent per year. The Institute of Security Studies estimates that with an estimated turnover in excess of R10 billion per year, the money spent on private security is approaching that of the South African Police Service's annual budget (R15.3 billion for the 99/ 2000 budget year). The broad private security industry employs over 400,000 persons, and there some 6,000 companies registered in South Africa. For every SAPS officer, there are four officers employed by private security firms. The private security industry has access to 80,000 vehicles while the South African Police Service's vehicle fleet numbers 37,000 vehicles.

There is a continuing debate over the use of the reserve police officers to patrol white suburbs (paid for by local traders). Amongst varying criticisms, it has been claimed that such policing represented a breach of the Constitution in ensuring that some citizens are protected better than others and that in particular cases, the reserve police are using extortion practices to ensure they are paid by local shopkeepers (*Woza*, 7 March 2000). In Johannesburg, private employment of police reservists in Johannesburg's 'highly successful "bobby on the beat" scheme have mushroomed elsewhere' only to be curtailed by the SAPS (*Mail and Guardian*, 19 October 2001). As a government spokesman said in relation to such a Stellensbosch patrol of the Central Business District, it was acceptable because 'If certain areas want to pay people as patrol officers, then obviously the richer suburbs will be able to pay for policing and the poor people will not be able to' (*Mail and Guardian*, 15 February 2002). It was however supported by senior Western Cape Police officers, both because it relieved their own resources and also that such a group might eventually become the basis of a newly incorporated municipal police.

In South Africa, private security policing falls under the aegis of community policing partnership approach in which security is seen as a cooperative effort to facilitate the process of problem-solving as well as to determine community needs and policing priorities through consultation. But when the unregulated private sector is the co-partner, there are major problems of equity which potentially undermine the civil liberties of the excluded (Nina 2000). White affluent areas receive technologically efficient private security policing; black townships come to depend on poorly paid and equipped state police officers.

Overview

What is clear from the work of the variety of commentators on the development of community policing in South Africa is the failure to solve the dilemma in communities where the police were perceived to be oppressors and where the police believe that the most constructive crime prevention is police-led '... (how) many members of the community would willingly give up their time and resources to assist the police in fighting crime?' (Pelser and Louw 2002, p. 5).

A decade after the first community policing proposals were launched, some lessons had been learned and others not. The import of community policing and its legislation in South Africa failed to address other contextual problems. Both donors and promoters of community policing did not recognize the diversity of South Africa's communities – not just in terms of race and different ethnicities but also in terms of social class. The term community may have little meaning in the gross inequalities and access to power between rich and poor.

Despite the above lessons, South Africa's police force is apparently considering adapting the Singapore NPP system for its own use. In similar words to many naïve senior officers in states in transition and in failed states, Superintendent Marius Smuts from South African Police Services said that since the system will appear quite new and different to most South Africans, it might take some time to convince them. 'But we are confident that this system will allow our police and the public to combat crime together,' he said. 'Hopefully we can achieve the same success as the Singapore Police Force.' Some had not learnt lessons.

There were some positive outcomes, such as the de-demonization between police and communities. Some relatively successful crime prevention campaigns had been launched. There had been progress in projects such as creating better treatment of victims (Shaw 2002). However, others have argued that there is little remaining community support for community policing crime prevention programmes[14]. At a different level of analysis, the crime prevention strategy did indicate a significant shift in the discourse on safety and security in South Africa. The focus changed from community policing to 'crime prevention' and the building of 'partnerships', both between government agencies and with outside organizations in business and civil society in an effort to stem the tide of crime. From the perspective of normative democratic police reform and effective law enforcement practices, however, 'crime prevention' and 'partnerships' are even further from addressing the basic needs of policing than community policing (van der Spuy 2000).

Despite the intentions of one of the major academic entrepreneurs in developing the new policing, Shearing, the 'police' have remained the Police. 'Policing problems' have remained Policing Problems – with various groups and communities excluded. For the SAPS, community policing was essentially a new tactic in the control of crime and in the construction of a police notion of social order. For many black people, community policing meant a new service role for the police including not just the prevention of crime but also a range of victim support and human rights' maintaining functions. In this second meaning, the social order of the township was a community construction as was the prioritization of problems – such as crime – with which the police should deal. The police thought otherwise, with community forums simply being a necessary additional resource for the police. There was a strong feeling that community policing has concentrated too heavily on the creation of CPF structures and gaining legitimacy for the SAPS, rather than improving the outcomes of policing in terms of better detection and crime reduction. Conversely, too many CPFs may have seen their role as one of control and direction of the police rather than as one of providing the community link in the chain of police accountability. Moreover, neither community associations nor the SAPS seem to have grasped the fact that there is more to community policing than establishing community forums.

There is also doubt whether the whole concept of community policing can work effectively in the disparate and divided communities that characterize South Africa and that have little in common in terms of needs and aspirations. While the more affluent white areas may still support community-driven solutions to crime, black people in poorer areas would prefer to see intervention by national government and more effective policing. Community policing can only have potential when the community has the relevant skills and resources to contribute to the fight against crime. These are patently lacking in the rural and poorer areas of the country. Most remaining CPFs are controlled, heavily influenced by, the police, or by white residents' associations. The SAPS by and large frequently sees community policing as a soft approach to the problem of crime. In this they may be supported by the community under the banner of community policing. While it may be argued that public order and crime fighting policing

> ... impedes community policing, it should be recognized that, if the concept of community policing is applied in the broadest terms, citizens as part of a consultative process, may in fact demand more forceful policing to ensure public order and safety in areas wracked by social violence.
>
> (Nina 2000, p. 4)

Finally, the lesson from community policing in South Africa, as in many other transitional societies, is that there is a major contradiction in the popular calls for community policing as a way of making the police more effective in fighting crime and community demands for increased police accountability through community policing structures. Effectiveness in crime control is deemed to be much more important than community policing as a vehicle for building human rights through community policing. Most community members see the two goals as contradictory. Pushing for enforcement strategies over prevention efforts through community policing is the norm because enforcement appears to be more effective at representing a tighter approach to combating crime. Many South African communities are more concerned about the non-delivery of services, including policing, than they are about questions of community accountability. Communities tend to view those groups who have the most need to be incorporated into the community forum structures such as youth gang members, as 'irredeemable' and NGO representatives who argue for their inclusion are viewed by community members as being 'soft on crime'. However, South Africa's democratic constitution, and a range of other measures associated with the country's new transparent and accountable structures, have succeeded in opening a previously closed organization to greater public scrutiny, study and interaction.

Notes

1 South Africa has produced over the last decade some of most competent academic studies of policing and crime prevention in the world. It should be noted therefore that, in several ways, the concept of 'community policing' has now largely been discarded in the current academic literature in that country and replaced by critically informed studies of 'community safety'.
2 Under apartheid, only one in ten members of the force were engaged in detecting and investigating 'real' crime. The rest were busy with regime maintenance.
3 In areas such as Tshwane, the old street committees of struggle (Brogden and Shearing 1993) were reinvented as CPFs (Sowetan, 2 July 2001).
4 By September 1997, approximately 1,200 community police forums and sub-forums had been established at the 1,221 police stations nationwide.
5 For example, the British and Dutch governments provided funds to teach community members about the mechanics of community policing, to help them develop strategies to decide on their needs, and to communicate these needs to the police (see Chapter 1). While many different Western donor countries contributed to the reform of the SAP, by far the largest was Britain's investment of some $9.4 billion for community policing projects (in addition to more marginal commitments [Malan 2000]). For example, the British DFID and the EU invested R6m in the Transkei in a 15-month community policing project in 1998.
6 The Community Policing Policy Framework and Guidelines, defining community policing as a collaborative, partnership based approach to low level problem-solving.
7 Financed by the British DFID in the Western Cape.
8 Over three million South Africans legally own 4.2 million firearms and it is estimated that a similar number of illegal weapons are circulating.
9 For example, in 1999, some 2.4 million crimes were recorded and only 200,000 ended in convictions – for example, car hijacking convictions were 2 per cent in 1999 and 3 per cent for aggravated robbery, and 8 per cent for

recorded rape. Crime itself appears to run at an extraordinary level, with murder of civilians (the only potentially accurate measure of the crime problem – for a period the Ministry curtailed publication of reported crime rates because of their unreliability) running at five times that of cities such as New York (Louw and Schonteich 2001).

10 Despite the fact that nearly two thirds of assault victims and of sexual victims knew the offender by name.

11 A few other regions of the world – such as the state of Sao Paulo in Brazil – are even more exceptional with some 270 police being killed per year in that province alone.

12 As we noted earlier, the relevant policy document on community policing was only developed three years after the transformation in the SAPS had begun.

13 In some parts of the country, the accused may spend as much as four years on remand before the trial, as they cannot afford bail.

14 Nedbank ISS Crime Index 2, 1998.

Chapter 7

Community policing in other transitional societies

... contemporary themes that enjoy unprecedented popularity (sourced from a burgeoning literature from the West) include 'community policing', 'sensitisation' and, of course, 'human rights'. As a result, from time to time, groups of (less than willing) officers are trooped in to well intentioned 'workshops' on these subjects, where they are harangued mercilessly by self-righteous orators who subject them to a second-hand wisdom that contains no suggestion of a familiarity with the situation on the ground, or the status of the terminally sick criminal justice system in the country.

(*The Times of India*, 17 December 2001)

Introduction

Societies across much of the world, faced with major dilemmas sourced in economic and political inequalities, often with bulging populations dislocated by poverty, racism, and Aids, have sought desperate help to curtail the rise in their crime problem – as recorded in the official crime data, measured in pioneering victim surveys, experienced by victims, and recognized by investors as major destabilizing factors and a threat to their possibilities of profit. A policing solution is sought. Community policing appeals. The last chapter dealt with the specific experience and relative failure of community policing in one such major country. But of course the South African experience, while much more intensively implemented and researched than elsewhere in a transitional society, is not the only example. In different parts of Africa, in several countries in Asia and across South America, varying types of community police have been planted, watered – and then died.

This chapter skirts discursively through transitional societies where community policing is being encouraged in its many guises. Chief amongst the instruments of COP change are the devices of community police forums, watch schemes, problem-solving policing and visible foot patrols.

An African study (Ruteere and Pommerolle 2003)[1] furnishes a detailed critique of the implantation of Western-style community policing in Kenya. This chapter places that case on a wider canvas. Utilising material from a range of countries, from Africa, the Indian sub-continent and Latin America, it argues that community policing is, at best, unproven practice. At worst, it is simply a practice that reinforces existing schisms and inequalities. Western emissaries promote it voraciously as the solution to a variety of ills. But, in reality, the experience of many locals demonstrates that Western-derived community policing merely serves to exacerbate social divisions and to co-opt local elites into existing divisive structures, which in turn serve to reinforce controls over Africa's 'dangerous classes'.

This chapter makes four points, drawing on varied secondary materials. Firstly, the experience of South Africa is not unique. Almost without exception, on the information available, the many development projects that have initiated COP schemes have simply served to reinforce schisms and to assist paramilitary policing agencies, coopting local business and political elites to reinforce social inequalities against those lower in the social scale. Secondly, evident in such schemes has been the combination of arrogance and incompetence in the application of a generalized policing model, with little operational relevance to relatively unique contexts in which the strategy has neither affinity nor contiguity. Thirdly, experts have portrayed COP, especially its key components of problem-solving, community forums, watch schemes and beat patrols, as a success story in the West. The evidence is otherwise. But this information is, not surprisingly, absent from the sales literature. Fourthly, and perhaps the key point of this chapter, is the extent to which COP is increasingly being sold to African and to South Asian societies, within an Anglo-American legacy, as a simplistic Human Rights solution to complex local issues. COP has become a *lex motif* of Human Rights.

Box 7.1 *Key features of policing in post-colonial societies*

- Centralised or regional policing systems.
- Policing traditionally bound up with the maintenance of central political rule.
- Policing concerned with imposing central notions of social order on locality.
- Strangers policing strangers.
- Co-existence of informal policing structure based on locality, communal or tribal tradition.
- State policing often badly paid, corrupt and badly resourced with resort to weaponry as primary feature of control.
- Confusion over legal powers of police due to colonial inheritance and local traditions.
- Minimal local accountability.

The post-colonial appeal in Africa for community policing

The attraction of community policing in Africa at both state and popular level is obvious. In the face of rising crime rates and of collapsing paramilitary police institutions, transitional society choices are limited.

Community policing was welcomed in Kenya as elsewhere as a solution to the increasing problem of crime and social disorder. Kenya seems to be heading along the South African path – first, recognition of the crime problems via a detailed habitat[2] victim survey. Crime in Nairobi would escalate if immediate remedial measures were not taken. Police incompetence (and consequent absence in public support) contributed to that failure – that euphemism for a politically directed, underpaid and corrupt police institution. The COP missionaries followed.

> Ours is a country ravaged by crime. The numerous victims of robberies, carjacking and other forms of violent crime in the towns and rural areas will no doubt welcome a programme that provides mechanisms to deal with this menace. The increased incidence of crime is not peculiar to Kenya. It therefore makes sense to learn from them how they deal with a similar problem and how they continue to cope today. With Britain's assistance, a new concept, a community policing and safety programme, will be launched in Nairobi tomorrow.
>
> (*The Nation*, 22 April 2001)

In Nigeria, as elsewhere, local elites saw it as the obvious solution (*The News* (Lagos), 19 June 2000). Current policing is often regarded as a hindrance rather than help. Orthodox reforms make the situation worse. Incompetent policing is 'reformed' simply by increasing numbers and firepower. The police academy is reportedly chaotic and under-resourced and there is a major problem in finding sufficient literate recruits (Alemika and Chukwuma 2000). The Nigerian Centre for Law Enforcement Education promoted COP through community forums but against a calamitous backdrop where the state police have been used by government to execute opponents, to detain suspects without trial and to earn part of their wages from roadblocks.

In Sierra Leone, with its civil war background, the police are paid a pittance and hence rely on corruption (e.g. through checkpoints) and on secondary jobs. The British adviser, Keith Biddle, described the condition of the police and of the police stations as appalling[3]. In Zambia, transition from socialism to capitalism created opportunities for serious violent crime – liberalising the economy resulted in increased unemployment and casual crime (*The Zambian*, 11 February 2003). In both countries, COP was signalled as the answer.

There are modernization claims. Other Nigerians (Igbinovia 2001) assume that COP is a logical component of political and economic development. Nigeria should follow the lead of Britain (modelled on the District Police Partnerships recommended by the Northern Ireland Patten Commission[4]) and expect appropriate technical and financial assistance, just as the Francophone countries of Africa would inevitably follow a French policing lead. COP for Nigeria was perceived as part of an inexorable process of modernization. Diffusion was based on training in the West, as in Swaziland, Sierra Leone, South Africa and Zambia. However, even countries outside the British colonial orbit have developed community policing schemes – such as Burkina Faso[5].

As in the West, official discourse describes both the intent and the practice of community policing in golden terms, especially structures such as that of neighbourhood watch schemes. In Kenya, as elsewhere, NWS were described as having had a major impact on crime in Britain (*The Nation*, 22 March 2001). From Tanzania to Malawi, from Gambia to Zambia, official rhetoric has disguised the realities and confusions of the new strategy. Amongst many other national examples, Namibia adopted COP as part of its policing policy at independence in 1990. Police forums were encouraged in many areas to share information and to discuss policing matters and a Windhoek NWS was established to promote dialogue between officers and the members of the community. However initial disenchantment with the project which had emphasized public accountability and police-public partnerships, meant that COP was reduced in the final Inspector General report on the project to one simply of ensuring the community '... assisting and cooperating with members of the Force, especially in information gathering' (quoted in Clegg *et al* 2000).

In Lesotho, between 1998-2003, the government developed a COP package as a means of improving relations between the police and the community. Zimbabwe (formally, at least) has Community Liaison Officers at each police station. The British sponsored COP in Malawi since 1995 (with later inputs from South Africa) as the basis for police reforms. Crime prevention panels were portrayed as the reinstatement of traditional peacekeeping structures destroyed under British colonialism and by the former President Banda. There were proposals for lay visitor schemes and for an independent police complaints commission. Donor cash paid for bicycles and whistles for the new community constables (Wood 2000). In Ghana, an International Criminal Investigative Training Assistance Program (ICITAP) initiated COP in 1998. It focused on community policing to promote crime prevention partnerships between the police and the public, to improve the police academy (incorporating community police training), and to enhance the public's opinion of the Ghana Police Service[6]. In Sierra Leone, COP (known as Local Needs Policing) was launched with the support of the DFID in 1998[7]. Under a Police Corporate Development Plan in Botswana, COP was introduced in the year 2000. Plans included the establishment of a toll-free telephone number to facilitate the reporting of rape and violent crimes against women, the development of NWS, and of Business and Farm Crime Prevention Schemes[8]. Tanzanian contributions to COP appear to have been limited to the development of the new Dar es Salaam City Auxiliary Police Force.

The failure to contextualize community policing

In practice, such COP schemes are often based on production rather than consumption priorities. Hence, in one South African case of appointment to a community policing forum

> ... the donor followed a checklist, appointing so many black members, so many white members, so many women, and so on. They did not consult enough, and what they failed to take into

account was that some of these were in fact extremely conservative individuals, opposed to many of the reforms to be implemented[9].

English-speaking Africa has had varied but uniformly ineffective experiences of Western community policing. Typically, Nigeria had been unable to establish representative forums because they were established by the police not by the communities (again a finding that merely mirrors experience in the West).

Local reaction has hardly been uncritical, as exemplified by the many Kenyan responses (*The Nation*, 18 August 2001). Little administrative and financial planning had occurred. It was suggested that the police were unthinkingly copycatting forms of policing practised in the West. Women's groups claimed that COP simply resulted in the harassment of women (a claim echoed by squatter groups), falsely accused of loitering with intent to solicit. COP reinforced historical colonial coercive practices especially in the control of '... refugee and migrant communities who are required to carry identity papers at all times because of harassment' (Ruteere and Pommerolle 2003, p. 7[10]). In a criticism that runs to the core of the community policing debate, one local commentator stated that the real need for community policing security practices was in squatter areas rather than for the privileged (Brogden 2005). The Kenyan police official response was that 'When people look suspicious, the police have a duty to stop them and ask them to identify themselves. They have a duty to answer'[11]. Scepticism was expressed elsewhere. The force was totally unequipped to strive for Western COP. The Kenyan police unilaterally decided to introduce COP without any discussion with the communities now expected to cooperate with the state police.

In Zambia, the NWS system appears to have largely disintegrated. Some official commentators see COP as a positive contribution to crime reduction, others as 'mob justice'. In an effort to connect the police with the community, the Zambian police established police posts in some rural areas and in Lusaka under the jurisdiction of a police station. However, some of these posts have reportedly been associated with Human Rights abuses by police officers – they are often manned by junior police (many recorded as inebriated) who maltreat civilians. Accountability and oversight are minimal. Wealthy suburbs are the sole location of the remaining NWS and COP patrols (*The Zambian*, 11 February 2003).

Organizational resistance to community policing, reflecting the impossibility of reforming policing when officers are grossly underpaid as well as undertrained, is reported in several countries. For example in Uganda, a female Community Liaison officer said:

> Some colleagues of ours are not supportive and not interested in community policing because it is assisting the public to become aware of the law and their rights. Some do not wish the public to know about community policing issues such as bond and bail. They say community policing is spoiling our things.

She noted pressure from her colleagues not to

> '… take the food from their mouths by informing the public of their rights to release on bond.'[12]

In Malawi it appears that COP is reserved for prosperous communities. In one case (Wood 2000), a local newspaper claimed that police had misappropriated money given by a local Asian community to introduce COP. While versions of COP have been around from 1995, the organizational structure of the Malawi police was a major impediment, as were other factors – arms smuggling across the Mozambique border, poorly paid police living in squalid conditions and a legacy of distrust incurred under the Banda regime. Private security proliferated because of a lack of police resources. COP was promoted in rural areas by a variety of imaginative devices – but the result has been a resurrection of traditional village policing styles under a community policing rubric. In Swaziland community police have been criticized for treating suspects brutally. The unit's status, mandate and powers are unclear and training inappropriate. In Namibia the community forums were jettisoned in 1996 because of flagging public interest.

What these experiences suggest is that while donor countries may direct their resources in developing policing in a transitional society, the preference is clearly for community policing. COP is both a band-aid for transitional governments as well as the panacea for all crime ills, and the key building block of the new democratic state. Successes are yet to be demonstrated.

The failure of community policing in Uganda

There is one rare evaluation study of community policing in a former British colony in Africa (Raleigh et al 2000). Community policing was introduced into Uganda in 1989, deriving from a Ugandan officer's experience on an Overseas Command Course at the Police Staff College in Britain[13]. In Kampala this was initially intended to be a pilot project to resolve conflict between different community groups and to combat increased instances of theft of electrical items. Between 1986 and 1990 a British Police Training Team (BPTT) was resident in Uganda and assisted in the basic training of recruits, promotional training, the education of direct entry graduate cadet superintendents, criminal investigation training, and rehabilitation of the police college at Kibuli and of the mechanical workshops.

These officers became the basis of the COP team in Uganda. They introduced the idea of 'sensitising the public' to policing. Local community police officers were appointed and provided with bicycles to enable them to 'mobilize the community', operating as beat officers to interact with the public and to discuss with them issues related to crime, security and welfare. This initiative faltered when the divisional head was transferred. In turn, this project was replaced with a larger British commitment when the state was emerging from the troubles of the Idi Amin years. The new COP project, by contrast,

> ... would seek to bring future British assistance to Uganda Police Force (UPF) under one umbrella so that it may be targeted to maximize the benefits of the Force. The fundamental reason for seeking to improve the capability of a police force such as the UPF was that ... economic growth depends on social stability, which in turn depends on an effective and respected police force. But all this had been conducted ... in an uncoordinated fashion largely responding to the needs of an institution in a state of collapse following the troubles of the 1970s and 1980s.
>
> (Raleigh *et al* 2000, p. 57)

Key Ugandan officers on the new project had been trained in community policing in the United Kingdom and believed that community policing practice observed in the UK could be applied to Uganda. During the first phase, community policing was pursued by the UPF on its own initiative in two or three districts of Kampala but faltered after only a few months.

The new development was the institutionalization of community policing within the UPF by means of a national system of Community Liaison Officers (CLOs). The initial mandate was optimistic.

> The social impact will come from the improved public confidence in the police; the greater incidence of crime prevention and detection resulting from a more efficient force and partly from the

planning, expansion, and improvement of community policing schemes; and the improved capacity for economic and social development[14].

The UPF regarded community policing as a promising way to bridge the gap between itself and the public, and to establish a new approach to policing based on mutual trust and cooperation. But no direct resources were committed.

DFID's subsequent Report was blunt.

> It seems doubtful if Community Policing, as currently practiced, has yet led to any substantive change in the public image of the UPF.
>
> (Raleigh *et al* 2000, p. 28)

Firstly, it was wrong to couple the development of a criminal intelligence system with community policing. Crime-fighting intelligence should be developed prior to COP not simultaneously. Secondly, in a classic critique of many such community policing projects, the Report stated that the UPF tended to regard community policing primarily as a means of instructing local populations, rather than of listening to them – in effect, failing at intelligence gathering while doing little to mitigate its authoritarian image. The UPF considered the public's role exclusively in terms of the help they could provide in the prevention of crime.

> The focus has been on sensitising the public on their role and what they can do to contain crime. There has been much less emphasis on listening to public priorities and concerns.
>
> (ibid p. 17)

Thirdly, the requirements of COP in an urban area were quite different from those in the rural areas of Uganda. But the same model was adopted in both contexts (especially problematic in the rural areas was the lack of transport for the new CLOs). Community policing in Kampala with easily patrolable beats and a dense concentration of people (DFID noted the absurdity of community-friendly officers carrying AK 47s) required very different processes from community policing in the scarcely populated rural areas of the northern and southern regions. Like criticisms of other COP projects, the DFID Report focused on the contradictions faced by a COP process, which aims to use a crime clear-up rate as an index of success – inevitably, the recorded crime rate also increased. There was a deep contradiction between the functions of COP as perceived by the seconded staff from Britain and by the local communities. The first saw COP as crime focused, the second perceived its function as about enhancing the image of the UPF.

Fourthly, resources both material and with regard to salaries undermined any individual motivation (for example, the local CLOs were not selected on the basis of training or commitment). Police salaries were very low, often late in arriving. Officers could not survive on their pay and hence relied on bribes. Accommodation was described as 'appalling', with one room often being shared with other officers' families. Pensions were low and often paid two or three months in arrears. 'So it is hardly surprising … if many feel that they "must make their pension while they are the desk'" (ibid p. 26). Indeed, after the first injection of funds from Britain, there had been no finance directed at sustaining community policing. A military structure of control was maintained with little local discretion. COP was centrally directed from Police Headquarters for District priorities. There was no local community consultation.

Finally, DFID points to the major issue undermining this and other exported COP projects. Totally insufficient thought had been given to the relevance of the UK model of community policing to Ugandan circumstances, and little consideration seems to have been given to differing community needs and priorities or to local conditions, customs and traditions. This was true both between Britain and Uganda and also within Uganda itself. Training for the different local conditions and values seems to have been simply based on British determination of what was appropriate.

The evaluators of the Uganda project completed their total criticism of COP in Uganda with mild irony.

Whether the concept of community policing, fostered by the project will take root in a way that genuinely enhances public perceptions of the role of the police remains for us an open question. Indeed the obstacles to a full realization of the benefits of community policing in Uganda remain formidable. In discussion with police and non-police sources alike, we found clear signs that the police regard community policing primarily as a means of instructing local populations, rather than of listening to them.

(ibid p. 18)

While community policing might be popular in local rhetoric, delivery of it had little actual substance[15]. In the Ugandan press, the police were widely portrayed as corrupt, inefficient and brutal. It was also a dangerous occupation[16]. Against a background of corruption by senior officers and in the CID, despite bizarre attempts to improve police community relations[17], nevertheless, COP policing is still fashionable in official discourse in Uganda[18].

Importing community policing to South Asia

There is almost identical evidence from the Indian sub-continent on the failure to be sensitive to the local context. In South Asia generally, especially in the former colonies and imperial territories, the community oriented policing system has rapidly become the alternative to the paramilitary inheritance of the former British colonial police. The British colonial past is the easy – and often justifiable – scapegoat for the need to change to community policing. As a response to rising recorded crime rates, one late colonial policing system is rapidly being replaced with versions of a second. Local elites, supported by key politicians and by police officers trained in the West, portray COP as a response to the crime problem. In Faisalabad in Pakistan (*Dawn*, 26 August 2001), as in Uttar Pradesh, the (new) system would help bridge the gap between the police and the public as a major break from the British colonial inheritance of paramilitary policing[19].

Failures in crime control provided the opening for the new dawn of community policing in the sub-continent.

> The police system is based upon antiquated systems and ideas of crime control, and has neglected the opportunities of systematic methods and technologies of crime analysis, of scientific investigation and documentation, of information processing, and of law and order mapping, projection and prediction. The sheer gap between contemporary policing practices in the West, and those that prevail in India is astonishing. Primitive policing practices are reflected in poor rates of conviction, in deteriorating efficiency and effectiveness, and consequently in a declining respect for the law.
> (*The Times of India*, 12 January 2001)

Initial official discourse and optimism reflected that of African societies. In Chennai crime prevention through community problem-solving rather than through traditional reactive policing was to be the new solution. According to the Chief Minister, community policing would

> ... indeed be a pleasurable experience. Imagine yourself being received by smiling plainclothes police personnel who will be manning the reception desk. No unnecessary talk or pleading with the 'para' constable holding the 303 rifle in front of the station. Hard to believe. But that's just what the city police are planning as part of an ambitious community policing scheme.
>
> (*The Times of India*, 4 August 2001)

Citizens were to become consumers – telephone numbers of officials to be contacted in case of complaints against the police were to be displayed prominently at police stations. Visitors to the Police Commissioner's Office were to be received by reception officials. Grievances would be addressed speedily. Station house officers had been directed to interact with the office-bearers of residents' associations and enlist their cooperation in crime control. Community problem-solving contacts would be enhanced. Similarly in Delhi

> The officers who attended the workshop will now be referred to as agents of change as they have been entrusted with the job of improving the day-to-day functioning of the police. The stress would be on informing and educating the public about crime, its causes and effects within society. It would also seek to mobilize individuals, families and various sections of the community – grassroots organizations, public and private bodies and other government agencies – in crime elimination, prevention and control – getting the community involved in self-policing, reducing petty crimes and disorder, and Community Liaison Groups formed[20].

As elsewhere, British policing missionaries were critical to the process. Amongst many other examples of British commitment to community policing in India, a Chief Superintendent from the West Midlands Police lectured in the Punjab on the benefits of community police structures such as Community Safety Bureaux (*Chandigarh Times*, 14 February 2002). Other British provincial forces played a similar role, with the South Yorkshire Police sending a group of its officers to Delhi in March 2002 to *inter alia* persuade their Indian colleagues of the benefits of community policing. COP in India also has international commercial sponsors – for example, a police department in Tamil Nadhu recently won the bizarrely named Night Vision Community Policing award sponsored by the ITT conglomerate. The British Council organized seminars on COP for police officers in Calcutta and Chennai.The Director General of the Punjab Police Service inaugurated a 'social orientation programme' on community policing with the primary function of dealing with the increasing crime threat. In Uttar Pradesh, the provincial government announced it was adopting a community policing system drawing on the practices in Singapore and Japan (while recognizing problems of local adaptation) – a team of officials had visited Singapore and Japan.

A Sri Lankan account combines a critique of the colonial policing past, together with an anecdote based on the English Tythingman, and conveys the British myth of policing by consent. But '... they never were citizens in uniform under community control as they were in Britain proper'[21]. Similar myths about the nature of policing in the West are replicated elsewhere in the sub-continent. In Delhi, the new Director General of Police welcomed the development of COP to replace the old para-military style, '... it is time to police by consent rather than police by coercion' (*The Times of India*, 14 February 2002). In Uttar Pradesh the senior police officer (recently returned from British community police training) stated:

> ... the police have tried many methods at solving crime. The vital thing lacking is the community's support ... with the community's help, desirable results can be obtained in solving crime. The concept of people's policing is based on the British view 'Every policeman is a citizen and every citizen is a policeman[22].

The British citizen-in-uniform myth is a common theme, as reiterated by an innovating Detective Inspector in Himachya Pradesh when launching a community policing scheme.

> ... the schema was based on the concept that every policeman was a citizen and every citizen was a policeman without a uniform
> (*The Times of India*, 20 September 2001)

This view ignored the lack of common law powers of arrest and prosecution in India[23]. Community consultation and problem-solving were to be the cornerstones of the new policing. Well-meaning injunctions are combined with a spurious claim to a British golden experience. Occasional caveats are attached. In Kerala

Community policing has proved a success in the US, Britain and Japan. But in these countries, the police are not politicised. But in our country they are. To forget this crucial difference while implementing the scheme will be foolhardy.

(*The Week*, 21 May 2000)

In Kerala, the provincial government had argued that community support for the police was possible because of the high rate of literacy, greater social mobility, urbanization, and effective transportation and communication. But there were local criticisms, which challenged the ruling Communist Party's claim that it would simply and desirably replicate Western COP schemes:

... the scheme will follow the high techniques of the Guardian Angels, the Portland burglary prevention programme, the Seattle community prevention programme, crime stoppers, and the koban system currently existing in the United States, Japan and Britain

but

The Kerala Congress President claimed 'The community policing project will turn the state police into the Marxists' hands'.

A senior officer noted

... in a country like the United States, the police force is a highly professional and competent body and the people are law-abiding and socially conscious[24]. That is why the neighbourhood watch scheme is a success in the US (sic!). People in a state like Kerala do not have much regard and respect for law. (*The Times of India*, 15 March 2001)

Two features dominate the Indian sub-continent provincial reaction to COP. Crime control is, of course, the *raison d'être*. But more importantly, community policing may sometimes be adapted through the development of police-community relations' schemes within traditional structures. Sometimes, however, these adaptations are more genuine than others. In Andhra Pradesh, the forums are incorporated within traditional Maithri committees consisting of 50-100 people nominated by the local station officer. In Pakistan (*Dawn*, 22 September 2001) senior officers proposed to incorporate the *mohallah chowkida* system in Karachi as part of the community policing system.

Orissa proposed a more specific and directed use of such forums

> ... a committee would be set up in each village and during violent incidents, police would consult the committee to nab culprits and restore normalcy in the area[25].

The Himachya Pradesh authorities had no doubt about the functions and proceedings of such forums (*The Times of India*, 20 September 2001). The schisms noted in Nairobi would be repeated with local notables and the police controlling the community forums:

> ... six respectable, non-political persons, and two police officers (with a police officer as Secretary). The (policeman acting as secretary) would be the key person in effect and would move around the sector at least one in three days and also organize night patrolling by the residents. He would win over the confidence of the residents by actively participating in social functions and make it a point to attend funeral ceremonies in the sector. He would maintain the record of each household in the sector and register all complaints received by him in writing – he would also maintain a beat patrol book of useful information in the area. The people's committee would collect information about illicit distilling, bootlegging, drug trafficking, criminal elements, accident-prone spots, assist the police in night patrolling, verification of antecedents, arranging watch over the house of residents who have gone out and check on suspicious persons moving around the area.

In Dacca (*Daily Star*, 19 August) in Bangladesh, one commentator expressed appropriate scepticism

> The manner in which members of the neighbourhood watch committees have been elected and the behaviour of some of them have raised questions about the success of community policing (especially) the lack of interest shown by the jurisdictional police in enlisting the support of the people to these committees.

In Chennai (in the above case), in the event, there was little public interest in the new schemes. Most projects had failed due to lack of public participation. Many of the new Community Liaison Officers had complaints pending against them.

Community forums simply served as an adjunct to traditional police goals, and had little in common with the critical lessons learned in the West. In Delhi, for example, the Nairobi pattern was followed, making the forums simply an adjunct of central business interests.

> The Inspector General said the experiment in community policing is being run successfully with the cooperation of the Defence Residents' Society, Delhi Mercantile Society, Chamber of Commerce and Industries, and other business communities and the problems are being resolved expeditiously[26].

In Surat, a city with a large migrant population ('dangerous classes'!), a Friends of the Police forum was expected to keep a watch on its neighbourhood and keep the police informed about groups and individual needs in their areas[27,28]. In Hyderabad, under the COP umbrella, Village Defence Parties (*Samitees*) were enlisted to evict encroachers from pavements and conduct house-to-house surveys of tenants in the detection of crime. Community Liaison Groups (CLGs) were formed of eminent 'and non-political persons'. Inevitably, the forums came to regard their primary function as correcting what they saw as a misrepresentation of policing in the local press rather than overseeing the police on behalf of the community (*Hyderabad Times*, 19 January 2000). Criticisms of the Western (and Japanese imports) have not been lacking. One sardonic senior police officer notes of the Kerala scheme that provincial government derived inspiration from the success (!) of the NWS schemes in the US but it failed to learn from its neighbours like Andhra Pradesh, Gujarat and Uttar Pradesh.

UNDP has promoted community policing in Delhi.

> A new community policing model will be introduced to the Delhi police which will aim at bringing the police closer to the common man (despite the fact that previous initiatives in developing police community liaison schemes have now become defunct – partly because they did not allow for a turnover in citizen members).
>
> (*The Times of India*, 17 December 2001)

The newspaper commented on the practice of imports and the experience of those imported schemes.

> The Delhi Police's favourite pastime seems to be community policing, at least if you go by the number of schemes that have been launched in the past. Some ten community schemes aimed at improving interaction between the police and citizens had been initiated over the past two decades.

A retired senior officer dryly noted that there was little purpose in the international contact, given the disparities in literacy levels and disciplinary structures. Other schemes launched by the Delhi police in the past years ' … have failed miserably. Most schemes appeared to be good on paper but could not be implemented with much success'. Other spokesmen agreed, adding

> … whether it was the 'neighbourhood watch scheme' or the 'senior citizens scheme' or even the highly publicized 'servant verification scheme', Delhiites have never benefited'.[29]

Hardly unique to India, many such senior police officers have been sceptical about the importation of community policing. In Uttar Pradesh, senior officers regarded COP as irrelevant to the Indian context. The criticisms of COP proposals in Pakistan were identical to those by informed observers and police officers in India, although often for more conservative reasons. Community policing was perceived as an infringement and interference in the domain of policing; senior officers arguing that the unpopular image of the police was a major and probably insurmountable handicap:

> … any genuine attempts in this regard would be seen as a new method of spying in a particular community, and that the quality of existing officers was so low and their exposure to police culture so great that they could not conduct the … sensitive and socially responsible tasks required by community oriented policing[30].

However the myth of the effectiveness of much of the community policing practices in relation to crime control represents a key theme of the salespeople, especially in relation to Neighbourhood Watch Schemes – that NWS work in the West is an effective means of achieving lower crime rates. Therefore they can be replicated in the East and South as a key part of the new community policing strategies. But the evidence on NWS is absolute. There is no evidence that they decrease recorded crime. Instead, they have two evidential effects. In the first place, they increase the reporting of minor misdemeanours to the police; misdemeanours which may have little to do with crime and certainly have little possibility of a policing resolution. Second, after a short period of such enhanced reporting, most NWS die away as the police increasingly come to believe that a deluge of such trivia requires no sensible police response.

Community policing elsewhere in transitional Asia

Aside from the Indian sub-continent, many other nation states in Asia have been in receipt of Anglo-American community policing. For example, Mongolia received $100,000 from COLPI for a three-year project implemented in Songino Khairan and Sukhbaatar districts of Ulaanbaatar. Each district police station appointed squads of community constables to be responsible for the development of policing partnerships. The project included the training of community beat officers, district area (*horoo*) governors, members of the committees and subcommittee, by members of Royal Ulster Constabulary. COP modules were established at the Police Academy combining theoretical knowledge with practical experience. Senior police managers and civil servants were taken to the Netherlands and to Northern Ireland to learn from the experiences of the police forces in those countries on COP. Remarkably, the International Society of Crime Prevention Practitioners presented its prestigious award to the Mongolian Police and the RUC for their cooperation and success. In Kyrgyzstan, the OSCE Ambassador

Box 7.2 *Reported success of COP in Mongolia*

The paradox of relying on statistical indices of the success or otherwise of COP can be illustrated from the Mongolian experience. Mr Bloed (Director of COLPI) described how COPLI's successful community policing project in Ulan Bator weathered an unexpected attack.

Four years ago the concept of community policing was virtually unknown in Mongolian. Today, it is the top priority in the government plan for police reform. Under the project, law enforcement officers in the capital were instructed to revise their policy towards first-time offenders. Instead of simply reporting the offenders, the police tried talking to them and issuing warnings. As a result, the number of imposed fines dropped from 750,000 in 2,000 to 400,000 in 2001. To the Minister of Justice, however, such a sharp decline could mean only one thing: that the police were not on the ball. He accused them of complacency in the face of rising crime rates. It took some effort but the national police chief eventually convinced the Minister that the new approach was essential to community policing ... Fortunately he could produce additional statistics showing that the number of reported crimes had also fallen.

(*Focus Newsletter*, 12 February 2002,
Centre for International Legal Cooperation)

Douglas Davidson urged community policing as both a local solution to internal conflict, and as an answer to social schisms in Central Asia and throughout the Caucasus[31]. Georgia is apparently the next such optimistic venture.

Community policing in Central and South America

Like Eastern Europe, and those areas of Africa influenced by the British policing tradition, Central and South America contain disparate experiences of the attempted implantation of community policing. At one extreme are major countries like Brazil and Argentina with a recent history of major social divisions, brutal military policing and serious economic problems. At the other, islands like Trinidad and Tobago are hardly prosperous but experience a relatively benign policing climate. All to varying extent have undergoing a *Pax Americana* through a latter-day Monroe doctrine of exporting community policing.

Brazil is at the extreme. During the 1980s and 1990s, it experienced a quadrupling of homicides at 36.2 per 100,000 (in 1995, 618 citizens were reportedly killed by the police) although little minor crime is reported to the (major) Military Police. Between 1995 and 1998, some 21 people were being killed by the police every month in Rio. In Sao Paulo, during the first four months of 2001, the police killed 248 civilians. Many police are relatively underpaid – police earn less than bus drivers (Huggins and MacTurk 2000) – and work part-time as private security officers (Beato 2003).

As part of a larger international remit, the Ontario Provincial Police has provided 'Customized Police Service' materials for Brazil[32]. Frequent missionary papers are given such as that by Charles Ramsay of the Washington DC Metropolitan Police (a force that has its own problems) in Rio de Janeiro[33]. The Washington Office for Latin America (WOLA) is also promoting community policing in Brazil. The Canadian International Development Agency (CIDA) reacted to the level of violence in Sao Paulo by sending senior officers to advise on new policing models. Inspector Haddow and Chief Superintendent Zanin (who was also charged with instructing the Brazilian police on the use of minimum force) waxed lyrically about the consequent development of community policing in the *favelas*. They claimed a 'huge' interest in community policing by their audiences and described how the concept of community policing was taking hold, and residents were gaining access to health services and other benefits they lacked before. Even the military police expressed interest in community policing. 'What really impressed me', Haddow blithely adds 'is that so many people are making progress in implementing the philosophy of community policing'.

Bizarrely, the development of community policing in one sector could be accompanied by increased repression on the other. In Brazil 'For many policemen, community policing was not anything new, and already existed through their links with local commerce associations … (sic!) (Bretas 2002, p. 175). As the International Crisis Group notes in the Argentine,

> At the same time as the state authorities were promoting police involved in fatal shootings, one leading NGO worked with the police in a large middle class neighbourhood on a model community policing initiative.
>
> (ICG 2003, p. 29)

In both Brazil and the Argentine, repression in a *favela* or working class district could be accompanied by reform in a more middle class context. Community policing development was uneven and skewed by socio-economic stratification.

In Brazil, police reform efforts are clearly commendable. But it is a little difficult at this distance to see such a policing agency – especially the military police hosts[34] – transform themselves into some small Canadian-style unit[35]. Given the description of the Brazilian police in a separate and euphoric account[36] as '… a force organized on the military model, and accustomed to excessive violence', a sum of $C1.8 million seems a drop in the ocean, no matter how well meaning the donors in the promotion of democratic policing and accountability in that country. Local commentators recognize the structural problems facing COP, but view it as a positive stopgap[37]. The externally-supported Vivo Rio program finances police efforts to improve community services by testing community policing:

> … in which officers spend time in the slum even when not responding to calls. That's tough in a place where criminals are heavily armed admits Oscar Valporto, communication coordinator for Viva Rio. But he says police are definitely more a part of the problem than a part of the solution. 'I don't think there's any police in the world that shoots as much as Rio police.'
>
> (*Lincoln Star Journal*, Summer 2001)

In 1994 Ruben Fernandez launched the first NGO experiment in community policing in Rio. Sixty police with high-school education (relatively new recruits and uncontaminated by previous police practices) received special training and were deployed on regular beats, consequently increasing community cooperation. The experiment received enthusiastic support from civilians and younger police officers, reportedly decreasing muggings, car theft and the activities of local drug dealers. But older officers boycotted it. Political considerations and the appointment of a new police commander ended the programme because it was claimed to be 'soft on crime'[38]. In its place, the commander instituted a series of police rewards for 'dealing' with crime and substantial pay increases for officers, typically awarded for killing 'suspects' (Neild 2002)[39]. The most detailed accounts are from the city of Sao Paulo. Civilian casualties at the hands of the police and major problems of violent crime gave rise to a community policing project through an Advisory Committee for the Creation of Community Policing[40]. It proposed a community policing model as the key organizing strategy for the police; improving quality of police instruction and training, and the recruitment and promotion system. It also proposed integrating the police with other agencies and improvements in the rights and statuses of police officers.

In 1997, the Commander of the Military Police formally adopted community policing. By August 1998 some 7,000 officers were formally engaged in community-based work, involving more preventive patrolling, the establishment of 24-hour police posts and the training of officers in COP[41]. But on the Advisory Committee, the attendance of both citizens and police soon declined. Although the establishment of the committee had been a significant achievement, relations between civilian members and police were difficult[42]. The police noted the problems expressed during meetings, but rarely conducted any rigorous follow-up. Dialogue on the councils did not appear to be highly productive – although representing a first step towards citizen involvement in police monitoring. The CONSEGS came to function more as venues for individual complaints about, and demands on, the police, rather than as a means of solving collective problems. They were often used for political purposes, and there was an evident lack of interest in them by both civilians and police, who were often unfamiliar with their purposes and procedures.

Mendes (2004) called for the introduction of *culturally acceptable* forms of community policing and the introduction of a professional model in order to deal with bureaucratic and police corruption. A colleague (Silva 2004) noted three obstacles to community policing – civilian oversight of the police would mean empowering lower socio-economic classes who were the target of police violence; Brazilian policing had derived from the Napoleonic state model not from local communities; and the major police agencies, as elsewhere in Latin America, reflected an authoritarian society with the police traditionally used as an instrument of repression, with neither professional nor community accountability[43].

Many of the small-scale COP projects have now been reversed by political intervention in response to perceptions of rising crime, for example, in Rio following the election of a new governor (coinciding with political support for alternative forms of policing such as private security). In the capitals of both Brazil and the Argentine, politicians standing on law-and-order programmes have reversed COP. Mendes (2004) concludes that the community councils in Brazil which seem to have most success are those in which the business community participates. But it is the poorest and most marginalized sectors of society that have the greatest security needs (Clegg *et al* 2000). In some districts, illegal enterprises such as drugs gangs provide the neighbourhood security from external threat, and supplant the state police. There is a common view that the prevalence of local inequalities, reinforced by a system of political contacts and bosses, is enhanced by a system in which the police, rather than answering to the law, answer to the preferences of a community that lacks any genuine autonomy.

Elsewhere in Central America there have been a variety of attempts, frequently supported by Britain and the United States, to develop community policing schemes.

> Analysts in the region have a tendency to either wholly ignore or uncritically import the crime-prevention experiences of other countries (e.g. US community policing).
>
> (Call 2002)

In Venezuela, the British Council provided British 'know-how' on COP. In Nicaragua Call notes a variety of apparently relatively successful schemes such Neighbourhood Watch Schemes and civilian review boards, developed with NGO support. In El Salvador, the United States Department of Justice has encouraged COP (such as funding for bicycles and radios). A USAID-funded community policing project has been adopted nationwide. ICITAP (March 1999) initiated a proactive flexible community oriented patrol strategy in the city of Mejicanos allegedly resulting in an immediate and significant decline in reported crimes. ICITAP taught COP principles – for example, integrating COP into patrol strategy. A COP presence is apparent in all the major metropolitan areas[44].

Similar accounts are evident from Costa Rica where Chinchilla and Rico (1997) reported a detailed community policing programme in a lower class area of the capital, involving permanent police beat patrols and a community forum representing the local community and local agencies. A succeeding community survey claimed decreases in local crime, enhanced feelings of security and positive views of the new police presence. On the other, there are anecdotal criticisms such as

> President Abel Pacheco ordered an investigation into police who abuse youngsters during a community policing meeting ... Nothing can justify the aggression directed at our socially at-risk sons and daughters at the hands of the agents of security and order[45].

The Washington Office for Latin America has acted as the coordinator for a variety of larger police reform attempts in Latin America. There have been few successes. In El Salvador, community policing initiatives have been limited and uncoordinated (Neild 2002). In one case, a collaborative effort started by the National Public Security Council in 1998 with specific social groups collapsed within two years when civil society groups withdrew due to the appointment of a new police chief with suspect paramilitary credentials. A much larger COP programme has suffered a similar fate. Community Oriented Police Patrol (PIP-Com) was designed and financed by the United States Justice Department's ICITAP. PIP-Com assigns police to regular patrols to increase police visibility in the community. It was linked to police information-gathering and police response to crime patterns. ICITAP claim significant results in crime levels from this programme. However, some local authorities and community leaders expressed scepticism about the programme and community involvement is negligible. Neild reiterates the argument made elsewhere, in regard to these El Salvador developments – that in essence there may be a contradiction given the different views on community policing – one reform group seeing COP as bringing about greater police effectiveness in the short term in relation to crime while the second, civil society, groups see community policing as being about improving accountability. As elsewhere, COP is stranded between the rock of accountability and the hammer of police effectiveness[46].

In Guatemala and Honduras, under the COP rubric, local security councils have been formed. In Guatemala, the Juntas Locales de Seguridad, and the civilian patrols they have initiated, have often been perceived locally as simply the re-emergence of new versions of 'stranger' policing on behalf of external authorities and have included members suspected of serious past abuse. In Honduras, as in several parts of Africa and in Guyana, community policing has resulted in the autonomous formation of community groups to monitor security. Some of these groups have been suspected as in Guatemala of links with the former right-wing paramilitaries. Call (2003) claims varied successes and failures for community policing in Central America, distinguishing between Nicaragua and Costa Rica where the police appear to have actively engaged the local police in COP schemes and Guatemala, Honduras and El Salvador where police-community relations are laced with distrust. Community based work alone is unlikely to advance the reform process. However, overall, Neild (2002) claims some positive successes for community policing in these countries, commenting generally on the Latin America experiences with COP that it has most often been adopted and most often been successful for minority communities who have long been marginalized from political decision-making. Nonetheless, the extreme inequities characteristic of Latin America suggest that the benefits of community policing may be far greater for already well-organized sectors than for those poor and marginalized communities whose need is greater. At worst, community policing simply offers another avenue for enhancement of elite interests.

A major British effort has been apparent in Guyana (*Stabroek News*, 25 August 1999). UK Caribbean Regional Police Adviser Paul Mathias says community policing in Guyana has been a 'resounding success'. He claimed the longevity of the schemes in Guyana and the ownership of them by local people contrasted with research findings in the US and Europe. COP was the 'the jewel in the crown of a force that has a poor public image'. He cited evidence that it had reduced the level of reported crime and of the fear of crime (thanks to local volunteers). It had apparently helped vulnerable groups such as 'women, peasants, farmers and the elderly.' However, Matthias' Report echoes concerns raised at community forums, noting in suspicion that some community groups were reportedly 'a cover for illegal activities' – criminal gangs allegedly had joined the forums in order to obtain firearm licences. He also questions the legality of vigilante groups formed under the auspices of the Community Forums.

In the wider Caribbean, COP has been introduced spasmodically, mainly in relation to a perceived increase in reported crime. In Trinidad and Tobago (Deosaran 2002) COP was introduced because of the admission that traditional law enforcement approaches were not working well and also because they could potentially link with civil notions of community and political decentralization. He claims that, since 1998, that country has been the most advanced in the development of COP, especially in relation to combating domestic violence. What was originally a separate branch of COP has been integrated within the wider policing structures (*Trinidad Express*, 21 June 2001). The Police Commissioners claimed that in future every police officer would be a community police officer. A note of scepticism is raised by Cain (2000) when she claims that the watch schemes initiated in Trinidad under the COP rubric flourished most effectively without police support and eventually assumed their own 'noncrime' *raison d'être*.

In Jamaica, COP was perceived as a response to the rising homicide rate and to everyday violence. The US Ambassador[47] launched a COP programme in a troubled inner city area of Kingston. The scheme included building a model police station, mentoring of schoolchildren by police and a prevention of domestic violence scheme. Police missionaries were apparent (*Jamaica Gleaner*, 31 January 2003) with Chief Inspector Leroy Logan of the Metropolitan Police promoting COP as part of a twinning strategy between Kingston and a London borough[48]. *The Gleaner's* optimism about the prospects for COP were in part countered by the Police Commissioner challenging 'commonsense' assumptions of community policing – 'though well-intentioned, outreach "Commissioner-for-a-day" and police and citizens fix-up projects tend to offer sizzle without providing much steak'. By the end of the year, more than three-quarters of the Jamaican police would have been trained in community policing.

Overview

Criticisms are very easy for the uninvolved of these varied attempts to implant a variety of community policing models in countries in the process of transition. Most of the unofficial commentary reflects the opposite to that of the official discourse. Critiques of the relevance of COP to transitional society are hard to verify. It may be, as Amnesty International reports,[49] that there has been some praise for these experiments. In South Africa, Malawi, and Botswana, they have apparently successfully demonstrated that local communities and police can cooperate in developing and implement crime reduction services for victims of crime, particularly of rape and domestic violence. Further, as Cain (2000) has reflected on her own initial criticism of the implementation of community policing in Trinidad and Tobago, Western critics may simply fail to recognize how, in practice, notions of 'community' may have a different meaning in other countries. Where communities have never before been given accountability powers over

Box 7.3   *Welcoming community policing in Jamaica*

A Caribbean Task Force on Community Policing was announced in Trinidad and Tobago on Friday with the aim of helping to reduce crime throughout the English-speaking Caribbean. The truth is that for too long too many members of the police force saw too many of the public, especially in the inner city communities, almost as natural enemies and treated them as such. So now, more and more police will walk their precincts, not only with their guns but with their smiles, not merely showing a friendlier face, but engaging the best crime-fighting responses that are available – the citizens who make up the community. The only way that Jamaica's crime problem is going to be tackled effectively is by community policing, which is the building of the trust between the community and the police.

(*Gleaner*, 31 January 2003)

the state police, such developments must be positive (Sita, Kibuka and Ssamula 2002). In her Trinidad study, most of the Western-initiated NWS soon disappeared from official (and police) view. But many of them remained relatively intact. The crucial difference from their early stages was now they had assumed many other community functions, and crime control was only a marginal activity. Further, in African cities, such as Dar es Salaam, informal structures of neighbourhood watch may develop and be regarded as effective, independently of state police participation. In practice, community policing, whatever the local official discourse, may be translated and adapted within local traditional structures. Some components of community policing can work if different foci and different measures of success are used to those that have been utilized in the West.

But in transitional societies, police reform can only work when at least two conditions are satisfied (Brogden and Shearing 1993). The key requirement is to rely on local experiences and practice in terms of 'what works'. Policing goods borrowed from the West must come with an attested success record. They must only be implemented when they are constructed through the benefit of local knowledge and sensitivity to local conditions and legitimation.

Notes

1 For an excellent newspaper critique of the Nairobi scenario, see the (Kenyan) *Financial Times*, 10 July 2001. That article notes *inter alia* the eulogistic view of the UK police trainers about the possibilities of transferring the COP model

to Nairobi, the contrasting views of the experiences from police and from squatters' leaders but also such gems as the reward for each new community constable of a drink of Coca Cola a day.

2 United Nations Centre for Human Settlements.

3 Interview with Keith Biddle www.sierra-leone.org/feature061701.html

4 Independent Commission on Policing in Northern Ireland, Northern Ireland Office, Belfast, 1999 (commonly known as the Patten Report).

5 www.nisat.org/security%20sector/ss_west_africa.htm

6 www.usdoj.gov/criminal/icitap/TextGhana.html

7 ICITAP Project Ghana http://www.usdoj.gov/criminal/icitap/ghana.html

8 http://www.gov.bw/government/chapter3.pdf

9 Quoted in Brogden (2004).

10 See also, *Financial Times*, 10 July, 2001.

11 Quoted in Ruteere and Pommerolle (2003). More recent examinations of COP development in Kenya are appearing regularly. There is an important study from the Institute of Security Studies in Pretoria which emphasises the continuing level of violence in the capital city – one in five of the inhabitants apparently regularly carrying weapons to 'defend' themselves. See also the thoughtful Paper *Police Reforms: East Africa* from the Commonwealth Human Rights Initiative at www.humanrightsinitiative.org/programs/aj/police/ ea/presentation_durban_cond

12 Quoted in Raleigh, Biddle, Male and Neema (2000).

13 The DFID Report complained that their specialist knowledge was in fact rarely utilized in Uganda.

14 Quoted in Raleigh *et al* (2000).

15 DFID (1999) conclude remarkably by suggesting that the Ugandans might learn from the experience of the Western Cape in South Africa.

16 In 1999, 307 police officers were killed (*The Monitor*, 9 January 2000).

17 Harmony Cares – an NGO offering counselling services – organized a 'community appreciation' function for the UPF in March 2003.

18 *ANB-BIA Supplement* Issue/edition Nr 457-01/06/2003. A recent empirical study on the develpoment of community policing in Uganda, produces conclusions markedly in contrast to the above. Bruce Baker, in a series of articles, argues that current developments in community policing are now much more positive, with considerable local support. He qualifies this view with a recognition that the Uganda Police are still perceived as conducting a variety of forms of serious abuse. Baker's work must be taken seriously, as differing markedly from the largely secondary evidence adduced in this text. However, the test of that development lies in the key question of whether this is a study of a *process* or of a *result*. Scepticism about the outcome remains. Given the level of reported violence in Northern Uganda, there are questions about the local context of such work. See amongst other articles B. Baker, Post-Conflict Policing: Lessons from Uganda 18 years on, *The Journal of Humanitarian Assistance*, 2004. The United States government has recently committed a substantial sum to promote COP in Uganda.

19 Inspector General of Police, Uttar Pradesh, 9 February 2000.

20 *The Times of India*, 12 January 2001.
21 K. Wickresmasuriya – retired senior officer in the Sri Lankan Police, May 1997.
22 http://www.sholay.com/stories/feb2000/10022000.htm
23 Not all senior Indian police officers subscribed to this community policing legitimating legend. One senior officer in Orissa – where the rural constable beat system was based on its British precedent – noted the clear lack of common law powers of the beat constable in India (as compared with Britain).
24 Including, of course, as an indication of such a law-abiding society, one of the highest imprisonment rates in the world (sic!).
25 Quoted in Brogden (2004).
26 *Ibid.*
27 The subsequent massacres of migrant Muslim workers in 2002 appear to have been led by those same community-friendly officers.
28 Across in Dubai as elsewhere, community forums were organized by the police not by citizen groups, '… the superintendents of the police stations who will head the councils would choose members of the public for each of the eight police stations' (*The Gulf News*, 15 July 1999).
29 Chairman of the Vasant Kunj Federation, 9 February 2000.
30 Seminar at the National Institute of Public Administration, Karachi, 6 June 2001.
31 At the OSCE (2002) Vienna Conference. Amongst many other schemes in Central Asia, the OSCE has launched small scale projects in Kyrgyzstan (March 2004).
32 Community Police Development Centre, Ontario Provincial Police 2000.
33 August 2000.
34 Military police provide public order and civilian police investigate crime – there are four times as many military police as civilian.
35 CIDPA Community Policing South American style 1999.
36 Canadian Co-operation in South America, Ottawa Human Rights Centre 1999 (pp. 3-4).
37 Dr Paulo Mesquita Neto of the Open Society Institute, New York, University of Oxford Centre for Brazilian Studies, 19 February 1999.
38 www.worldpaper.com/archive/1998/July 98/castilho.html
39 Quoted in Mendes (2000).
40 Involving Human Rights agencies, community councils, business and industry.
41 Communities Security Councils (CONSEGS), autonomous in manner and function, were established by state government decree, convened monthly and forwarded their minutes to the Public Security Council Coordinator.
42 See Note 33.
43 Although that same lack of professional organization may paradoxically have prevented organized police resistance to the concept – Mendes (2004). A thoughtful critique of COP developments in Brazil and Argentina (and which illustrates several of the criticism made above) is in C. Smulotovitz, Community Policing in the Southern Cone: Results, Problems, Policies, *Woodrow Wilson Centre Update on the Americas, 2002, August.*

44 The claim that COP has reduced the level of reported crime across El Salvador must of course be treated with appropriate scepticism.
45 *A.M. Costa Rica*, 20 August 2002.
46 Neild (2002) – in Central America – furnishes the most systematic account of the development of community policing projects available internationally.
47 21 January 2002.
48 Leroy remarkably claimed as part of the same thesis that COP had been successful in defeating drug culture in a London black community, a decrease in the murder rate, a three-fold increase in the clear-up rate especially in firearms offences.
49 Amnesty International (2000). Amnesty's substantive evidence is sparse – http://web.amnesty.org/library/Index/ENGAFR030042002?open&of-ENG-SWAZ

Chapter 8

Community policing in failed societies

Police Lt. Robert D. Gariepy is brushing up on his Russian. The 28-year old veteran of the Haverhill Police Force will travel to Volgograd, Russia, in two weeks as part of Project Harmony, a law enforcement program. For two weeks, Lt. Gariepy, and 28 others from the United States, will educate Russian officers about community policing, the prison system, and other concepts of American justice.

(*Eagle-Tribune*, 13 April 1998)

In a time when the public distrusts the government and a lot of people live in poverty, it would be naïve to think that concepts like Community Oriented Policing themselves can noticeably reduce crime. That is why community policing may be a useful element only within the framework of general and complex improvement of economic and social situation in the country.

(Haberfeld, Walancik, Uydess and Bartels 2003, p. 7)

Introduction

'Failed' societies, unlike those we have described as transitional, are essentially states in which the primary reason for transformation is due to the collapse of structures of political governance. Although such a collapse may have been impelled by underlying economic causes, the public face of existing police structures and other key organs of government have been disappearing into a void, without immediate replacement by new legitimate agencies. In that vacuum appear a variety of competing agencies of civil society – from mushrooming private security to organized international crime. In this text, the term 'failed society' is intended to encompass those societies of the previous Soviet system which straddle a chasm between the disappearance of their command economies and the chaotic onrush of a free market system. Self-evidently such a confusion has led to major problems for, amongst other agencies, that of the policing system. Certainties of life, predictability in security, in employment and in welfare, gave way to the uncertainties of an anarchic market. The economic safety net was dismantled and people enjoyed the freedom of individual expression but at a major cost. In most cases, living standards were subjected to deep depression as the chaotic free market undermined social stability. Freedom from basic wants was replaced with freedom to want. A very few were vastly enriched while many others were plunged into a state of poverty and anomie (Skolnick 1999).

Box 8.1   *Key features of policing in Eastern Bloc countries*

- Generally closely modelled on the policing system of the former USSR.
- Policing included a variety of political and administrative duties.
- Powerful secret police.
- Militarized and centralized civil police.
- Accountable primarily to a ruling political party with no local accountability.
- Crime matters secondary to political function.
- Minimal welfare functions.

The transition of the countries of Eastern Europe from a security police committed to defending the political order of the state to one formally committed to the personal security has been dramatic. The political and ideological tutelage imposed by the Soviet Union had left a distinctive mark on the different national policing systems which were modelled according to the Russia militia (Koci 1996)[1]. Virtually overnight (in some cases) these systems collapsed. Given the collapse of political structures not merely did the state police fall into relative chaos – one without political legitimacy – but so did the opportunism for a rampant market capitalism in which opportunities, both legal and illegal, mushroomed. Corruption and white-collar crime were the most evident growth. At the local level, anarchy of social life, subjection to arbitrary and anarchic police dictates, as well as that of the criminalization of

alienated youth and of an expanding underclass, were evident
Regulation had disappeared not just from the market but also from the
normative structure of social and economic life. Crime mushroomed[2]. In
turn, conservative politicians took up the slogan of 'fighting crime' to
slow down the pace of reform.

Especially problematic was the lack of certainty both for the rule
enforcers and for the ruled in terms of what social regulation was to
guide the emerging democratic and economic structures. Policing
agencies were severely under-resourced to counter the new economic
order, often poorly paid, and utilizing equipment several decades out of
date (Williams and Serrins 1993). The wider criminal justice process –
from prosecution to the penal system – was faced with identical
problems. Further, the police were increasingly forced to commit a major
volte-face – being required (publicly, at least) to face a different master
than that of a centralized state. They were now expected to meet the
needs of people as victims and offenders on the basis of a curious notion
of citizen rights. Coercion as the symbol of state authority was to be
mitigated by a degree of consent. Zvekic (2002) has used International
Victim Survey data to show that citizens of Eastern Europe, of all the
countries surveyed, have least respect for the police – on average less
than 25 per cent of all citizens were satisfied and almost 50 per cent
dissatisfied.

> … unless the police develop legitimacy and public consent, crime is
> likely to become rampant. If the police are not able to cope with
> these problems, then people will call for return to the old
> authoritarian structures.
>
> (Feltes 2002, p. 4)

Further, as Koci (1996) says succinctly

> If one in three is a victim of crime in Hungary, the people have the
> right to question the real meaning of freedom. Does it mean
> freedom to be robbed and victimized?

A further problem was apparent. Existing policing systems had much in
common with the Napoleonic model, although more extreme. They were
centrally administered and directly subordinate to the Ministry of the
Interior. Paramilitary police organizations ensured that individual police
officers enjoyed very little discretion in powers and in practice, and few
skills in citizen interaction. Cooper's (1996) account of policing in the
German Democratic Republic immediately prior to merger with the

Federal Republic provides an illustrative account. In that country, the police were primarily committed to implement socialist legality – that is protecting the political order of the state. Interpersonal crime was a second order priority. Policing emphasized protection for the state and society over the rights of the individual in the belief that the achievement of socialist society was the best protection of rights. Collective rather than individual rights were the priority. However, crime fighting remained an important function. Official ideology held that crime and socialism were incompatible and that any remaining crime was a pathological relic of the previous political order. Consequently, crime was often perceived as a function of faulty socialization, a problem that could in part be resolved by educational practices. Community cooperation with the police in that education role was integral to the policing system. Interpersonal violence – household abuse aside – was relatively rare.

> One person I spoke to stated only half-jokingly that the most common crime was 'theft of baby carriages'. For the average police officer, this absence of violent crime meant that he or she rarely confronted the situations faced by policemen in any large Western city.
>
> (Cooper 1996, p. 6)

A kind of community policing was practiced by default. For example, in Berlin, only police officers' residences might have access to home telephones. Consequently, almost independently of his/her role as a functionary on behalf of the state, local police practice frequently involved neighbourhood problems such as calls for assistance for non-crime matters. Aspects of community policing were practiced *de facto* rather than *de jure*.

Eastern bloc countries were not however a unitary phenomenon but possessed their own distinctive economic, cultural, political and economic features. Although the policing system derived historically from the Napoleonic model of policing and the more recent Soviet model, their different characteristics entail different priorities of policy development in considering the development of new policing. Distinctive characteristics remained. Development of new policing systems must take account of other local traditions than the Soviet one (Koci 1996). The legitimacy, the structure and the functions of the police are socially determined by underlying factors in the different societies. For example, Feltes (2002) notes major economic disparities between those societies – between the extremes of ten per cent inflation in Hungary and Slovenia and more than 1,000 per cent in Estonia and Russia, and with similar disparities in incomes.

Clearly, different Soviet bloc countries were not confronted with a crisis of an identical order. In the relatively Western countries such as Hungary and the new Czech Republic, the processes of transition were relatively ameliorated by access to Western technologies and through a relatively non-authoritarian state structure. In others, such as Byelorussia, one centralized state was replaced with another. Changes in the upper echelon of the power structure, and especially in the functions and composition of the police agencies, were sometimes more apparent than real. That was not always the case. For example, in the Russian Federation, the violent suppression of nationalist rebels in Chechnya confusingly regarded as a 'policing operation' is partly carried out by police officers of the Ministry of the Interior. Police officers might still conduct violent internal security functions.

In this void emerged a variety of Western entrepreneurs. That intervention was not just one of the exports of McDonald franchises and Western currency and investment, it also encompassed both the technological and the legal aspects of reform. Policing exporters seized a variety of opportunities in a hugger-mugger of interventions. Especially important were the advocates of Human Rights[3].

The input of community policing

Community policing was of course only one of the criminal justice strategies introduced within the former Eastern bloc societies. It has also appeared as an unthoughout add-on to wider surveys of security needs (Yusufi 2003). But it was a crucial one in that, above all else, it represents a benchmark for social change and one in whose development ultimately rests upon a positive relationship between police and public. As elsewhere, the concept of community policing was used in its widest sense, frequently intended to increase the role of the community in developing public safety and local responsiveness. There was internal support for such a development.

> ... for some of the locals, particularly those viewing Western material Utopians with the emblematic notion of the sunrise, images of policing were also rosy-tinted. The redoubtable 'bobby' on the beat is perceived as a potent symbol of a law enforcement agency, focused on serving the needs of the public, as well as somebody who treats everybody equally and fairly.
>
> (Beck and Chistyakova 2002, p. 134)

In the Ukraine, as elsewhere, the evidential material is limited to a few primarily Western sources. The difficulties are considerable (Povolotskiy 2002). The police had only received a third of their pay in the last two years (the average salary is $30-50 a month). Basic resources such as radios and cars (often out of fuel) are absent. Local police had undergone a complete change of personnel in the two previous years. The police structure was state centralized. Most people believe they take bribes. The key problem is perceived as an absence of resources.

The major entrepreneurial venture has been by the Scarman Centre of the University of Leicester funded by the British Council. To give those entrepreneurs their due, despite a blunt assumption by their taskmasters in the UK, the innovators were realistically aware of the magnitude of the task (police resources remained at a minimum and training schemes had remained largely unaltered since Soviet days). Apart from the larger structural factors, they were faced with the limited value of the criminal justice tools[4] in the definition of crime, in its assumptions of both police-public relations and the manifestation of police culture.

The project had the particular merit of recognizing its limits in its emphasis on a 'context-driven aproach'. But necessarily its aim was Utopian, given the history of the Ukrainian militia. These included developing community meetings, police surgeries, NWS, and security and crime prevention for the community. It also optimistically built in an evaluative component measuring effects of police and community relations on the level of reported crime. Police training was to be supplemented with a community policing module (Beck and Chistyakova 2002). Police reform starts from a low base. One-third of members of the public responding to the surveys carried out in Kharkov stated that they did not trust the police, while a further one-quarter was unsure. This trend was accentuated for younger respondents, particularly young men[5].

Box 8.2 *Aims of British Council Community Policing Project in the Ukraine*

- To identify and understand the context within which community policing might take place within Ukraine.
- To introduce a number of context specific forms of community policing within limited geographical areas, which might include, amongst others, developing community meetings, police surgeries, neighbourhood watch schemes and crime prevention advice to the community.
- To evaluate the effect such schemes have on the relationship between the community and the police and on the level of reported and recorded crime.

Community policing in Russia starts from an equally awkward base. Lack of confidence in state law enforcement machinery has been expressed in numerous opinion polls, in the context of increases in the recorded crime and accompanying enhanced fears of insecurity. In the changing environment, the state police (UVO) and the public order police (MOB) have to deal with both the problems of high-policing and local low-policing (Brodeur 1983). The Militia is faced with largely insurmountable problems in changing its function and character. Thus a 1991 law guaranteed a range of new citizen rights against police oppression and encouraged a more open legal culture, with the by-product of constraining traditional police practices. The militia suffers from poor material conditions, an increasing turnover of policing staff, widespread corruption, and lack of training reform, leading to a deep organizational and professional crisis, especially evident amongst the street level neighbourhood police whose mixture of local policing and social control was a key feature of the Soviet period.

Consequently, there was a rise in private and voluntary policing initiatives to fill the vacuum. On the one hand there has been a rapid development of private security agencies which provides 'policing' for the business class often in competition with the UVO. Many of the new private police are former state police officers encouraged to join by higher salaries. Over recent years there have been several grassroots

Box 8.3 *A typical eulogistic account of community policing in the Russian Federation*[6]

A day and a night's work, community policing style (Tatarstan)
Nobody knows how many hours Nuriahmetov has to put in every day. He is first seen in 'his' neighborhood between 7 and 8 in the morning, and he never leaves before 11 in the evening. Which still doesn't tell you much about how he does it, because community policing is more a way of life than a 9 to 5 office job with piles of papers and files of visitors. His superiors blame him mildly for being too meticulous. A strong believer in the fact that in real life small details always count, he tends to disregard these criticisms.

In any Russian town, wherever there is a community police officer, he is easily recognizable, especially by his peaked cap. Which is both good and bad. Good because people always know where to seek assistance if they need it. But on the other hand, it gives an easy notice to the bad guys to get lost. Well aware of this treacherous deficiency of his uniform, Nuriahmetov has learnt with time, when needed, to take the cap off and to blend into the crowd.

attempts at community policing – for example, in Moscow and St Petersburg initiatives have occurred to restore the *dobrovovolnye narodyne druzhiny*, a body of auxiliary volunteers that existed from 1958 to the fall of the Soviet Union. Given the absence of a legal basis and lack of material incentives, such variants of community policing remain localized and not very popular, despite widespread demand for more security. The development of neighbourhood committees has given way to limited new forms of local policing, such as prevention committees (*soviet profilaktiki*) aimed at securing crime control on an inter-agency basis. They often have pragmatic close ties with state policing agencies. The few experiments to develop municipal or local policing have largely failed.

There have been varied, marginal inputs by Western countries attempting to encourage community policing in Russia, often as part of a larger enterprise to democratize the Russian police. For example, the British DFID has sponsored a one-dimensional community policing programme in St Petersburg.

Box 8.4 *Outline of DFID Project on COP in Russia*[7]

> The primary objective of Phase I of the Community Policing Project was to expose future Russian senior police officers and their trainers to the systems, structures and methods required to police a democracy ... The expected benefit of the project is that it will improve the content and delivery of the training of future senior police officers by exposing them to the concepts and experiences of democratic, accountable, community based and ethical policing. The project will enable them to identify the advantages of a democratic community based policing model over their present police system.

Typical of several small entrepreneurial ventures was the adoption of police departments on the island of Sakhalin by Olympia Police Department in Washington State, pioneering COP[8]. But the Russian situation is intractable given both structural factors relating to the state and to the several different policing agencies.

Poland – a case study of failure

Poland furnishes the best documented account of the attempt to develop community policing in a former Eastern bloc country. The overnight introduction of a market economy to replace the existing command economy contributed to the development of major disparities in income and in property-holding. Market driven social and economic inequality became a major and defining feature of the new Polish society. Like many failed societies, Poland is characterized by relatively high and rising rates of recorded crime. During the last decade, the number of recorded crimes doubled[9]. The collapse of the previous social and political order resulted in a high level of crime. Simultaneously, the police institution was heavily affected by the transition with many senior and often experienced officers being dismissed because of previous political loyalties. Given that for most of Poland's history policing had been conducted by a foreign power, distrust of the state police is a major legacy[10] (Haberfeld, Walancik, Uydess and Bartels 2003, p. 18). As in the GDR (above) the primary function of the police was to safeguard the integrity of the state and political rule. The national state police was supported by a Citizen's Militia, tied tightly to the ruling Communist Party. In turn, this new state police was supplemented by a large voluntary reserve (ORMO). These structures were dissolved by the Police Service Act of 1990 and the state attempted to restore a version of the policing system of the independence period.

During the later days of the previous system, anti-state activities – including theft of state property – had been considered as legitimate forms of social crime[11].

> Since everything, or almost everything ... belonged to the government, it was considered to be quite appropriate to act against this governing body. One of these patriotic activities included plain theft of government property, from stealing a light bulb to car parts.
>
> (Haberfeld *et al* 2003, p. 23)

Petty criminality had to some extent been condoned and institutionalized when directed against the state monopoly in trade, work and industry. Further, dislocation of social structure, and the relatively privileged access to consumer goods for a few, created new opportunities for criminality. Crime rises were confronted by a policing agency renowned for inefficiency. As elsewhere in the former Soviet bloc, salaries of public officials such as the police had been relatively easy for the state to control in the context of rampant inflation – many officers reportedly survived in poverty with concomitant few policing resources. Policing could not compete with other forms of employment. Consequently there was a major shortage of competent recruits. Many police officers had to work in second jobs in order to supplement their income.

The community policing experiment

Modernization and community-oriented reforms were introduced to the Polish police in early 1990s, blessed by support from the Chicago Police Department (towards the end of the decade). Critical to the reform process was the attempt to develop accountability to local authorities through financial and consultative constraints, in effect redefining the police as a crime preventative agency on behalf of local communities. In that process, the state resurrected its own District Constable version of the Tythingman myth to legitimize community policing developments[12].

Formally revived under the Police Act of 1998, the District Constable function was reconstituted as the basis for local policing. He/she was to be the key link between the public and the police. The District Constable, in a clear formulation of specific community policing functions, was required to establish contact with all appropriate citizens in the area – such as crime victims, key local government, political, educational and safety officials. Constables were expected to spend some two-thirds of their working time on active patrol of the district to discuss local problems with community members. The older system of district constables had been criticized because of the inordinate time spent on bureaucratic matters. Whatever the local support for the function, financial support from the locality had only rarely been forthcoming in the face of other priorities. Lack of clarity of the legal powers of the Constable had denied them the authority to engage in preventative matters. They had little training or expertise in inter-agency work and cooperation was therefore difficult. While a District Constable had been formally allocated for every 2,500 citizens, in practice populations of twice that size were the norm. Organizationally, the post was frequently occupied by the less qualified and lower ranked police officers, relatively new to policing.

Linked with the role of the District Constable under the 1990 Police Act were a range of preventative crime functions – for example, promoting situational safety techniques, preventative programmes with high risk groups such as women, children and the elderly, and encouraging inter-agency security and safety functions and encouraging victim support. Coincidental with these proposed functions was the development of a national Safe City project, again involving inter-agency links and cooperation. An imported Crime Stoppers programme was also developed.

The decentralization process was a major step in police reform.

Since the financing of the local police is dependent on local civil
authorities, they have real supervisory power over the police in
their territories.

(Haberfeld *et al* 2003, p. 151)

New preventative functions were to be a primary responsibility of the
locality. Local government was given limited rights to determine the
appointment of chief officers and the length of their tenure.

In the event, the evidence of the effects of these reforms on developing
COP suggests little progress. There was evidence of continuing conflict
between local authorities and police managers over who actually
controlled local police policies[13]. Again paralleling nineteenth century
debates in Britain, influence by the local authority over the financing of
local policing was cited by police representatives as limiting
effectiveness and contributing to partisanship – for example, by
directing police resources to areas from which the local representatives
were elected. Haberfeld *et al* argue[14] that the elected authorities were
perceived as incompetent and inefficient in conducting their relationships with the local police. Repeating much older arguments about
police perceptions of local accountability (Brogden 1982), a typical police
chief claimed:

> ... in practice ... one (local council) provided extra money for
> uniforms of field police officers on time, another did it on time but
> provided only half of the required sum and still another provided
> nothing at all because he thinks there are more urgent matters.
>
> (quoted in Haberfeld *et al*, 2003)

Police autonomy was challenged and the police could provide chapter
and verse to justify the retention of that autonomy over police finance
and policy, as well as over police operations. Consequently, little
practical commitment was given by the police to public consultation in
the decentralization process critical to COP. Further, given that local
authorities have other priorities than policing, on many occasions
finance which the police regarded as their prerogative in combating
crime was utilized for non-crime matters which the local authority
regarded as of prior importance to the locality.

COP practice on the ground differed from official rhetoric.

> ... it is seven years since the ... programmes started being
> implemented. So what are the results? Not much information can
> be found. It may be assumed that most of these initiatives remained

on paper only. This alone allows us to say that the measures mentioned above aimed at implementing the community policing philosophy in Poland have mostly been unsuccessful.

(Haberfeld *et al* 2003, p. 99)

In only a minority of cases had the Safe Cities programmes been implemented with little evidence of inter-agency cooperation – few were involved apart from the police. Only the Crimestoppers programme allegedly had a degree of success.

Overview of the Polish attempt to develop COP

During the early transition period, the new Polish government attempted to develop an indigenous form of community policing. To that end, it sought to revitalize the mythological past in which the local District Police Officer played critical preventative roles. It also attempted local authority financial supervision. In the context of a badly paid, badly trained, and badly resourced police with an indigenous public order function, a centralized structure and a rising recorded crime rate, such a development was problematic enough. But these complexities were further exacerbated by a failure to recognize that local crime prevention work is part of a larger matrix of affairs, relating to the security and quality of life of the local populace, which only partially concerns the police. Community policing does not stand on its own but is ideally a part of a larger tapestry of social affairs. In Poland, the police regarded crime fighting, the police *raison d'être*, as the expenditure priority. The local authorities had a larger concern and often refused to submit to the police notion of the problem. This refusal was often regarded by the police as partisanship, failing to appreciate that local authorities and citizens have other priorities than simply that of prevention and reaction to crime.

Critically, the writers also note that COP – both in its indigenous source and in the influence from abroad – was developed in Poland without any previous groundwork. Historical mythology was deemed adequate for the cultural change proposed in policing. There was little investment in police recruitment, training and resources. In particular, there was no consideration of whether local communities either knew what COP meant or whether they actually wanted community policing. State character and the existing police-public relation were largely ignored. There was little evidence that people actually understood and supported what was being proposed. A survey of police officers found that only a minority had ever heard of COP – even in its indigenous form. This finding was replicated in a more extreme form by a survey of non-police officers. Only a minority of officers regarded local consultation as desirable. Most police officers considered meetings with local residents not as a necessity for local policing but rather as a criterion for occupational promotion.

While community control of the criminal justice system is not a new or radical concept in Western democracies this was not the case in Eastern Europe. While it is possible to be sceptical about the first statement, the second is unarguable. A key feature of Western development of COP is the assumption that the locals actually desire a closer relationship with the state agencies of criminal justice control. In Poland, community consent to policing and to the wider criminal justice system was absent. There was widespread cynicism about the value and possibilities of transforming that negative relationship. This reality has frequently been ignored by both those seeking to export community policing and those seeking an alternative to the present structures. Local Eastern European communities recognize more fully than do the Anglo-American exporters the degree of resistance by insiders to any change in the nature of their accountability.

In Poland, objections to COP arose from other actors in the criminal justice system – COP threatened all the justice agencies with new forms of public relationship, transparency, and accountability – challenging their existing professional expertise and autonomy. This reaction was especially severe in the absence of a tradition of civic or non-state involvement in Eastern Europe – COP by its very nature requires active community, agency and citizens' involvement – indeed, empowering in relation to the police. Haberfeld *et al* conclude that the prospects for community-oriented policing were highly negative given the position of both professional and potential consumers. In early 2003 the Polish government formally terminated the community policing programme[15].

Community policing in South Eastern Europe

Community policing has been recommended as a blanket solution to problems of security problems in Southern East Europe (Yusufi 2003). Many COP inputs have been made, often with no evident forms of assessment or accounts of need. Some of the projects that are located under the community policing heading are occasionally difficult to reconcile with core (broadly sketched) practices – for example, the US Institute of Peace provides a range of negotiation and mediation training under the COP rubric in Bosnia. Some projects, however, are more specific.

The Romanian Police Law 1994 had reorganized the police into three agencies: the National Police (an institution with a civil profile); the gendarmerie (retaining paramilitary structure and functions); and the Public Guards (a new proximity police based on community principles). Together, they were decreed to be a public service rather than an instrument of coercion. Police powers were reconstructed towards a Human Rights emphasis and police officers were no longer to regard themselves as military cadres but encouraged to use discretionary 'human qualities'. The US Department of Justice granted assistance to community police training with senior Romanian officers being given brief secondments for that purpose to the United States (under the auspices of the University of Louisville), as part of a larger police democratization project. Soros has committed his funds here as elsewhere in the development of COP as part of a larger package of community safety measures (with COP in the city of Iasis furnished by the Metropolitan Police[16]). The project aims to be a 'customer-oriented' approach which apparently here, as in Poland, it is not[17]. Police General Dr Pavel Abraham apparently established community programmes in 1994 under the rubric of the Institute for Crime Inquiry and Prevention. Coincidentally the Swiss Agency for Development and Cooperation has funded an incremental COP project.

> By means of a Train-the-Trainer System the project aims at progressively promoting community policing to become a recognized part of police work in the town of Potesti, and thus to put the police into a position to better ensure public safety and contact with the population.

In its variety of commitment to a problem solving orientation, the project seems stranded on it own Utopian discourse, material being based on a 'daily contract with the population, on opinion polls, and on problem analyses', concepts and strategies which seem at considerable variance with the nature of the Romanian context. The Geneva police have assisted in drafting a Romanian Community Policing Guide and the appointment of Community Liaison Officers.

Hungary has been the scene of several COP attempts. Friedman (who has considerable experience elsewhere on COP in transitional societies) comments:

> Recently touted by public officials as a step in the right direction –

some even suggest it as a panacea for solving crime – community policing has been neither understood or not well, or not fully implemented.

(Friedmann 1996, p. 1)

He argues that increasingly the police in a failed society such as Hungary will be judged no longer so much on their coercive potential but on the service they supply and not by the power they exert. Recognizing context (if in a somewhat golden history vein), he urges Hungarian officials in developing community policing to draw on a traditional sense of Hungarian community rather than on the individualism that characterizes American society. Hungarian commentators were prescient, noting the failure to plan to dismantle the militaristic hierarchy and to decentralize the policing structure from the outset.

In the Czech Republic, the Canadian International Development Agency has been training the Prague police in community policing, as well as in larger projects[18]. Considerable specification has gone into these schemes. In Lithuania the concept of community policing has been well known for some two decades[19]. Early patrols with civil volunteers were based on the concept. COP formally commenced with the passing of the Police Act 1990 which created limited municipal policing[20]. The Canadian International Development Agency has funded a COP project (organized by the Toronto police) since 1998 and training of community police has occurred under the Tempus PHARE programme since 1999.

Similar overseas promotion of community policing has occurred in Bulgaria, in part prompted by evidence of police attacks on the Roma community. The International Helsinki Federation for Human Rights depicted the Bulgarian police as an institution still adhering to past militaristic traditions and as an instrument for repression. In Bulgaria, as indeed elsewhere in central Europe, policing intervention has often been coupled with support from a Human Rights culture with regard to the 'policing' of the large Roma minority, whose experiences are most evident in the transitional period. The Roma, as representative of a larger underclass, still suffer the brunt of a repressive and violent occupational ideology committed to exercise discriminatory control over those with least recourse to rights. Physical ill-treatment at the time of arrest and during interrogation is common[21] and cited as the rationale for the promotion of community policing as human rights work. Since 2001 the Soros Open Society Foundation (COLPI) has organized a Community Policing programme with $180,000 of funding – supporting *inter alia* training modules on COP at the Bulgarian Police Academy and a major conference on developing community policing was held with the

Ministry of the Interior in Sofia in April 2002. Simultaneously, four other NGOs launched a project entitled Police – a Community Oriented Structure. The function of the latter was formally directed to the quality of police-public relations, to develop new standards of public order and to develop a measure of police accountability to the wider public. Under that umbrella, seminars were held throughout Bulgaria. The British Council has supported a variety of community policing programmes since 1996 – for example, in the city of Plodiv, supported by ex-Metropolitan police officers and funded by several NGOs. However, in Bulgaria the police reportedly still adhere to 'traditions from the past' and behave as an instrument for repression rather than a community oriented service provider[22].

Slovenia has a recent tradition of carefully informed critique of policing styles. Meško (1999) claims that while community policing is no longer in its infancy, it still remains problematic – regarded as inferior work by other officers – and community police officers still combine their functions with roles as coercive agents of the state. In Albania, initiatives towards community policing faced similar major handicaps in the light of the past widespread police brutality and the misuse of the police force by politicians, facts that have damaged the image of the police and ruined the basis for mutual trust between citizens and police. Corruption and a low level of professionalism were further factors. This has led to a low level of reported crime[23]. New legislation promoted a radical change in police-public relations[24]. Community policing was portrayed as a major vehicle for solving communal ills. In the event, this proposal was supported by marginal overseas training inputs.

Apart from the direct effects of the Balkan civil war, the Croatian police were highly unpopular with the civil population. Taking bribes was allegedly regarded as an acceptable and normal part of police work, and police brutality was common, with few victims considering it worth their while to complain. In the year 2000 some 3,000 police were dismissed for such infractions. Especially noticeable to foreign agencies was the Croatian violent treatment of minorities. The Ministry of the Interior introduced a post-Balkan war pilot project on community policing coupled with proposals to decentralize the national police. More recently[25], the OSCE launched community policing projects in Zagreb, Split, Sisak and Pozega, in an attempt to reduce the rate of recorded crime.

A similar prompting of community policing because of concern about the police treatment of minorities has occurred in the former Yugoslav Republic of Macedonia (FYROM). In some 90 per cent of the cases of police misconduct, as recorded by NGOs, the victims were members of

Box 8.5 *Introduction to cooperation on community policing between Croatia and the Sussex Police*[26]

The Croatian government is encouraging its police to become more active in the communities and form local partnership groups, which will focus on problems specific to local communities. The concept of community policing is in its infancy in Croatia but the government is supportive of widespread change and is identifying legislative barriers to partnership activity. It is still illegal for agencies to share information in Croatia. In contrast to Britain, Croatia has too many officers, although it is widely recognized that officers' educational levels are inadequate and that many are unwilling to take on a decision making role. Croatia has sought to join the EU as soon as possible. Before being accepted as a member, it must pay special attention to minority rights and the concepts underlying community policing are seen as instrumental to achieving this.

---

the Albanian or Roma communities. Police officers who represent another ethnic group than the local population were perceived by the community in which they worked as external occupiers. A Community Policing Conference in Skopje regarded COP as the answer (15 May 2002), the US Ambassador Kay Eide describing COP reform as critical in the process of integration into European and Euro-Atlantic structures. The OSCE organized three regional seminars on community policing in December 2002, following from COP workshops in the spring of that year run by ICITAP. However, the Director of the Public Security Ministry claimed that COP was not a novelty – relevant projects had been prepared before the conflict (such as a decision to include 500 ethnic Albanians in the state police). Other commentators disagreed – COP had never been present in the new state. There had never been any support for it primarily because of the public order definition of the police role and because the centralization required by community policing might undermine the centralized state structure.[27]

Since July 2001 the OSCE has supported police reform in Serbia, where much violence against minorities has been reported. The impediments are again obvious including the existence of three legally separate police forces in the former Yugoslavia: Federal, Serbian and Montenegrin. The police had traditionally been the servant of the ruling political party and during the transition period were forbidden to cooperate with municipalities in the hands of opposition political parties. The police were in any case grossly under-equipped and under-paid and what equipment was available had been largely destroyed by NATO bombardment. The military structure of policing had been totally closed to any lateral influence, with military ranks, and military sciences emphasized at the Police Academy. The police remain heavily armed. Police powers are concentrated in the Minister of the Interior. There is no substantive accountability system. After democratization, many of the better qualified police found jobs in the private sector. There were few women officers. Police corruption was endemic and most crime remains unrecorded. An early (1996) victim survey in Belgrade suggested that most people regarded the police as inefficient at crime control. There was a prevailing view that the police were totally incompetent in relation to crime. During the period of transition, agents of state security often collaborated with organized crime.

A major Report in 2000[28] proposed the immediate introduction of community policing, with training in Serbia by external experts and secondments from the UK.

> ... aiming to develop the relationship between the people and the community, the Serbian Ministry of the Interior, with the support of the OSCE Mission ... initiated a programme to reform the police in Serbia. This programme is based on the Community Policing concept"[29].

Box 8.6 *Official discourse on COP in Serbia*[32]

Community policing in practice

As a senior police officer committed to modern policing concepts, Captain Dragan Manoljovic is a stakeholder in the Ministry of Interior's comprehensive programme to improve community policing in Serbia ... according to Captain Manoljovic, the policeman's first task was to encourage trust ... The progress in Zvezdara's schools illustrate what has been achieved to date ... the police conducted a survey to determine how children perceive security at school and in their community. The outcome revealed extensive problems with drugs and violence, the presence of firearms and the existence of gangs. Police also found children requesting information and advice on how to improve their security. 'We implemented an educational programme for students, parents and teachers and organized regular meetings with police officers.' ... uniformed but unarmed policemen were posted in schools as a means of establishing contact and building confidence. Other police officers, in plain clothes, taught crime prevention methods. Together with visits to police stations and the provision of emergency telephone numbers, the programme led to a significant drop in criminal offences.

British police advisers advised that the Yugoslav police convert from a 'State Police Force' to a 'Community Police Force'[30]. A range of recommendations included the formation of consultative groups, court user groups, lay visitors, and both external and independent inspectors (p. 16). The Open Society Foundation (June 2001) had proposed a 'Model Police Law' whose main recommendation was the development of COP, emphasizing the role of NGOs in training community police officers[31].

Overview

I think we need to be careful about simply assuming that, for example, because community policing works well in Prince George's County (in the US) therefore we will send it to Bosnia[33].

If anything community policing projects in failed states face an even more uphill task than in transitional societies. Centralized state structures are not just passive towards the implications of decentralized policing but their officials may actively oppose it. Police organizations suffer from problems similar to those of the transitional societies – demoralized, over-armed, ill paid, badly resourced and with little tradition of the lawful use of discretion. Police roles committed to serving an internal security function are unable to be changed to meet the primacy of crime concerns of citizens and communities.

However the principle problem is the lack of popular demand for community policing. An absence of public consent to policing ensures the pragmatic view that police action is inevitably coercive. There is little reason to believe that a change to a more community friendly structure is either possible or desirable.

The medley of projects that have descended upon failed societies have often been driven by a Human Rights perspective, committed to the thesis that COP can be the major tactical weapon in the Human Rights armoury. Such a view, as in South Africa, presumes too much about local populations' prioritization of the crime problem rather than of the rights problem. Reaction to COP exposes the fundamental contradiction between policing as a form of democratization and policing as public order maintenance or crime fighting.

Notes

1 I.e. a highly centralized national police force whose legitimacy derived from the party in power and whose functions and structure were determined by the ideology ruling the country.

2 However, the extent of the crime increase may have been amplified by political rhetoric. As Biryukov and Sergeyev (1997) say of Russia, a mass media that had previously concentrated on 'good news', now as in the West gave much more space to crime.

3 See, amongst many others, International Helsinki Federation for Human Rights Community Policing and the Balkans, 31 October 2002.

4 Such as the relativistic character of the International Victim Survey and its often inappropriate measures of the local context – see Brogden 2000 for a similar comment on Northern Ireland.

5 Other agencies have also been exporting COP to the Ukraine – for example, the Greenfield Wisconsin police.

6 Dmitri Aksenov http://www.ogoniok.com/win/200291/91-30-31.html

7 DFID project profile 'Policing in a Democracy: Community Policing' in St Petersburg, 1998.

8 Project Harmony is involved in a wide-ranging scheme to train community police officers across both the Russian Federation and the Ukraine.

9 Although remarkably – subject to major problems of recording such as a general unwillingness of victims to report crimes to the police – often lower than in Western countries.

10 In the relatively brief period of autonomy between the Wars, the police officer was still regarded as a symbol of an authoritarian power.

11 The concept of social crime here is a curious variation on the use of the theme within criminal justice history – see Hay (1975).

12 This development drew heavily on the notion of the District Constable of Czarism years. 'An Uchastkovyj was very familiar with the area of which he served for many years. He had his secret informers in the underworld of a district. He knew personally most potential and real criminals, especially recidivists in the area' (Haberfeld *et al* 2003, p. 91). That figure appears at various times in recent Polish history and constitutes the basis for the movement in the 1990s towards forms of community policing.

13 Paralleling in Britain the distinction between the local authority's power to influence police policy and its inability to affect police operations.

14 Their evidence on this question is drawn only from the police and not from the local communities.

15 Primarily because of the central versus local authority issue. However, local community policing transfers continue – such as in the US Charlotte Mecklenburg exchanges with the city of Wroclaw.

16 Funders also included the World Bank, the CIDA, the UK Embassy and the European Commission.

17 See Association Liaison Office for University Cooperation in Development, 2001.

18 A detailed, qualified statement on the Czech plan on police reform, drawing
    on a variety of external experience is www.mvcr.cz/2003/odbor/phare.doc
    TH Zech specification on the overall programme of community policing
    development, is at http://osf.cz/coop/projekt_eng.html
19 A. Sakocius at OSCE – The Role of Community Policing in Building
    Confidence in Minority Communities, Vienna, 2002.
20 The Siaulia City Police project was praised highly by the EU.
21 International Helsinki Federation (2002).
22 OSCE 2002 *op.cit.*
23 International Helsinki Federation (2002).
24 Law no. 8553, 25 November 1999.
25 International Helsinki Federation (2002).
26 www.janes.com/security/law_enforcement/news
27 A recent account of COP developments in Macedonia is in D. Lesjak,
    Community Policing in the Former Yugoslav republic of Macedonia, *Helsinki
    Monitor*, 2004, 15, 187–192.
28 Centre for European Policy Studies, Brussels, 6 November 2000 – E. Babovic.
29 OSCE, 10 October 2002.
30 Quoted in Caparini and Day 2001.
31 See also IHF (2002).
32 www.osce.org/features
33 Chuck Wexler, Executive Director, Police Executive Research Forum,
    comment in Burack *et al* 1997.

Chapter 9

A new beginning? Community policing in Northern Ireland

> The proposed revisions for the policing services in Northern Ireland are the most complex and dramatic changes ever attempted in modern history.
>
> (Oversight Commissioner T.A. Constantine 2003)

Introduction

At first sight considering the development of community policing in Northern Ireland, in a volume devoted to such developments internationally, is bizarre. The mini-statelet of Northern Ireland has a population of 1.6 million. Located within one of the fastest growing economies in the Western world, it has little in common with the former countries of the Soviet bloc or of the 'developing' societies of Southern Asia and of Africa. Relatively, it is highly prosperous as judged by factors such as employment and car ownership. There have been frequent comparisons with transitional South Africa[1]. But the differences are huge. Northern Ireland has a much higher resource base, much smaller polity, minute population and police establishment, different qualities of civil society institutions and reported crime rates. Its visible ethnic minority composition is less than one per cent.

Yet it remains a test case for the development of COP. It is a trial of the extent to which one can transform a paramilitary policing structure – in this case, a direct legacy of colonial policing – into one based upon the principles of COP. Relatively, more resources have been committed to police reform than in any other jurisdiction. Eminent scholars from

David Bayley to Clifford Shearing to George Kelling have conducted a variety of local tasks in relation to COP. International practitioners such as Thomas Constantine have been contracted to oversee implementation changes. Resources and international expertise on community policing have not been in short supply. Similarly, at ground level, there have been the types of COP missionary work of inter-functionary contact seen elsewhere[2]. If COP cannot be developed in Northern Ireland in terms of financial and expert commitment, it cannot work in any society that is undergoing police transformation.

The context – a divided Western society

For historical reasons Northern Ireland is especially important as a model of divided societies. Until 1922 policing in Ireland generally was governed from Dublin Castle – the nineteenth century source of Britain's first colonial style police institution. The Irish Constabulary had given birth to many of the colonial style police forces discussed in earlier chapters. While there is debate about whether such policing was directly different from the original Metropolitan police style and organization, Ireland generally until 1922 was policed by the prototype for paramilitary policing agencies across the world (Brogden 1987). The model of policing developed in nineteenth century Ireland involved a centralized force organized and trained on military lines, and based on the colonial 'strangers policing strangers'. Although all of Ireland was ruled from London until 1922, and Northern Ireland still remains within the orbit of the Westminster Parliament, the development of policing reflected the particular colonial status of Ireland rather than the situation of the rest of the UK (Brogden 1987). It was a policing agency directed by the central state whose primary commitment was to defend the state against the locals rather than police by any notion of local consent. The police in Ireland were faced with a population that, by and large, was hostile to colonial rule (Smyth 2002). Local hostility was complicated by a medley of socio-economic, political and religious factors.

After partition the Unionist government instituted a new police force in the statelet of Northern Ireland. The Royal Irish Constabulary, disbanded in the South after the 1920 Anglo-Irish treaty, was replaced in the North by the Royal Ulster Constabulary (RUC) in June 1922. One-third of the new force was to be composed of Catholic ex-members of the RUC, to offset the Protestant majority. However that quota was never reached and the RUC became a predominantly Protestant institution, in a society divided 60:40 in terms of religion and politics. The new centralized force was under indirect political control, and with a primary function of defending the state. Officers were armed and enjoyed wide-ranging powers of arrest and detention[3]. An auxiliary force called the 'B Specials' supported the RUC.

Between 1955 and 1962 the RUC responded to deal with the minor IRA border campaign. But street demonstrations and riots in 1968-9 over sectarian dominance stretched the RUC to the limit. Failure to police the demonstrations impartially led to Catholic complaints of serious misconduct. Three Royal Commissions, Cameron (1969), Hunt (1969), Scarman (1972) were critical of the RUC and B Specials. Cameron criticized the RUC for a breakdown in discipline. Scarman was critical of the sectarian conduct of the B Specials. Hunt called for the RUC to be disarmed and the B Specials disbanded. The Ulster Defence Regiment was created to relieve the police of its paramilitary functions. Hunt's proposals angered Protestants and led to sectarian reaction and the killing of the first RUC officers in the Troubles.

RUC disarmament was short-lived and, by late 1971, sidearms were again issued. Subsequently, deep divisions over nationality, identity, and ethnicity, the result of a colonial past, fuelled the armed conflict between the Irish Republican Army (IRA, supported by its political arm Sinn Fein) and the British state with which the Protestant majority wished to retain a political and constitutional union[4]. As the IRA campaign intensified, the British government shifted responsibility for internal security from the army to the RUC. This strategy led to controversy. The RUC was accused of using violence during interrogations and providing loyalists with classified information on republican suspects.

By the beginning of the 1990s it had become clear that there could be no clear-cut military victory for either side and protracted negotiations led to the declaration of a ceasefire in September 1994. During the course of the Troubles, 301 police officers were killed, mainly by the IRA. The RUC was responsible for 52 deaths, the majority of them being Catholics. Physical conflict was replaced by deep political divisions over policing. A divided society such as Northern Ireland appears to have missed the high road to modernization, thus allowing the debris of history to dominate internal police development (Smyth 2002). The nationalist communities called for radical police reform. Unionists vehemently opposed those proposals. Out of this imbroglio came the Belfast Agreement of 1998. Subsequent referendums in both Northern Ireland and the Republic of Ireland demonstrated substantial popular support for its proposals. While policing was not dealt with by what was essentially a political agreement, the centrality of policing to the reform process was acknowledged and a commission established to deal with police organizational and practice reforms in Northern Ireland (short of disbandment).

Policing prior to Patten – conflicting views

Policing in Northern Ireland has always been paramilitary in character. Until the early years of the present century, policing was a centralized function. Police officers – unlike those elsewhere in the UK – were often heavily armed and utilized a variety of armoured vehicles in patrol work. The police-population ratio of one officer to 106 of the population (excluding others involved in security work such as the British Army and private security agencies) was the highest recorded in the Western world. The police themselves were almost entirely recruited from not just the Protestant community but from its more affluent strata (policing in Northern Ireland is a lucrative occupation). The small minority of policewomen was concentrated in the voluntary part-time reserve. Criminal intelligence work was normally subordinated to the counter-terrorism priority of the Police Special Branch (some ten per cent of the force), an agency that was prioritized in terms of manpower and technology.

Attitudes to the police were – depending upon the source – either highly favourable to the police or grotesquely exaggerated in their negative character (Mulcahy and Ellison 2001). In support of the latter, it is clear that an armed insurrection in a population of 1.6 million could not have been sustained for 30 years in a policing context of considerable technological sophistication and substantial resource base without con siderable local support for those who physically confronted the British state.

Box 9.1 *Contrasting views of the need for police reform[5] – Unionist and Nationalist*

> The Federation does not embrace the concept of community policing simply because it is in vogue to do so. Throughout the history of policing, effective policing has always been the preserve of those working closely with the community.
>
> The militarised, tooled and armed-to-the teeth police force that maraud around our streets in their daft-looking white Daleks has got to go.

In support of that former view, the Police Federation quoted a 1998 Belfast case.

The success of the Markets Unit in winning the UK Award for Community Police Officer of the Year is only the tip of the iceberg of effort which goes into community policing in Northern Ireland.

While that case has been cited in the Patten Commission and internationally in support of the golden age view, it has been impossible to substantiate the claim – all the evidence for its success comes from police sources, which quote anonymous informants. Anecdotal evidence directly from that staunchly republican area casts severe doubts about this unlikely award. Nevertheless the Federation claims:

> Despite the brutal murders of community police officers who are the most vulnerable to attack, our members have consistently tried to deliver community policing. The terrorists see our ability to work within the community as a major threat to their power base and it is therefore not surprising that they have specifically targeted community police officers for murder.

Resistance to police reforms was considerable with the majority Protestant community and the police appealing to golden age notions of the past – police violence over the previous 30 years was portrayed as an aberration from the normality of policing in Northern Ireland. Once the threat from terrorism was over, policing would return to a 'normal' trajectory of development and modernization[6]. That golden age romanticism has several sources (Mulcahy 2000). It includes the memories of older officers of a Northern Ireland where police officers patrolled on bicycles and crime was a rarity. An RUC Superintendent talking of policing on bicycle prior to the Troubles[7]:

> When I joined, the experience was very good. Things were normal in '65; in actual fact in '66 and '67 we weren't even carrying guns in those days … We cycled about, normal like, probably the way the Guards have done for years down South.

Mulcahy adds that the public is absent from such memories and their absence is taken as an unspoken consent to policing:

> Such characterization of pre-Troubles policing offers an implicit non-sequitur: since political conflict is not mentioned, there must have been none.
>
> (1999, p. 284)

The second element of the golden discourse draws on the official crime data in Northern Ireland, data that has always represented the country as a being a tranquil location with relatively little crime. Repeatedly in official commentaries the overall tranquillity is emphasized. In police memoirs and official statements:

> … all identify such indicators and crime detection rates as a measure of the uncontentiousness of its social landscape … even at the height of the conflict, the [RUC] was doing exactly what a normal police force would be doing: preventing and investigating crime.
>
> (Mulcahy 2000, p. 285)

The official imprimatur of relatively low crime and victimization rates, and high detection rates, 'proves' that the external picture of a jurisdiction racked by civil war was a myth. Such data served to legitimate an image of an essentially untroubled society in which only a minority of pathological terrorists disturb the social world of the vast majority, both Protestants and Catholics (Brogden 2000).

Together, these and other elements flesh out a model of policing that has at its core a very traditional concept of community. It harks back to a mythical past, and proposes the idealized police community to be accepted as the model for, and reality of, the present day (Mulcahy 2000). As far as the police agency was concerned and particular policing agencies in Northern Ireland and Britain, the RUC was an heroic force that has been destabilized by terrorists and also by partisan accounts from agencies within the international community such as Amnesty International.

The criticisms of the golden age view are many. For example, Ellison and Smyth's (2002) detailed study of pre-Troubles Northern Ireland has cast severe doubt upon that nostalgic account. If there had been a form of community policing in Northern Ireland prior to 1969, it was contingent upon the principal role of the RUC in combating and suppressing political dissent from the minority population. All policing even at that period came secondary to the security role of the RUC. Further, the notion that the society was largely crime free and tranquil during the Troubles has been dissected in detail (Brogden 2000). Much crime was rarely recorded by the police. Opinion polls of support for the police were grotesquely distorted, lacking direct opinion from the minority community and the introduction of data-gathering devices such as the International Victim Surveys merely demonstrated the relativity of that technique. The existing Police Authority simply acted as the public relations machinery of the RUC and had in no way functioned as an agency of even token accountability[8]. Local consultative committees (CPLCs) were partisan in character and rarely reflected local views (Weitzer 1995)[9]. The weight of the new political opinion and of academic scholars was that these measures and agencies were totally insignificant as a measure of the RUC as a reflection of 'modern' policing.

The Patten Commission and the proposals for community policing in Northern Ireland

Against this dissenting background, the Patten Commission began its work. It had the dead weight of the old establishment, the Unionist majority, undermining its commitment to police reform. For example, the Northern Ireland Police Federation had commissioned its own survey of a view of police reform and concluded that only a modicum of change was necessary – police officers had always conducted community policing. Conversely, Nationalist and Republican opinion called almost unanimously for the disbandment of the RUC.

Patten, in conception, in proposals and indeed in its accessible discourse, was by any measure of policing reform, a radical document. It had received submissions from quite different sources. The Commission consulted widely, both internally and internationally. It held many public meetings across Northern Ireland. Individual members saw community policing as the popular key to reform[10]. The Commission included several international policing experts (including Clifford Shearing). It proposed a style of policing – community both in name and in practice – that was far removed from the traditional militaristic style and function of the Royal Ulster Constabulary. The Report[11] (subsequently referred to as 'Patten') made far-reaching and radical recommendations for the reform of policing. Patten clearly acknowledged the importance of reforming the RUC as critical to the Belfast Agreement. Although Patten noted the 'unique' problems facing a police agency in Northern Ireland, the point was also made that the challenges posed in police transformation were, in general, common to policing transition elsewhere. The Report stressed the sensitivity of the policing issues and the necessity to consider it separately from wider societal changes:

> ... the issue of policing is at the heart of many of the problems that politicians have been unable to solve in Northern Ireland, hence the fact that we were able to consider the question ourselves.

(p. 2)

From the outset, Patten acknowledged that there

... had been a failure to find an acceptable democratic basis for the
rights and aspirations of both unionist and nationalist communities
(p. 2)

with regard to policing. It highlighted community policing as the way
forward.

The participants recognize that Northern Ireland's history of deep
division has made it [the question of policing] highly emotive
... They believe that the agreement provides the opportunity for a
new beginning to policing in Northern Ireland with a police service
capable of attracting and sustaining support from the community
as a whole.
(Belfast Agreement 1998, p. 22)

The principles of Patten

According to Patten 'policing is a matter for the whole community and
not something the community leaves to the police'. The principle of
consent was to be the core of the new service. Patten's proposals on
accountability were designed to dismantle the inherited paramilitary
colonial model of policing and to make policing a matter for the society
as a whole.

The key proposal was to establish a community policing structure and
function[12]. Central to the concept were the recommendations of
decentralization and accountability. The Report rejected the centralized,
hierarchical and specialized RUC model. Its objective was to
fundamentally alter the relationship between police and community and
establish policing as a 'collective responsibility', not something which
the community 'leaves the police to do'. Structures should be developed
to transform the 'defensive, reactive, and cautious culture of the RUC,
replacing it with one of openness and transparency' (p. 25). Patten
recommended a devolved police service as part of a framework of
interlocking agencies and organizations proactively developing
initiatives to deal with a range of clearly identified local problems. The
police should be accountable, representative, effective and efficient, free
from control of any one section of the community and operate within a
Human Rights framework.

By introducing accountability structures at local and regional levels, the new mechanisms would allow a continuing constructive dialogue between police and the community, making policing with the community 'a core function of the police service and the core function of every police station' (p. 43). In Shearing's words, the Commission intended that '... policing is, and should be, more than the police' (*Guardian*, 14 November 2001). The Report recommended two levels of accountability and participation – a Policing Board with its own budget and proactive powers to hold the police accountable, including oversight of practices. By accepting this concept of 'operational responsibility', Patten rejected the traditional doctrine of 'operational independence' under which the RUC and police forces in the rest of the UK had traditionally operated autonomously. The Policing Board would have the power to call the Chief Constable to account on many issues including the right to investigate all aspects of operational policing. The grounds which the Chief Constable could invoke to avoid scrutiny were strictly limited to 'national security', to sensitive personnel matters and to cases before the courts. The Board was to negotiate the policing budget with the government and then allocate it to the Chief Constable. Financial powers were also proposed to allow the Board to monitor police performance against the allocated budget. These proposals were to be accompanied by the maximum degree of transparency. The proposed Policing Board would have the role of negotiating the structure and practice of policing in consultation with other agencies and the public.

Local accountability and responsibility was to be achieved by establishing district and community policing structures including similar civilian budgetary powers. District Policing Boards (DPPs) would have a direct input into policing arrangements, and have the power to raise money to provide extra policing services (up to a maximum of five per cent of the total budget to address its own local concerns) – policing outside the control of the Chief Constable. Further, there were to be changes in the religious affiliation of members of the new police service, attempting to make a more equable balance between Catholics and Protestants and to increase the number of female officers. Finally, problem-solving policing was to be promoted as a key feature of community policing.

The two-tier alternative

The only significant alternative to the Patten Commission's proposal was a call from several writers and academics for a two-tier structure of policing in Northern Ireland.

Box 9.2 *Popular nationalist support for a two-tier community policing model*[13]

> 'Why not recruit a local reserve force of unarmed community police to help rid our lives of the curse of death-driving and mugging of older people. And brawling outside and inside pubs and clubs, and all the other antisocial activity that a normal police force would be tasked with ...'

The call for a radical restructuring of the RUC on tiered lines is best captured in the words of a member of the British Parliamentary Select Committee on the RUC. Labour members of that committee claimed:

> The RUC has developed around its security role, almost a pseudo-military one at times. It will not be easy for the force to transform itself into what is more commonly understood to be a civilian police force. If we are serious about wanting a force accountable to the whole community, creating a second tier of policing based more in a traditional community, civilian, community policing might offer a way forward[14].

A similar argument for a two-tiered community policing structure was detailed by Brogden (1998) and McGarry and O'Leary (1999, p. 96).

> The effect of any of the models described ... should be ... to hand more control over policing to different localities in Northern Ireland, and to create policing units with which these bodies can identify. This approach has several advantages over the *status quo*. It would make it much more likely that Northern Ireland would have formal policing; it would satisfy the demands of local communities ... for greater control over policing and it would be likely to contribute to a higher rate of Catholics and nationalists to become police officers ...

Patten came out strongly against two-tier policing (or indeed against any local structures) on the basis that a tiered structure might well lead to increased existing social divisions. Further, the Unionist press argued that the second tier could become a cover for paramilitaries to retain sole control over their communities. In effect, the Report turned a central argument of the proponents of local policing on its head, implicitly rejecting the experience of countries such as Belgium and Switzerland where tiered police forces are a regular part of federal arrangements, designed to reduce the possibility of ethnic conflict.

The process of Patten

Two procedural stages modified practice. Patten announced its proposals. After partisan lobbying in Parliament, the subsequent Bill published by the government had considerably watered down the proposals. However some of these elements were subsequently restored in the final legislation. Like other such Reports, there was a long way between the principles enunciated and final implementation.

There were of course difficulties at the outset. Despite its progressive agenda, there were key problems with the Patten Commission report in its own right. It assumed the feasibility of moving directly from paramilitary policing to COP. It did not for the most part confront the deeply stratified nature of Northern Ireland society by politics, class and religion (the obvious principle implicit throughout this text is that you cannot alter policing without a favourable political and economic context). You cannot use policing as the lever of political and social change. In Northern Ireland, these problems are as evident as elsewhere. The Unionist majority in Northern Ireland opposed many of the more symbolic proposals (having already successfully prevented a complete reconstruction of policing as desired by the Nationalist minority) such as the retitling of the RUC as the Police Service of Northern Ireland.

The subsequent parliamentary Bill, according to Shearing, the key academic member of the Commission, rejected the 'core principles' of the Patten report. Following his own conception of 'policing' (as partly embodied in the Report), he reiterated that 'policing' was a larger social function and not simply the task of a body called the 'police'. He claimed that:

> ... the core elements of the Patten Commission's Report have been undermined everywhere ... The Patten Report has not been cherry-picked – it has been gutted.
>
> (*Guardian*, 14 November 2000)

These problems were compounded, as Shearing indicates, by the changes that occurred during the legislative process. The Bill failed to follow Patten in the following areas according to the critical Statewatch:[15]

- *Locally based policing.* There was no legislative provision for the development of a non-hierarchical, decentralized policing service. The only concession was the statutory provision for District Policing Partnerships and for each police district to have a designated district commander. There was no provision in the Bill for the devolution and control of finances and personnel to the District Command level. This was considered to be an operational matter and is left with the Chief Constable. Patten also recommended that four District Policing Partnership Boards should be set up in Belfast (where half the population live). The Bill, however, provided for *up to four* and the decision on the number and the boundaries is left with the Chief Constable.

- *Accountability.* Patten recommended that 'the statutory primary function of the Policing Board should be to hold the Chief Constable to account'. As noted above, to emphasize the importance of this function, Patten recommended that the concept of 'operational independence' of the Chief Constable should be replaced by 'operational responsibility' to reflect the need for retrospective accountability. The Bill failed to incorporate this innovative principle in the general functions of the Chief Constable. The Bill also denied the automatic right of the Policing Board to request reports and to establish enquiries although later modified in the legislation. In addition, the final decision over Policing Board requests was to rest with the Secretary of State, including the euphemism that it would serve no useful purpose. No retrospective enquiries were to take place into policing (thus sweeping out of the Board's remit many of the major controversies that had partly given rise to the Patten Report). These provisions effectively placed the Secretary of State and not the Board in control of the police.

- *Transparency.* Patten recommended that the police take steps to improve its transparency and proposed the principle that everything should be available to the public unless it was in the public interest – not the police interest – to hold it back. The Bill largely ignored this principle. Moreover, there was no provision for the Police Board to keep itself informed about the most contentious area of policing – the trends, proportionality and patterns in use and outcome of police powers, and police decisions to charge.

- *Policing as a community function.* Primarily through the inputs of Shearing, the Patten Commission had attempted to construct a model of policing that was larger than the function associated with the state

221

police. Shearing's view, repeated in a variety of recent work, is to assume that both civil and private commercial bodies can also 'do' policing. The Bills and the subsequent legislation emasculated the subtlety of this approach in Patten, constructing policing simply as a state function.

- *Independent supervision.* Patten recommended that an Oversight Commissioner be appointed 'to supervise the implementation of our recommendations'. This proposal was included in the eventual legislation but limited to overseeing the changes 'decided by the government'. Patten also recommended an Ombudsman – an independent institution to provide an effective mechanism for holding the police accountable to the law. The institution is now in place, but it has no retrospective powers[16].

In the final legislation, some of the key elements of Patten were restored. The final Implementation Plan (in August 2001) entitled The Community and the Police Service promised to:

> … amend the Police Act to clarify that policing with the community
> is to be a core function of the police service and its officers
> (Recommendation 44)

although some may argue that this amendment still falls short of Patten's unambiguous recommendation that policing within the community should be the core function of the police service. On accountability, the Plan goes some way to restoring Patten's proposal for some of the legal amendments curtailing the Police Board's powers to block inquiries into policing practice (section 59, Police Act). The powers of the DPPs to raise limited finance for extra policing have been restored. However, Patten's recommendation that 'community partnerships' are an essential part of everyday policing and local problem-solving, a recommendation which is not contained in the Police Act, reappeared in a very diluted form in the Plan which vaguely talked of 'consultation with community representatives'. Ex-prisoners[17] can sit on the Policing Board and as elected members of local DPPs but cannot be appointed until five years after release and a pledge to non-violence. Further, they could assume those functions only if the IRA was dissolved. On 4 November 2001 the RUC changed its name to the Police Service of Northern Ireland (PSNI) as part of the larger mosaic of reforms under the Belfast Agreement.

Overview

Critical evidence is lacking on the new community policing in Northern Ireland.

Box 9.3 *Local policing from official sources*[18]

> Official sources furnish a Utopian view of practice. Typical of that official view is a description of local community policing structures (as envisaged by Patten) in Craigavon. In that District, a joint plan was agreed between the local Board and the local police Chief Superintendent. The latter controls expenditure, relying on performance indicators and joint targets. Each neighbourhood would have a dedicated policing team with lead responsibility for policing in its area. Members of that policing team would remain at least three and ideally five years in the same neighbourhood. All probationary police, during the operational phases of probationary training, would do team policing in the community. Where possible, policing teams would operate on foot. Problem-solving policing would be the key practice with civilian members of the DPP members and other community leaders also trained in the same techniques.

Given the deluge of publicity emanating from state and policing quarters in Northern Ireland regarding the claimed success of the new community policing, it is hard to find more objective views. Certainly, the old RUC has gone. Militarism is no longer evident on the streets of Belfast. Transparency in operations and in explanations is more evident – the old justifications for secrecy have largely vanished. A degree of accountability has been established – although more evident via the new office of Ombudsman than necessarily by the new formal structures of accountability. The opinion polls on policing continue as before to reflect roughly the same views on policing as they did in the latter days of the RUC – with the continuing differences between Catholics and Protestants. In practice, policing on the ground has been reduced to problem-solving which has become the defining feature of COP practice. Problem-solving is central to community policing for the PSNI[19]. In 2003 the PSNI won two out of the three Home Office awards for problem-solving policing in the UK – for a late night assault reduction strategy in Derry and for an interagency campaign against youthful alcohol misuse in central Belfast.

Alternative evidence is anecdotal and the same stories about police naïveté in such practice have an international currency:

Box 9.4 *Apocryphal stories about community policing reform*

In Zambia, police officers of the Schools Liaison Unit visit schools to talk about crime and safety. They have visited most schools in Lusaka and are planning to go to other parts of the country. The head of the unit admitted that during their early visits, children tried to escape through classroom windows because they were so afraid.

In Belfast, as part of the new community policing programme, the new Schools Liaison Officer – previously excluded from some Catholic Schools – came round to give a ritual talk about not going with strangers. In particular, they emphasized that children should not climb into the cars of strangers as the consequences might be unpleasant. One young man retorted from the back row that he had undergone just such an experience – being picked up by strange people in a strange vehicle who promptly beat the hell out of him, 'and it was youse!' he said.

The Oversight Commissioner, while praising the general thrust of COP practice, noted the major failure of the traditional core of the militaristic policing practice to change as typified by the delay in restructuring the archaic and huge Special Branch under the control of the Criminal Investigation Department. Membership of the DPPs is still without formal representation from Sinn Fein, the second major political party in Northern Ireland. There have been claims that Catholics have been intimidated by their own community from taking part in civilian policing structures[20].

Critically, sectarian disputes seem to have diminished little with the annual summer marching season commonly resulting in many police injuries – few observers had predicted the continuing need for a paramilitary capacity of the new police service to police such confrontations. A new factor has emerged with one national newspaper describing Belfast as the most racist city in Europe (*Guardian*, 11 September 2004) – a police service committed to opposing sectarianism appears to find racism a novelty that is beyond its brief. Political impasse show no signs of being overcome – the wider terrain within which policing operates is characteristic of an armed truce, though none of the serious paramilitaries seem inclined to resume conflict. In the eight years since the IRA ceasefire of 1996, 170 people have been murdered by paramilitaries, another 11,000 have suffered terror related incidents, nearly 2,600 people have received 'punishment beatings', some 5,500 illegal firearms have been seized and 1,100 explosive devices uncovered. In the year 2003, 1,200 people were forced to move home for security or sectarian reasons. Policing progress is inevitably contiguous on larger factors.[21] But Patten does seem to have removed policing as a cause of conflict and relocated it as a symptom of wider changes.

However, there are at least two serious causes for concern about the new policing. Firstly reform of policing (as elsewhere in Northern Ireland) has frequently largely been reduced to the introduction of Human Rights legislation. In that context, that perspective represents a conservative resolution to matters which often have a structural base. New Human Rights legislation and implementation is not the resolution to sociological problems. Secondly, the primacy of problem-solving in the PSNI's notion of COP raises questions. Much policing appears to be directed towards that practice. While the following account may be atypical, there is reason to believe that the new policing of Northern Ireland is following what Manning (1988) described as the conservative version of COP – in which police officers intervene in social contexts beyond their remit and expertise.

One of the authors of this text was involved in a minor incident at his home in a mixed Belfast suburb which escalated into a police problem-solving incident. Clumsy disposal of peat ashes from an open fire led overnight to a minor conflagration which set fire to his neighbour's wooden fence. That initial incident was largely settled by the author agreeing compensation to the neighbour. But the following day two police officers arrived and claimed that a second neighbour's fence had also been damaged, involving alleged damage of some $100. The author disputed this occurrence. Subsequently, he received a phone call from the lead community officer threatening a charge of criminal damage if he did not pay that sum. A formal interview at the police station under the procedures of the Police and Criminal Evidence Act bizarrely resulted in the police officer producing photographs of the alleged damage, taken by the Scene of Crime Unit of the PSNI. A lengthy debate occurred in the interview over these photographs. Eventually, the police were forced to withdraw the charge.

But three points were curious about this incident. It occurred at a time when, in a different part of the city, homes of Catholics were regularly being firebombed in the continuing sectarian strife. (On that police resourcing paradox, the lead officer commented that they merely 'took notes' of such incidents!). Police resources were extraordinarily stretched. The cost of the fence-burning investigation was in the region of some $5,000. Different communities received different styles of policing. Critical was the attempt by the police officer to use the threat of criminal action to ensure the success of civil allegation, a matter quite outside her jurisdiction. One swallow does not make a summer. But as an indicator of the ascendancy of a conservative version of problem-solving through COP, it has larger implications for the nature of police reform in Northern Ireland.

Notes

1   Amongst many other naïve such comparisons on policing and transition, see Brocklehurst, Stott, Hamber and Robinson (2001). In reality, the single basis for comparison was that police reform was politically motivated rather than crime-related.
2   For example, between the Ballymena police and the police of Medina, Ohio.
3   Enshrined in the Special Powers Act (1922), the Public Order Bill (1951) and the Flags and Emblems Act (1954).
4   The terms 'Protestant' and 'Unionist' are virtually synonymous (Smyth 2000).
5   http://www.policefed-ni.org.uk/patten section4.htm; and G.O. Caireallain 'Will we ever get proper policing? Irepaqnclcik.com. 31 January 2003.
6   For a detailed and cynical account of the police view of the function and character of community policing prior to the Patten Commission, see http://www.research.ofmdfmni.gov.uk/managingdisorder policecommunityrelations.htm
7   Quoted by Mulcahy (2000).
8   See amongst other caustic comments on the police authority, that of the Northern Ireland Parliamentary Affairs Committee 1997.
9   The Patten Report pointed out that only 29% of respondents to its public attitude surveys had actually heard of the CPLCs, let alone be able to influence local policing by accessing such non-accountable local agencies.
10   For example, Dr Maurice Hayes, speaking as a member of the Patten Commission to CAJ Conference 'The Patten Commission: The way forward for policing in NI', Belfast, 8 October 1999.
11   Entitled *A New Beginning: Policing in Northern Ireland*, 1999.
12   The – highly accessible – Report is essentially an outline of fundamental COP structures and practice.
13   G.O. Caireallain 'Will we ever get proper policing?' Irepaqnclcik.com. 31 January 2003.
14   Steve McCabe, MP Northern Ireland Parliamentary Affairs Committee, 24 February 1999.
15   http://www.statewatch.org/news/oct00/09patten.htm
16   There were also minor variations over the timetable of change with regard to the composition of the new police service and over the contribution of the Human Rights Commission to overseeing relevant codes. But here the differences are minor in character.

17 The point here has similarities with South Africa in that many of those previously convicted had been involved in the different paramilitary organizations.
18 Craigavon District Policing Plan (2003-4).
19 56 Police Analyst posts had been established by 2003.
20 For example the (11 September 2003) resignation of Fermanagh District Policing Partnership member Cathal O'Donal after threats from Real IRA. Smilar threats had been made to Denis Bradley, Deputy Chair of the Policing Board and Marion Quinn of the DPP in Derry.
21 Typical of the external events that affect police transition was the remarkably effective and organised robbery of some £26 million from the Northern Bank, in Belfast on Boxing Day, 2004, presumed to have been conducted by paramilitaries in search of funding.

Chapter 10

Transforming policing

... police reform resembles the famous story of the five blind men feeling different parts of an elephant, each man holding an entirely different perception to the other. This lack of shared concepts means that policymakers and practitioners have no unequivocal answer to several key questions such as 'How is success measured?' and 'Who are the relevant actors and counterparts?'

(Call 2003, p. 2)

... democratic police forces are not supposed to be insular, self-contained, or cut off from the communities from which their power derives. Openness to the free and the poor should be a master ideal of democratic policing.

(Skolnick 1999, p. 2)

Introduction

Community policing has always been a vague concept, ready in Shearing's words (as quoted earlier) to be 'cherry-picked'. In the process of implementation universally, the curate's egg of community policing has been broken up and addled pieces distributed. Indeed, outside the United States, it is difficult to discover where community policing has been successfully developed. Community policing in developed societies from Western Europe to Australasia has been rendered down to the entrails of problem-solving policing, a variety of community forums and watch schemes, and beat practices. Adaptation and application has followed local exigencies. The lack of measurable success cannot however be blamed on that piecemeal process. Blaming locals for failing to apply the concept in its totality is a little like the thesis that eighteenth century Britain would have been a more peaceful place if the application of capital punishment under the law had been mandatory rather than discretionary, with all villains consigned to the scaffold. It is no defence of COP to blame its faults on *ad hoc* application.

The evidence in this text of the experience of community policing is varied in quality. It is a long way from the detailed research analyses such as Skogan's in Chicago through the varied studies of community policing in South Africa, to the much qualified and descriptive newspaper and related accounts of its implementation in transitional and failed states. However, together they represent formidable indictments. Crucially, they have not met the criterion of Skolnick's (quoted above) in relation to access to those at the bottom of the social scale.

However, we need to place the development of community policing on a larger canvas – one that perceives it as part of a discredited practice of exporting used goods from the Western supermarkets of policing and other legal institutions to so-called developing and transitional societies. Community policing has been transmitted without the 'warts' and without reference to context and to history.

A legal export tradition – 'the West knows best'

Such a legalistic strategy of stimulating social change through legal export has a long history outside policing. In the 1960s and 1970s, the *law and development movement* involved many liberal Western jurists and legal scholars concerned about the social and political stability of the so-called 'developing world'. The general assumption of that movement was that law was central to the development process. Progress could not occur without appropriate legal provisions. Law was a key instrument of social reform with lawyers and jurists acting as social engineers. In law, as later in policing exports, a gap between the ideal of law and of law-in-action was widely noted in the developing societies. One partial resolution was to educate lawyers and judges from those countries in the values and procedures of Western legal systems. To mix metaphors, law would be the catalyst, the lubricant, and the rock, on which social change in other state structures could be based in the developing societies.

That movement eventually foundered on major obstacles. Critics argued that the law and development movement did not take account of the importance of traditional laws, of customary codes and of local indigenous legal structures. The reform movement focused on the formal legal system to the exclusion of custom and other informal ways in which developing societies order their affairs. It failed to recognize the essential diversity of legal codes and agencies. There was too little participation in planning by locals who would carry out the roles or be affected by them. External experts drew up the plans for legal reform, supervized their implementation and evaluated their effectiveness according to Western legal criteria. Behind the development enterprise was the naïve belief that the American legal system (and American legal culture generally) could be easily transplanted to developing countries (Trubek and Galanter 1974).

In policing, this evolutionary approach (that there is a unilinear path) to modernization has a variety of exponents. It has had a curious historical trajectory – from its Comteian-Reithian background, to Monkkonen's (1981) Weberian account of the diffusion process of the Metropolitan model, to the law and development movement, to Zvekic (1996) in Eastern Europe. Liang's (1992) trenchant critique of the equation between the development of state policing and notions of social progress are well known. His quote from the Prussian official Dr Wilhel Avegg, after the 1914-18 war, sums up the motif of that evolutionary history, '… every single police decree must constitute a step forward in the progress of a culture'. Somehow the connection between the inquisitorial policing of the criminal class of the Victorian urban rookeries, the Criminal Tribes repression in imperial India, Zero Tolerance policies in New York, and the British Anti-Social Behaviour legislation – amongst many other examples – is ignored in the view of state policing's inexorable contribution to the development of civilized standards.

The failings of that approach are increasingly acknowledged. The domestic and international political contexts of police reform (especially since 9-11) demonstrate that policing – societal roles, organizational relationships, and the canteen culture of rank and file officers – is almost intractable (Marenin 1998). History and social context add to the complications. Call (2003) lists many tensions facing national and international actors in the process – between police and other state and civil society agencies, adaptation to local realities versus external models, the competing international interests, pruning tainted personnel[1], and top-down versus bottom-up reform. State police reform may be impossible where there is a tradition of state police oppression and that agency is largely irrelevant to the majority population (Hills 2000). Is a new relationship possible (Neild 2000)?

The four primary components of community policing in the West that are most evident in the export drive – community forums, neighbourhood watch schemes, problem-solving and beat patrolling – have not worked anything like as successfully as appears in the international sales literature. For the most part, where such schemes have been established by the police and by local business elites in Africa and in the Indian sub-continent, they have simply exacerbated social schisms. For the most part, COP materials are shoddy goods, with few health warnings attached. They have invariably not been tailored to the particular needs of African, Asian, Latin American and Eastern European societies – failing to heed the health warnings of Bayley that reforms must be adapted to the local context (Mendes *et al* 2002)[2]. Certainly, the major exporter of policing, the ICITAP, can no longer be faulted in terms of its concerns for context and locality[3]. Policing cannot be developed independently of major structural change in the larger society. As Clegg *et al* say in their excellent report on policing for the British DFID

> ... poorer communities are unable to play a significant part in community policing unless major efforts are made to provide them with the basic necessities of survival and development ... Policing does not occur in a vacuum and expecting a reformed police force to effectively uphold rights and maintain order in a highly stratified society is unrealistic.
>
> (2000, pp. 8–18)

In considering the implications of these varying critiques, we need to be careful. On the one hand there are organizational explanations of the failures – mainly in terms of the mode of implementation (as in much of the DFID Report on Uganda) – that cannot be summarily dismissed as inconsequential. The implication of those aberrational criticisms is that COP will work only if the correct procedures and resources are ensured. The core argument in this article, however, is that the problem is systemic. COP, as designed in the West, is simply largely irrelevant to most transitional and failed societies, not simply a product of ineffective implementation. Some virtues emerge from this catalogue – the importance of diversified policing, the recognition that policing is not simply a function of the state police alone, and that community policing is not universally applicable.

The lessons from the export of community policing

The first lesson which that mass of material should teach police scholars is that the export and import of COP – whether it may be from a small homogeneous community in the United States to a dilapidated and socially divided American city, or from Newport News to Nairobi – is largely unsuccessful. A second lesson is that few components of community policing have passed the historical test of the last two decades. While this text has deliberately drawn on sceptical sources in developing an overview of community policing as a necessary antidote to the partisan multitude of success stories, there is little good news in practice. The several success stories may be very contextually limited to minor programmes. A third lesson is that it remains curious what exactly the objectives are of community policing – is it a crime reduction programme as perceived in the importing context, or is it at the other extreme a new experiment in governance (although an old one if one considers the practice of Japanese and Chinese registration police) in which the agencies of the state remodel themselves in a post-modern world to develop new modes of relationship with citizens and communities? The best one can say for COP is that it cannot be worse than a crime control form of policing that was expressed in rhetoric but rarely successful in practice. Nor could COP be worse than the corrupt, murderous forms of policing that characterize many countries of import.

We list three final conundrums for COP exponents:

- *Community policing and the problem of inequality* – who does community policing serve? Police forces have invariably, some times directly, often obliquely, been designed and utilized to maintain the existing social order – economic and social inequality. This is true as much for Peel's vaunted and mythologized first Metropolitan Police with its target of the 'dangerous classes' as it is of the paramilitary police forces of transitional and failed societies.

- *The functions of community policing* – are human rights concepts compatible with questions of police effectiveness? As the South African experience especially demonstrates, is a 'rights basis approach' appropriate as in South Africa where the majority population may regard those rights as an obstacle to the control of crime? Despite the views of those such as David Bayley, insecurity may only concretely be alleviated by emphasis on police structures and practices that might often ignore *individual* human rights concerns in favour of *collective* rights.

- *Community policing as autonomous from state policing institutions* – can community policing be conducted by citizen groups independently of the state police? The spirit of community policing implies invoking community involvement, indeed locating policing as a community matter rather than as a state function, as part of a safety security continuum in which the state police are merely one actor in that process. The evidence from a variety of developing societies is that there are many community groups – some traditional in character, some reacting to the new circumstances of the modernization process that have the commitment to and need to conduct policing functions. The energy of these informal policing structures is critical and is in direct response to local needs. But they are often subject to major problems of accountability.

Democratic policing

More thoughtful and accomplished scholars of international policing have largely discarded COP as the appropriate approach to policing transitional and failed societies. In the past five years, often learning from United States and Canadian experiences in Latin America, a severe reappraisal of the value of COP has been conducted. A euphemistic conception of democratic policing has replaced COP in their varied works (Bayley 1997; Neild 2002). Central to the latter have been the emphases placed on a commitment to the twin pillars of accountability and transparency in developing reformed policing structures in transitional societies.

However democratic policing is an oxymoron. Whether it be the policing of a majority on behalf of an economic and political elite or the policing by a majority of a minority such as in contemporary notions of the criminal class[4], policing remains the case in which some people are to be required by a state police to do something that they do not want to do. Whether it be the mythical source of COP in the original Metropolitan police formed to 'control the dangerous classes of the metropolis', 'the broken windows' version of COP directed at (typically) 'squeegee' merchants on the street corner, the new community police of Nairobi harassing street hawkers and itinerants on behalf of the new community forum, or the current British version of COP armed with inquisitorial street powers under the Crime and Disorder Act and equipped with a range of presumptive powers such as the ASBOs, the primary function is one of suppressing one group on behalf of another. The key functions (Cain 1979) remain as true now as they were within the mythical Peelite Metropolitan Police.

The most useful contribution to the debate on policing models that meets the criteria of democracy is one that hangs around a notion of tiering (Brodeur 1983; Brogden 1999; and especially Liang 1992). The latter argues that any state police – especially one primarily committed to the policing of the state (as in anti-terrorist work) needs to be counter-balanced by low policing[5], and by parallel policing – through private security and regulatory agencies. For Liang, it is the tension between such agencies that sustains democratic policing.

Box 10.1   *Inequality and democracy in policing*

> ... a system (of law enforcement) that can prosecute only ordinary street crimes and that cannot prosecute crimes involving prominent or powerful people is a weak system of criminal justice. A weak system that does not deal with corruption of the sorts that are rampant in Moscow, that cannot deal with the wealthy and powerful (as was true until recently in Guatemala and Italy), and that cannot prevent systematic violence or intimidation by its own security forces (as has been true at one time or another within the last decade in South Africa, Israel, Spain and Northern Ireland) is an open announcement that there is inequality in fundamental political rights and is an open announcement to disloyalty towards the democratic institutions of each of these countries.
>
> (Shearing 1997)

As Klockars phrases it, community policing is the latest in a long tradition of circumlocution whose purpose is to conceal, mystify and legitimate police distribution of non-negotiable force (1988). COP is undemocratic whatever its commitment to openness, local accountability and working with communities. Inequality and anti-democratic practices are built into state policing of whatever hue – community policing in reinforcing inequality is not an aberrational by-product of practice. State COP is not an enabling institution to support the quality of life of all. It is and will always be, whatever its whimsical reference to a notional community, committed to the key practice of suppressing the activities and practices of one group on behalf of another, if in more discursive and subtle form.

It may be that the new ideas on non-state policing may play a role in constructing some notional democracy into policework – although you cannot reinvent the wheel of early forms of informal justice – as Johnston and Shearing (2002) most recently argue. Further, as the critical scholar Garry T. Marx has pungently stated, the development of democratic policing should be seen as a process rather than as a product – a contribution to larger social change. But COP as presently exported seems most usefully summed up in the words of Kappeler and Kraska (1998, p. 294):

> ... community policing reforms are less likely to stem from the threat of crime or the desire to be more responsible to a concerned public than from the necessity to reconstruct governmental controls in times of high modernity.

Even where that process of development is elevated in the interests of 'democratic policing' that latter term is itself culturally bound (Manning 2004) and ignores history and context.

'Community policing' is an oxymoron. Further, it is difficult to see how a notion of democratic policing, however well intended, can coexist with state police histories of the support for social and economic inequality.

Notes

1 In the South African and Northern Irish experiences, the most effective personnel retired or took work in the private sector whilst the more undesirable police remain.
2 See, for example International Crisis Group (2002), on the central Asian states.
3 http://www.usdoj.gov/criminal/icitap/transitionTo DemocraticPolicing.html. Transition to Democratic Policing ICITAP Development Program.
4 One recalls Lea and Young's (1984) nightmare scenario of a democratic majority using the police to suppress an indigenous minority – Northern Ireland before the Peace Process is an obvious example.
5 As in Fouche's concept of the policing of the streets.

Bibliography

Albritton, J.S. (1995) The technique of community-oriented policing: an alternative explanation, in P.C. Kratcoski and D. Dukes (eds), *Issues in Community Policing*, Cincinnati: Anderson.

Aldous, C. and Leishman, F. (2000) Enigma variations: assessing the role of the koban, *Nissan Occasional Papers*, No 31.

Alemika, E. and Chukwuma, I. (2000) *Police Community Violence in Nigeria*. Lagos: Centre for Law Enforcement Education.

Alpert, G.P. and Dunham, R.G. (2001) *Community Policing: Contemporary Readings*. Prospect Heights: Waveland Press.

Amnesty International (2000) *Policing to protect human rights: a survey of police practice in countries of the Southern African Development Community, 1997–2002.*

Anderson, D.M. and Killingray, D. (eds) (1991) *Policing and Decolonisation: Politics, Nationalism and the Police*, 1917–65. Manchester: Manchester University Press.

Anderson, D.M. and Killingray, D. (eds) (1992) *Policing the Empire: Government, Authority and Control*, 1830-1940. Manchester: Manchester University Press.

Bayley, D. (1985) *Patterns of Policing: A Comparative International Analysis*. New Brunswick, NJ: Rutgers University Press.

Bayley, D. (2001) *Democratizing the Police Abroad: What to Do and How Not to Do It*. Washington DC: National Institute of Justice, US Justice Department.

Bayley, D.H. (1976). *Forces of Order: Police Behaviour in Japan and the United States*. Berkeley: University of California Press.

Bayley, D.H. (1989) *A Model of Community Policing: The Singapore Story*. Washington DC: National Institute of Justice.

Bayley, D.H. (1991) *Forces of Order, Policing Modern Japan*. Berkeley: University of California Press.

Bayley, D.H. (1992) *The Best Defense*. Police Executive Forum Publications: State University of New York.

Bayley, D.H. (1992A) The state of the art in community policing: an international perspective in J. Vernon and S. McKillop (eds) *The Police and the Community: Proceedings of a Conference, 23–25 Oct. 1990.* Canberra: Australian Institute of Criminology.

Bayley, D.H. (1994) *Police for the Future: Studies in Crime and Public Policy.* Oxford: Oxford University Press.

Bayley, D.H. (1995) A foreign policy for democratic policing, *Policing and Society*, 5, 79–93.

Bayley, D.H. (1995) Who are we kidding? Or developing democracy through police reform, in *Policing in Emerging Democracies, Workshop Papers and Highlights*, Washington DC: US Department of Justice.

Bayley, D.H. (1997) The contemporary practices of policing: a comparative view, in J. Burack, W. Lewis and E. Marks (eds) *Civilian Police and Multinational Peacekeeping – A Workshop Series: A Role for Democratic Policing.* Washington DC: Police Executive Research Forum.

Bayley, D.H. and Shearing, C.D. (2001) *The New Structure of Policing: Description, Conceptualisation and Research Agenda* National Institute of Justice. Washington DC: US Justice Department.

Beato, C.C. (2003) Public safety in Brazil, paper given at Conference on Safety and Security: University of Montreal, Montreal.

Beck, A. (2002) International and regional initiatives: providing appropriate regional assistance: http://www.kas.org.za/Publications/SeminarReports/Crimeandpolicingintransitionalsocieties/content2.pdf/

Beck, A. and Chistyakova, Y. (2002) Crime and policing in post-Soviet societies: bridging the police/public divide, *Policing and Society* 12, 2, 123–137.

Bennett, T. (1994) Community policing on the ground: developments in Britain in D. Rosenbaum (ed) *The challenge of community policing: Testing the promises.* Thousand Oaks, CA: Sage.

Biddle, K., Clegg, I., and Wheaton, J. (1998) *Evaluation of ODO/DFID Support to the Police in Developing Countries.* London: DFIDS.

Biryukov, N. and Sergeyev, S. (1997) *Russian Politics in Transition.* London: Ashgate.

Blair, I. (2003) Enabling the police to police: a London initiative in multi-tiered policing, paper given at Conference on Safety and Security: University of Montreal, Montreal.

Body-Gendrot, S. (2004) From zero tolerance to zero impunity: policing New York City and Paris, paper given at Conference *Paris – New York: the Two Cities Culture, Politics and Visions for the Future.* New York: New York University, Center for European Studies.

Boostrom, R. (2000) *Enduring Issues in Criminology.* San Diego, CA: Greenhaven Press.

Bowling, B. (1999). The rise and fall of New York murder: zero tolerance or crack's decline? *British Journal of Criminology*, 39, 4: 531–554.

Braiden, C. (1992) *Enriching Police Roles Police Management: Issues and Perspectives.* Washington DC: Police Executive Forum.

Bratton, M. and Landsberg, C. (1999) *From Promise to Delivery: Official Developmental Assistance to South Africa, 1994–8.* Johannesburg: Centre for Policy Studies. Research Report No 68.

Bretas, M.L. (2002) Police and community in Rio de Janeiro: an historical overview, in E.P. Mendes, J. Zuckerberg, S. Lecorre, A. Gabriel and J.A. Clark (eds). (2002) *Democratic Policing and Accountability: Global Perspectives* Aldershot: Ashgate.

Brocklehurst, H., Stott, N., Hamber, B. and Robinson, G. (2001) Lesson drawing: Northern Ireland and South Africa, *Indicator SA*, 18, 1, March.

Brodeur, J.P. (1983) High policing and low policing: remarks about the policing of political activities, *Social Problems*, 30.

Brogden, M.E. (1982) *The Police: Autonomy and Consent.* London: Academic Press.

Brogden, M.E. (1987) An Act to govern the internal lands of the island, *International Journal of the Sociology of Law* 15, 7.

Brogden, M.E. (1991) *On the Mersey Beat.* Oxford University Press: Oxford.

Brogden, M.E. (1998) *Two-tiered policing: a middle way for Northern Ireland?* Belfast: Democratic Dialogue.

Brogden, M.E. (1999) Community policing as cherry pie, in R.I. Mawby (ed) *Policing across the World.* London: UCL Press.

Brogden, M.E. (2000) Burning churches and victim surveys: the myth of Northern Ireland as a low crime community, *Irish Journal of Sociology.*

Brogden, M.E. (2003) The failure of community policing in South Africa, *Liverpool Law Review*, 24, 3 157–180.

Brogden, M.E. (2005) Horses for courses and thin blue lines? Community Policing in Transitional Society, *Police Quarterly*, 8, 1, 64–98.

Brogden, M.E., Jefferson, T. and Walklate, S. (1988) *Introducing Policework.* Unwin Hyman: London.

Brogden. M.E. and Nijhar, S.K. (2000) *Crime, Abuse and the Elderly.* Cullompton: Willan.

Brogden. M.E. and Shearing, C.D. (1993) *Policing for a New South Africa.* Routledge: London.

Bullock, K. and Tilley, N. (2003) *Crime Reduction and Problem-oriented Policing.* Cullompton: Willan.

Buono, V.M. del (2003) The Poor's Search for Security Conference on *In Search of Security.* Montreal: University of Montreal.

Burack, J., Lewis, W. and Marks, E. (1997) *Civilian Police and Multinational Peacekeeping – A Workshop Series: A role for democratic policing.* Washington DC: Police Executive Research Forum.

Cain, M. (1979) Trends in the sociology of police work. *International Journal of the Sociology of Law 7*, 143–167.

Cain, M. (2000) Orientalism, occidentalism and the sociology of crime, *British Journal of Criminology*, 40, 239–260.

Cao, L. (2001) A problem in no-problem policing in Germany: confidence in the police in Germany and USA, *European Journal of Crime, Criminal Law and Criminal Justice* 9, 33, 167–179.

Call, C.T. (2003) Challenges in police reform: promoting effectiveness and accountability, workshop on UNDP, Justice and Security Sector Reform: Developing Guidance for the Field, United Nations Development Program.

Call, C.T. and Barnett, M. (1999) Looking for a few good cops, *International Peacekeeping*, 6, 4.

Caparini, M. (2002) Police reform: issues and experiences. Fifth International Forum, Geneva Centre for the Democratic Control of Armed Forces, Zurich, 14–16 October.

Caparini, M. and Day, G. (2001) Workshop on democratic control of policing and security sector reform. Geneva: Geneva Centre for the Democratic Control of Armed Forces.

Cardarelli, A.P. and McDevitt, K. (1995) Towards a conceptual framework for evaluating community policing, in P.C. Kratcoski and D. Dukes (eds) *Issues in Community Policing*. Cincinnati: Anderson.

Cardarelli, A., McDevitt, J. and Baum, K. (1998) The rhetoric and reality of community policing in small and medium-sized cities and towns. *Policing: An International Journal of Police Strategies and Management*, 21, 3, 397–415.

Carrier, R. (1999) Dissolving boundaries: private security and policing in South Africa, *African Security Review* 8, 6.

Carriere, K. and Ericson, R.C. (1989) *Crime Stoppers: A Study in the Organization of Community Policing*, Research Report of the Centre of Criminology, University of Toronto.

Cawthra, G. (1997) Sub-regional security co-operation: the Southern African development community in comparative perspective, *Southern African Perspectives*, 63.

Champion, D.J. and Rush, G.E. (2001) *Policing in the Community*. London: Prentice Hall.

Chan, J.B. (1997) *Changing Police Culture: Policing in a Multicultural Society*. Cambridge: Cambridge University Press.

Chen, X. (2002) Community and policing strategies: a Chinese approach to social control, *Policing and Society*, 12, 1, 1–13.

Chinchilla, L. and Rico, M. (1997) *La prevencion Communitaria de delita: Perpecyve para Americana Latina*. Miami: Center for the Administration of Justice, Florida State University.

Chukwuma, I. (1994) *Above the Law*. Lagos: Civil Liberties Organization.

Clark, J.A. (2004) Human Rights and democratic accountability: toward useful Brazil-Canada dialogue on addressing institutional violence, in E.P. Mendes, J. Zuckerberg, S. Lecorre, A. Gabriel and J.A. Clark (eds) *Democratic Policing and Accountability: Global Perspectives*. Aldershot: Ashgate.

Clegg, I., Hunt, R., and Whetton, J. (2000) *Policy Guidance on Support to Policing in Developing Societies*. Swansea: Centre for Independent Studies, University of Wales.

Cole, B. (1998) Post colonial systems, in R.I. Mawby (ed) *Policing Across the World*. London: UCL Press.

Cooper, B. (1996) The fall of the wall and the East German Police, Conference on policing in Central and Eastern Europe. College of Police and Security Studies, Slovenia.

Council of the European Union (2003) Community Policing: best practice concerning neighbourhood and community policing. Brussels, 7521/03.

Crank, J. (1995) The community-policing movement of the early twenty-first century: what we learned, in J. Klofas and S. Stojkovic (eds) *Crime and Justice in the Year 2010*. Belmont, CA: Wadsworth Publishing.

Crawford, A. (1998) *Crime Prevention and Community Safety: Politics, Policies and Practices*. London: Longman.

Crawford, A. (2003) Plural policing: policing beyond the police in England, *Conference on Safety and Security*, University of Montreal, Montreal.

Critchley, T.A. (1978) *A History of Policing in England and Wales*. London: Constable.

Deosaran. R. (2002) Community policing in the Caribbean: context, community and police capability, *Policing: An International Journal of Police Strategies and Management* 25, 1, 125–146.

Dixon, D. (1999) Beyond zero tolerance, Third National Outlook Symposium on Crime in Australia, 22–23 March, Canberra.

Donzelot, J. and Wyvekens, A. (2000) Le 'Community Policing' aux Etats-Unis un mode alternatif de reglement des conflist urbaines. Paris: Centre d'Etudes Politiques Sociales.

Dupont, B. (2002) Implementing community policing in a centralised criminal justice system: another French paradox. Working paper, University of Montreal.

Dutton, M.R. (1992) *Policing and Punishment in China: From Patriarchy to 'The People'*. Cambridge: Cambridge University Press.

Dvorsek, A. (1996) Applicability of Western police experience: desires and possibilities from the viewpoint of the Slovenian police, in M. Pagon (ed) *Policing in Central and Eastern Europe: Comparing Firsthand Knowledge with Experience from the West*. Ljubljana, Slovenia: College of Police and Security Studies.

Ellison, G. and Smyth, J. (2000) *The Crowned Harp: Policing in Northern Ireland*. London: Pluto Press.

Emsley, C. (2000) *Gendarmes and the State in Nineteenth Century Europe*. Oxford: Oxford University Press.

Erickson, R.V. and Shearing, C.D. (1986) The scientification of police work, in G. Boohme and N. Stehr (eds) *The Knowledge Society*. Boston, MA: Reidel.

Feltes, T. (2002) Community-oriented policing in Germany: training and education. *Policing: An International Journal of Police Strategies and Management*, 25, 1, 48–59.

Ferreira, B.R. (1996) The use and effectiveness of community policing in a democracy, in M. Pagon (ed) *Policing in Central and Eastern Europe: Comparing Firsthand Knowledge with Experience from the West*, Ljubljana, Slovenia: College of Police and Security Studies.

Ferret, J. (2004) The state, policing and Old Continental Europe: managing the local/national tension. *Policing and Society*, 14, 1, March 49–65.

Finch, A.J. (1999) The Japanese police's claim to efficiency: a critical view, *Modern Asian Studies* 33: 483–511.

Fintzer, G. and Korinek, L. (1995) Criminality and the fight against crime in Hungary, *The Kriminalist* 27, 498–505.

Friedmann, R. (1992) *Community Policing: Comparative Perspectives and Prospects.* London: Macmillan.

Friedmann, R. (1996) Community policing: some conceptual and practical issues. *Home Affairs Review* 34, 6, 114–23.

Fruhling, H. (2002) Changing the police in transitional countries: the case of Latin America. Paper presented at the Conference In Search of Security: Montreal.

Glensor, R. and Peak, K. (1996). Implementing change: community-oriented policing and problem solving. *Law Enforcement Bulletin*, 65, 7, 14–21.

Goldstein, H. (1960) Police discretion not to invoke the criminal process. *Yale Law Review*, 60, 543–594.

Goldstein, H. (1990) *Problem-Oriented Policing.* London: McGraw-Hill.

Goris, P. and Walters, R. (1999) Locally oriented crime prevention and the 'partnership approach'. *Politics, Practices and Prospects*, 22, 4, 633–645.

Grinc, R. (1994) Angels in marble: problems in stimulating community involvement in community policing, *Crime and Delinquency*, 40, 3, 437–468.

Haberfeld, M., Walancik, P. and Uydess, A.M. (2003) Teamwork – not making the dream work: community policing in Poland. *Policing: An International Journal of Police Strategies and Management*, 25, 1, 147–168.

Haberfeld, M., Walancik, P., Uydess, A.M. and Bartels, E. (2003) *Community Policing in Poland: Final Report.* Washington DC: US Department of Justice.

Harring, S. (1983) *Policing in a Class Society: The Experience of American Cities, 1865-1915.* New Brunswick, New Jersey: Rutgers University Press.

Hay, D. (1975) *Albion's Fatal Tree: Crime and Society in Eighteenth-century England.* London: Allen Lane.

Heymann, P.B. (2000) The new policing, *Fordham Urban Law Journal*, XXVIII, 407–456.

Hills, A. (1996) Towards a critique of policing and national development in Africa, *Journal of Modern African Studies* 34, 2, 271–91.

Hills, A. (2000) *Policing Africa: Internal Security and the Limits of Liberalization.* Boulder, Co: Lynne Rienner.

Holdaway, S. (1994) Recruitment, race and the police subculture, in M. Stephens and S. Becker (eds) *Police Force, Police Service: Care and Control in Britain.* London: Macmillan.

Holm, T.T. and Eide, E.P. (eds) (2001) *Peacebuilding and Police Reform*. London: Frank Cass.

Holmberg, L. (2003) Personalized policing: results from a series of experiments with proximity policing in Denmark, *Policing: An International Journal of Police Strategies and Management*, 25, 1, 32–47.

Huggins, M.K. (1998) *Political Policing: Institutionalising Security through US Assistance to Latin American Forces*. Durham: Duke University Press.

Huggins, M.K. (1998) US foreign police training in Latin America: an international protection racket. *Contemporary Justice Review*, 1:4.

Huggins, M. and MacTurk, J. (2000) Armed and dangerous: where the military and police can't keep order, private security takes over, editorial in *Connection to the Americas*, Resource Center of the Americas, Fall.

Igbinovia, P.E. (2001) The future of the Nigerian police, *Policing: An International Journal of Police Strategies and Management* 23, 4, 538–554.

Independent Commission on Policing in Northern Ireland (1999) *A New Beginning*. Belfast: Northern Ireland Office.

International Crisis Group (2002) *Central Asia: The Politics of Police Reform*. Asia Report No 42.

International Crisis Group (1st draft March 2003) *Crime, Public Order and Human Rights*. Geneva: International Council on Human Rights.

International Helsinki Federation for Human Rights (2002) Conference on the Role of Community Policing in Building Confidence in Minority Communities. Vienna, October.

Ivkovic, S.K. and Haberfeld, M.R. (2000) Transformation from militia to police in Croatia and Poland: a comparative perspective, *Policing*, 2, 194–217.

Jacobs, J. (1961) *The Death and Life of Great American Cities*. New York: Vintage Books.

Jenks, D. (2004) The Czech police: adopting democratic principles, in M. Caparini and O. Marenin (eds) *Transforming Police in Central and Eastern Europe: Process and Progress*. Geneva Center for the Democratic Control of Armed Forces, Geneva: Transaction.

Jenks, D., Costelloe, M. and Krebs, C. (2003) After the fall: Czech police in a post-Communist era, *International Criminal Justice Review*, 13, 90–109.

Johnston, L. (2000) *Policing Britain*. Cullompton: Willan.

Johnston, L. (2003) From 'pluralisation' to 'the police extended family': discourses on the governance of community policing in Britain. Paper given at Conference on Safety and Security. Montreal: University of Montreal.

Johnston, L. and Shearing, C.D. (2002) *Governing Security: Explorations in Policing and Justice*. London: Routledge.

Jones, A.A. and Wiseman, R. (2001) Europe Emphasizes Rehab, not Arrest, *Links* September, 1–2.

Kappeler, V.E. (1996) Making police history in light of modernity: a sign of the times? *Police Forum*, 6, 3, 1–6.

Kappeler, V.E., Blumberg, M. and Potter, G.W. (1996) *The Mythology of Crime and Criminal Justice*, 2nd ed. Prospect Heights, IL: Waveland Press.

Kappeler, V.E. and Kraska, P.B. (1998) Police adapting to high modernity: a textual critique of community policing, *Policing: An International Journal of Police Strategies and Management*, 21, 2, 293–313.

Kelling, G. and Coles, C. (eds) (1996). *Fixing broken windows: restoring order and reducing crime in our communities*. New York: Touchstone.

Kelling, G. and Moore, M. (1988). From political to reform to community: The evolving strategy of police, in J. Greene and S. Mastrofski (eds) *Community Policing: Rhetoric or Reality*. New York: Praeger.

Kilpin, J. (1999) *Training Needs Analysis for the ICD*. Johannesburg: Centre for the Study of Violence and Reconciliation.

Kilpin, J. and Harrison, K. (2003) *The Future for Policing and Crime Prevention in the SADC*. Montreal: International Crime Prevention Centre.

Klockars, C.B. (1985) *The Idea of Police*. Beverly Hills, CA: Sage.

Klockars, C.B. (1988) The rhetoric of community policing, in J.R. Greene and S.D. Mastrofski (eds) *Community Policing: Rhetoric or Reality*, pp. 239–258. New York: Praeger.

Koci, A. (1996) Legitimation and culturalism: towards policing changes in the European 'post socialist' countries, in M. Pagon (ed) *Policing in Central and Eastern Europe: Comparing Firsthand Knowledge with Experience from the West*. Ljubljana, Slovenia: College of Police and Security Studies.

Lau, R. (2004) Community policing in Hong Kong: transplanting a questionable model, *Criminal Justice*, 4, 1, 61–80.

Laufer, S. (2001) The Politics of Fighting Crime in South Africa since 1964 in Steinberg (ed) *Crime Wave – the South African Underworld and its Foes*. Johannesburg: Witwatersrand University Press.

Lea, J. and Young, J. (1984) *What Is to be Done About Law and Order?* Harmondsworth: Penguin.

Leigh, A., Read, T. and Tilley, N. (1996) *Problem-Oriented Policing: Brit POP*. Crime Detection and Prevention Series, Paper 75. London: Police Research Group, HMSO.

Leishman, F. (1998) Policing in Japan: East Asian archetype? in R.I. Mawby (ed) *Policing across the World*. London: UCL Press, 109–126.

Leishman, F., Cope, S. and Starie, P. (1997) Globalization, new public management and the enabling state: futures of police management, *International Journal of Public Sector Management*, 10, 6–7, 444–460.

Levy, R. and Zauberman, K. (2002) Police and public in Paris. Paper for *Paris-New York Conference*, New York University, 25–27 April.

Lia, B. (2000) The establishment of a Palestinian police force in the West Bank and Gaza Strip, in T.T. Holm and E.B. Eide (eds) *Peacebuilding and Police Reform*. London: Frank Cass.

Liang, H.H. (1992) *The Rise of Modern Police and the European State System since Metternich to the Second World War*. Cambridge: Cambridge University Press.

Loader, I. and Mulcahy, A. (2003) *Policing and the Condition of England: Memory, Politics and Culture.* Oxford: Oxford University Press.

Louw, A. and Schonteich, M. (2001) Playing the numbers game, in Steinberg (ed).

Louw, A. and Shaw, M. (1997), *Stolen Opportunities: The Impact of Crime on South Africa's poor.* ISS Monograph Series, 14, Halfway House: Institute for Security Studies.

Lyons, W. (1999). *The Politics of Community Policing: Rearranging the Power to Punish.* Ann Arbor: University of Michigan Press.

Malan, M. (2001) Peacebuilding in Southern Africa: police reform in Mozambique and South Africa, in Eide and Hold (eds).

Manning, P. (1988) Community policing as a drama of control, in J. Greene and S. Mastrofski (eds) *Community Policing: Rhetoric or Reality.* New York: Praeger.

Manning, P.K. (1993) Community-based policing, in R.G. Dunham and G. P. Alpert (eds) *Critical Issues in Policing: Contemporary Perspectives.* Prospect Heights, Illinois: Waveland.

Manning, P.K. (2004) Some observations regarding a democratic theory of policing. http://www.policeuseofforce.org/pdf/Manning%20.pdf

Marais, E. (1992) The police-community relationship, in L. Glanz (ed) *Managing Crime in the New South Africa: Selected Readings*, pp. 113-136. Pretoria: HSRC.

Marenin, O. (1989) The utility of community needs surveys in community policing, *Police Studies*, 12, 2, 73–81.

Marenin, O. (1996) United States police assistance to emerging democracies, in O. Marenin (ed) *Policing Change, Changing Policing.* New York: Garland Press.

Marenin, O. (1998) The goal of democracy in international police assistance programs, *Policing*, 21, 2, 159–177.

Marenin, O. (2001) The role of unilateral support for police reform processes: the case of the United States, in T.T. Holm and E.B. Eide (eds) *Peacebuilding and Police Reform.* London: Frank Cass.

Marks, M. (1995) Community policing, Human Rights and the Truth and Reconciliation Commission, Paper presented to the National Secretariat of the South African Police Union, Roodeplaat Training Centre, 25 July.

Marks, M. (2000) Transforming police organizations from within, *British Journal of Criminology* 40, 557–573.

Marquis, G. (1997) The Irish Model and nineteenth century Canadian policing, *Journal of Imperial and Commonwealth History*, 25, 193–218.

Marshall, G. (2004) The legal regulation of policing, in T. Newburn (ed) *Policing: Key Readings.* Cullompton: Willan.

Mastrofski, S. (1988) Community policing as reform: a cautionary tale, in J. Greene and S. Mastrofski (eds) *Community Policing: Rhetoric or Reality.* New York: Praeger.

Mawby, R.I. (1990) *Comparative Policing Issues: The British and American System in International Perspective.* London: Unwin Hyman.

Mawby, R.I. (1999) Approaches to comparative analysis: the impossibility of becoming an expert on everywhere, in R. Mawby (ed) *Policing across the World*. London: UCL Press.

McGarry, J. and O'Leary, B. (1999) *Policing Northern Ireland: Proposals for a New Start*. Belfast: Blackstaff Press.

Mendes, E.P. (2002) Raising the social capital of policing and nations: how can professional policing and civilian oversight weaken the circle of violence?, in Mendes *et al*.

Mendes, E.P., Zuckerberg, J., Lecorre, S., Gabriel, A. and Clark, J.A. (ed) (2002) *Democratic Policing and Accountability: Global Perspectives*. Aldershot: Ashgate.

Meško, G. (1999) Police and crime prevention – a look from the other side, paper given at the Annual Conference of the British Society of Criminology, Liverpool.

Miller, W.R. (1999 ed) *Cops and Bobbies: Police Authority in New York and London, 1830-1870*. Ohio State University Press.

Mistry, D. (1997) *A Review of Community Policing*. Johannesburg: Centre for the Study of Violence and Reconciliation.

Mistry, D. (2000) The dilemma of case withdrawal, in G. Mair and R. Tarling (eds) *British Society of Criminology Papers*, 3, Liverpool.

Monjardet, D. (1996) *Ce que fait la police. Sociologie de la force publique*. Paris: La Découverte.

Monkkonen, E. (1981) *Police in Urban America, 1860-1920*. New York: Cambridge University Press.

Moore, M. (1992) Problem-solving and community policing, in M. Tonry and N. Morris (eds) *Modern Policing. Crime and Justice: A Review of Research*, Volume 15. Chicago: University of Chicago Press.

Mulcahy, A (1999) Visions of normality: peace and the reconstruction of policing in Northern Ireland, *Social and Legal Studies* 8/2, 277–95.

Mulcahy, A. (2000) Policing history: the official discourse and organisational memory of the Royal Ulster Constabulary, *British Journal of Criminology*, 40/1, 68–87.

Mulcahy, A. and Ellison, G. (2001) The language of policing and the struggle for legitimacy in Northern Ireland, *Policing and Society*, 11, 3–4, 383–404.

Murphy, C. (1988) The development, impact, and implications of community policing in Canada, in J. Greene and S. Mastrofski (eds) *Community Policing: Rhetoric or Reality*. New York: Praeger.

Neild, R. (2000) *Themes and Debates in Public Security Reform. A Manual for Civil Society: Community Policing*. Washington DC: Washington Office on Latin America.

Neild, R. (2001) Democratic policing, *Conflict, Security and Development*, 1,1 Summer.

Neild, R. (2002) Sustaining reform: democratic policing in Central America, *Citizen Security Monitor*, October.

Newham, G. (2000) *Transformation and the Internal Disciplinary System of the South African Police Service*. Occasional paper, Johannesburg: Centre for the Study of Violence and Reconciliation.
Nina, D. (2000) *The 'Rainbow Paper': Safety and Security in the Next Millennium*, Community Peace Foundation: University of the Western Cape.

O'Connor, T. (2000) *Community Policing: A List of Programs*. North Carolina: Wesleyan College, http://faculty.ncwc.edu/toconnor/comlist.htm
Oliver, W.C.M. (2001) *Community-Oriented Policing*. Upper Saddle River: Prentice Hall.
Opolot, J.S.E. (1992) The resilience of the British colonial police legacies in East Africa, Southern Africa, and West Africa, *Police Studies*, 15, 2, 90–99.
Oppler, S. (1997) Partners against crime *Crime and Conflict*, 9 Winter.

Peak, K. and Glensor, R. (2nd ed.) (2002) *Community Policing and Problem-Solving: Strategies*. Upper Saddle River, NJ: Prentice Hall.
Pelser, E. (1999) *The Challenge of Community Policing in South Africa*, Occasional Paper No 42. *Pretoria:* Institute for Security Studies.
Pelser, E. and Louw, A. (2001) *Evaluation of the Western Cape Community Safety Forums*, Project Report, Pretoria: Institute for Security Studies.
Pelser, E. and Louw, A. (2002) Evaluating community safety forums, in E. Pelser (ed) *Crime Prevention Forums*. Pretoria: Institute for Security Studies.
Pelser, E., Schnetler, J. and Louw, A. (1999) *Not Everybody's Business: Community Policing in the SAPS' Priority Area*, Monograph 71, Pretoria: Institute for Security Studies.
Polish Ministry of Justice (1995) *Crime Control in Poland*. Warsaw: Oficyna Naukowa.
Povolotskiy, A. (2002) Reform of the police in the Ukraine: the need for cooperation between the police and the public in tackling crime. Paper given at Conference on Crime and Policing in Transitional Societies: Johannesburg.
Prateep, P.V. (1996) Friends of the police movement, Conference on Policing in Central and Eastern Europe, College of Police and Security Studies, Slovenia.
Prinsloo, J. (1996) Institutional attitudes towards policing in South Africa, *Conference on Policing in Central and Eastern Europe*. Slovenia: College of Police and Security Studies.
Punch, M. (1977) The secret social service, in S. Holdaway (ed) *The British Police*. London: Edward Arnold.
Punch, M. (2004) The Belgian disease: Dutroux, scandal and 'system failure', in R. Sarre, D. Das and H.J. Albrecht (eds) *Policing Corruption: International Perspectives, Proceedings of the IPES Conference* (2001). Poland: Lexington Books.
Punch, M., van der Vijver, K. and Zoomer, M. (2002) Dutch 'COP': developing community policing in The Netherlands, *Policing: An International Journal of Police Strategies and Management*, 25, 1, 60–79.
Raleigh, C., Biddle, K., Male, C., and Neema, S. (2000) *Uganda Police Project Evaluation*, Evaluation Report FV 591. London: Department for International Development.

Reed, W.R. and Reed, E.R. (1999) *The Politics of Community Policing: The Case of Seattle Garland.*

Reiner, R. (1992) *The Politics of the Police.* Brighton: Harvester.

Rigakos, S.R. and Papanicolaou, G. (2003) The political economy of Greek policing: between neo-liberalism and the Sovereign State. *Policing and Society* 13, 3, 271–304.

Robertshaw, R., Louw, A. and Mtani, A. (2001) *Crime in Dar es Salaam.* Pretoria: Institute for Security Studies.

Robin, D. (2000) *Community Policing: Origins, Elements, Implementation, Assessment.* Edwin Mellen Press.

Rosenbaum, D. (1994). *The Challenge of Community Policing: Testing the Promises.* Thousand Oaks, CA: Sage.

Ruteere, M. and Pommerolle, M.-E. (2003) Democratizing security or de-centralizing repression? The ambiguities of community policing in Kenya, *African Affairs*, 102, 1–18.

Sadd, S. and Grinc, R. (1994) Innovative neighborhood oriented policing: an evaluation in eight cities, in D. Rosenbaum (ed) *The Challenge of Community Policing: Testing the Promises.* Thousand Oaks, CA: Sage.

Scharf, W. (2000) Community justice and community policing in post-apartheid South Africa, paper presented at the *International Workshop on the Rule of Law*, Institute of Development Studies, University of Sussex, 1–3 June.

Scharf, W., Saban, G. and Hauck, M. (2001) Local communities and crime prevention, in Steinberg (ed).

Schonteich, M. and Louw, A. (2001) *Crime in South Africa: a country and cities profile,* Paper 49, Pretoria: Institute for Safety and Security.

Sergeyeb, V. M. (1998) *The Wild East: Crime and Lawlessness in Post Communist Russia.* New York: M.E. Sharpe.

Shaw, M. (1995) Urban conflict, crime and policing in South African cities, *Africa Insight*, 25, 4, 216–220.

Shaw, M. (ed) (2001) *Crime and Policing in Transitional Societies.* St Augustine, Germany: Konrad Adenaeur Siftung.

Shaw, M. (2002) *Crime and Policing in Post-Apartheid South Africa: Transforming Under Fire.* Bloomington: Indiana University Press.

Shaw, M. and Shearing, C. (1998) Reshaping security: an examination of the governance of security in South Africa, *African Security Review*, 7, 3, 3–12.

Shearing, C. (1995) Towards democratic policing: rethinking strategies of transformation, in US Department of Justice, Policing in Emerging Democracies: Workshop papers and highlights. NIJ Research Report. Washington: National Institute of Justice.

Shearing, C. (1998) *Changing Paradigms in Policing: The Significance of Community Policing for the Governance of Security.* Occasional paper No 34, Pretoria: Institute for Security Studies.

Shearing, C.D. (1997) *Toward Democratic Policing: Rethinking strategies of transformation and highlights.* Washington: National Institute of Justice, US Department of Justice.

Shearing, C.D. (2003) Refiguring the public and the private within a nodal governance, framework paper given at Conference on Safety and Security, University of Montreal: Montreal.

Shelley, L. (1996) *Policing Soviet Society.* London: Routledge.

Silva da Tatigiba, J.C. (2002) Proposal: interactive policing: the Brazilian experience in Mendes *et al.*

Singh, J. (2002) *Inside Indian Police.* New Delhi: Gyan Publishing House.

Sita, N.M., Kibuka, P.E. and Ssamula, M. (2002) *The Involvement of (Local) Communities in Crime Prevention: The Case of African Countries.* www.unicri.it/workshop2002/9-%20Masamba%20Sita.doc

Skogan, W. and Hartnett, S.M. (1997) *Community Policing Chicago Style.* Oxford: Oxford University Press.

Skolnick, J. (1966) *Justice Without Trial.* New York: Wiley and Sons.

Skolnick, J. (1973) The police and the urban ghetto, in A. Niederhoffer and A. Blumberg (eds) *The Ambivalent Force: Perspective on the Police.* San Francisco, CA: Rinehart.

Skolnick, J. (1999) On democratic policing, *Ideas on American Policing.* Washington: Police Foundation.

Skolnick, J. and Bayley, D. (1986) *The New Blue Line: Police Innovations in Six American Cities.* New York: Free Press.

Skolnick, J. and Bayley, D. (1988) *Community Policing around the World.* Washington DC: National Institute of Justice.

Skolnick, J. and Bayley, D. (1988) Theme and variation in community policing, in M. Tonry and N. Morris (eds) *Crime and Justice: A Review of Research*, Volume 8. Chicago, IL: University of Chicago Press.

Smyth, J. (2002) Community policing and the reform of the Royal Ulster Constabulary, *Policing: An International Journal of Police Strategies and Management*, 25, 1, 110–124.

Stanley, W. (2000) Building new police forces in El Salvador and Guatemala, in Steinberg, J. (ed) (2001) *Crime Wave: The South African Underworld and its Foes.* Johannesburg: Witwatersrand University Press.

Stenson, K. (1999) Crime control, governmentality and sovereignty, in R. Smandych (ed) *Governable Places: Readings in Governmentality and Crime Control.* Aldershot: Ashgate.

Szikinger, I. (1996) Continuity and change in Hungarian policing in the mirror of public security detention, in M. Pagon (ed) *Policing in Central and Eastern Europe: Comparing Firsthand Knowledge with Experience from the West.* Ljubljana, Slovenia: College of Police and Security Studies.

Taylor, R.W., Fritsch, E.J. and Caeti, T.J. (1998) Core challenges facing community policing: the Emperor still has no clothes, newsletter of the Academy of Criminal Justice Sciences, 17, 1, 1–5.

Travis, J. (1998) Policing in transition, *Fourth Biennial Conference: International Perspectives on Crime, Justice, and Order.* Budapest.

Trojanowicz, R. and Bucqueroux, B. (1990) Community Policing. Cincinnati: Anderson Publishing.

Trubek, D.M. and Galanter, M. (1974) Scholars in self-esteem: some reflections on the crisis in law and development, *Wisconsin Law Review*, 1062–1101.

Tupman, W. and Tupman, A. (1999) *Policing in Europe: Uniform in Diversity*. Exeter: Intellect.

Van den Broeck, T. (2002) Keeping up appearances: a community's perspectives on community policing and the local governance of crime, *Policing: An International Journal of Police Strategies and Management*, 25, 1, 169–189.

Van der Spuy, E. (1997) Regionalism in policing: from lessons in Europe to lessons in Southern Africa, *African Security Review*, 6,6.

Van der Spuy, E. (2000) Foreign donor assistance and policing reform in South Africa, *Policing and Society*, 10, 342–366.

Van der Spuy, E., Geerlings, J. and Singh, A. (1998) *Donor assistance to crime prevention and criminal justice reform: South Africa, 1994–1998*, Report for the National Crime Prevention Secretariat, July.

Van Vuuren, J. (1996) The evolution and status of community police forums in South Africa, *Southern African Journal of Criminology* 9.1.

Virta, S. (2002) Local security management: policing through networks, *Policing: An International Journal of Police Strategies and Management*, 25, 1, 190–200.

Waddington, P.A.J. (1999) *Policing Citizens*. London: UCL Press.

Walker, S. (1999) 'Broken windows' and fractured history, in W.M. Oliver (ed) *Community Policing: Classical Readings*. Upper Saddle River: Prentice Hall.

Walker, S. (2000). Does anyone remember team policing? Lessons of the team policing experience for community policing. *American Journal of Police*, 12 (1), 33–55.

Weisburd, D. and McElroy, J. (1988). Enacting the CPO role: findings from the New York City pilot program in community policing, in J. Greene and S. Mastrofski (eds) *Community Policing: Rhetoric or Reality*. New York: Praeger.

Weisburd, D. McElroy, J. and Hardyman, E.P. (1988) Challenges to supervision in community policing observations on a pilot project, *American Journal of Police*, 7: 29–50.

Weisburd, D., McElroy, J. and Hardyman, P. (1989) Maintaining control in community-oriented policing, in D. Kenney (ed) *Police and Policing: Contemporary Issues*. New York: Praeger.

Weisburd, D., Shalev, O. and Amir, M. (2003) Community policing in Israel: resistance and change, *Policing: An International Journal of Police Strategies and Management*, 25, 1, 80–109.

Weitzer, R. (1995) *Policing Under Fire: Ethnic Conflict and Police-Community Relations in Northern Ireland*. New York: University of New York Press.

Westney, D.E. (1987) *Imitation and Innovation*. Cambridge: Harvard University Press.

Williams, J.L. and Serrins, E.S. (1993) The Russian militia: an organisation in Transition, *Policy Studies* 16, 4, 124–128.

Wilson, D. (2000) Toward community policing: the police and ethnic minorities in Hungary. Princeton: Project on ethnic relations.

Wilson, J.Q. (1968) *Varieties of Police Behavior: The Management of Law and Order in Eight Communities*. Cambridge: Harvard University Press.

Wilson, J.Q. (1983) *Thinking about crime*. New York: Basic Books.

Wilson, J.Q. and Kelling, G. (1982) Broken windows, *The Atlantic Monthly*. March, 46–52.

Wilson, J.Q. and Petersilia, J. (eds) (2002) *Crime: Public Policies for Crime Control*. Oakland: Institute for Contemporary Studies.

Wong, K.C. (2001) Community policing in China: philosophy, law and practice, *International Journal of the Sociology of Law*, 29, 2, 127–147.

Wood, B. (2000) Community safety and firearms control, *Malawi Security Sector Reform*, Pilot Project Report.

Wyvekens, A. (1996). Justice de proximité et proximité de la justice. Les maisons de justice et du droit, *Droit et Société*, 33, 363–388.

Yusufi, I. (2003) *Security Sector Reform in SE Europe*, Interim Policy Paper, July, International Policy Fellowship, Budapest http://www.policy.hu/yusufi/researchreport.pdf

Zhao J. (1996). *Why Police Organizations Change: A Study of Community-oriented Policing*. Washington: Executive Police Forum.

Zhao, J. Lovrich, N. and Thurman, Q. (1995) Community-oriented policing across the US: facilitators and impediments to implementation, *American Journal of Police*, 1, 11–28.

Ziegler, M. and Neild, R. (2002) *From Police to Governance: Police Reforms and the International Community*. Washington: Washington Office on Latin America.

Ziembo-Vogl, J. and Woods, D. (1996) Community policing: practice versus paradigm, *Police Studies*, 19, 3.

Zvekic, U. (1996) Policing and attitudes towards private police in countries in transition, *Conference on Policing in Central and Eastern Europe*. Slovenia: College of Police and Security Studies.

Zvekic, U. (2002) Citizens, crime and criminal justice in Central and Eastern Europe, paper given at Conference on Policing in Transition, Johannesburg.

Author Index

Subject Index